The Nature of Supreme Court Power

Few institutions in the world are credited with initiating and confounding political change on the scale of the United States Supreme Court. The Court is uniquely positioned to enhance or inhibit political reform, enshrine or dismantle social inequalities, and expand or suppress individual rights. Yet despite claims of victory from judicial activists and complaints of undemocratic lawmaking from the Court's critics, numerous studies of the Court assert that it wields little real power. This book examines the nature of Supreme Court power by identifying conditions under which the Court is successful at altering the behavior of state and private actors. Employing a series of longitudinal studies that use quantitative measures of behavior outcomes across a wide range of issue areas, Matthew E. K. Hall develops and supports a new theory of Supreme Court power. Hall finds that the Court tends to exercise power successfully when lower courts can directly implement its rulings; however, when the Court must rely on non-court actors to implement its decisions, its success depends on the popularity of those decisions. Overall, this theory depicts the Court as a powerful institution, capable of exerting significant influence over social change.

Matthew E. K. Hall is assistant professor of Political Science at the University of Notre Dame. He earned his Ph.D. in political science, with distinction, from Yale University. His work has appeared in *American Politics Review,* the *Journal of Empirical Legal Studies,* and the *Journal of Law and Policy.*

The Nature of Supreme Court Power

MATTHEW E. K. HALL
Saint Louis University

CAMBRIDGE
UNIVERSITY PRESS

CAMBRIDGE UNIVERSITY PRESS
Cambridge, New York, Melbourne, Madrid, Cape Town,
Singapore, São Paulo, Delhi, Mexico City

Cambridge University Press
32 Avenue of the Americas, New York NY 10013-2473, USA

Published in the United States of America by Cambridge University Press, New York

www.cambridge.org
Information on this title: www.cambridge.org/9781107617827

First published 2011
Reprinted 2012
First paperback edition 2013

A catalogue record for this publication is available from the British Library

Library of Congress Cataloging in Publication Data
Hall, Matthew Eric Kane.
The nature of supreme court power / Matthew Eric Kane Hall.
p. cm.
ISBN 978-1-107-00143-5 (hardback)
1. United States. Supreme Court – History. 2. Political questions and judicial
power – United States – History – Sources. 3. Judgments – United States – History.
4. Constitutional history – United States. 5. United States – Social conditions – Sources.
I. Title.
KF8742.H35 2010
347.73′26–dc22 2010031356

ISBN 978-1-107-00143-5 Hardback
ISBN 978-1-107-61782-7 Paperback

This book is dedicated to those who revere the courts as guardians of our personal freedoms and to those who revile the courts as saboteurs of democratic self-government. May the struggle to balance personal liberties and majority rule persist forever, for only this constant tension ensures that both will long endure.

Contents

Figures

Tables

Preface

When I was a sophomore in college, my friend and mentor Professor Laura Beth Nielsen assigned me to read Gerald Rosenberg's *The Hollow Hope* as part of a seminar on legal studies. Professor Rosenberg's compelling and controversial book piqued my interest in the role of courts in our society. Time, reflection, and my continued study of law and politics have only sharpened my interest in his project and my objections to his thesis. In many ways, this book is my term paper for that seminar, now eight years overdue.

I have been aided in this project by the helpful contributions of numerous scholars, including professors Paul Brace, Daniel Butler, Bradley Canon, Alan Gerber, Jerry Goldman, Mark Graber, Thomas Keck, Andrew Martin, Kenneth Scheve, Stephen Skowronek, and Peter Swenson, as well as my graduate school colleagues Stephen Engel, Judkins Mathews, Joshua Pheterson, Joseph Sempolinski, and the members of the Yale Graduate Student Colloquium on American Politics. I am indebted to each of them for their thoughtful suggestions and critiques.

I was fortunate to be directed through this process by an exceptional group of diverse scholars: professors Bruce Ackerman, Donald Green, Gregory Huber, and David Mayhew. These men have shaped my approach to the world around me – the questions I ask and the way that I answer them. I am grateful for their many invaluable insights, and it is my fervent hope that this manuscript reflects their influence on me.

Finally, I am thankful to my friends and family, without whose love and support I would never have been able to complete this work.

Neither Force, Nor Will

> The judiciary, on the contrary, has no influence over either the sword or the purse; no direction either of the strength or of the wealth of the society; and can take no active resolution whatever. It may truly be said to have neither FORCE nor WILL, but merely judgment; and must ultimately depend upon the aid of the executive arm even for the efficacy of its judgments.
>
> Alexander Hamilton[1]

In June of 2007, the United States Supreme Court handed down its decision in *Parents Involved in Community Schools v. Seattle School District No. 1* (2007; hereafter *Parents*). In his plurality opinion, Chief Justice John Roberts declared that the Fourteenth Amendment requires school districts to assign students "to the public schools *on a nonracial basis*" (*Parents* 2007, 84) and therefore prohibits the race-conscious programs in the Seattle and Louisville school districts designed to promote racial diversity. Sharon Browne, the principal attorney for the parents challenging the school's assignment process, called the rulings "the most important decisions on the use of race since *Brown v. Board of Education*" (Rosen 2007) and predicted that, like *Brown*, the Court's ruling would have "a tremendous impact on the rest of the nation" (Lambert 2007).

However, several legal scholars disagreed: "School districts are going to continue to do indirectly what they tried to do directly," said Peter H. Schuck of the Yale Law School. "There will be another layer of bureaucracy," said David A. Strauss, University of Chicago law professor, "but I wouldn't expect a large-scale retreat from what public schools have tried" (Rosen 2007). According to Michael Klarman of the University of Virginia School of Law, "Just as *Brown* produced massive resistance in the South and therefore had little impact on desegregation for a decade, this decision is going to be similarly inconsequential … I don't think the court decision will make much difference either way" (Rosen 2007).

---

[1] *The Federalist 78.*

The juxtaposition of these viewpoints is particularly interesting because they differ, not only in their predictions regarding the effects of the *Parents* ruling, but also in their understandings regarding the effects of the *Brown* ruling. The traditional view of the Court's decision in *Brown v. Board of Education* (1954) suggests that "*Brown* really did transform society by stopping *de jure* segregation, and without *Brown*, schools would look very different" (Rosen 2007).[2] This view suggests the Supreme Court is a powerful institution, capable of promoting justice and protecting minority rights by enforcing its interpretation of the Constitution. However, the view of *Brown* advanced by Schuck, Strauss, and Klarman is consistent with a very different understanding of the Court. This alternate view depicts the Court as an almost powerless institution that may issue high-minded rulings but lacks the power to ensure that those rulings are actually implemented. These competing views weave in and out of the most prominent histories of the Supreme Court and the most prevalent scientific examinations of the Court's influence.

The U.S. Supreme Court was described as a relatively weak institution even before it existed. Arguing for the merits of the new federal Constitution in *The Federalist 78*, Alexander Hamilton assured his readers that "the judiciary, from the nature of its functions, will always be the least dangerous branch to the political rights of the Constitution; because it will be least in a capacity to annoy or injure them ..." According to Hamilton, a

> simple view of the matter suggests several important consequences. It proves incontestably, that the judiciary is beyond comparison the weakest of the three departments of power; that it can never attack with success either of the other two; and that all possible care is requisite to defend itself against their attacks. (Hamilton 1961)

Hamilton's description of a weak judiciary was borne out during the early years of the Supreme Court. The justices were originally forced to "ride circuit," travelling from town to town to hear lower-court cases. The first chief justice, John Jay, resigned from the Court to become governor of New York. When President Adams offered Jay a second appointment as chief justice, Jay refused, citing his poor health and arguing that the Court lacked "the energy, weight, and dignity which are essential to its affording due support to the national government" (Johnston 1890–93, 285). In the 1803 case *Marbury v. Madison*, Chief Justice John Marshall, speaking for the Court, strategically retreated in the face of political opposition from the president and Congress. Although *Marbury v. Madison* is widely credited with establishing the power of judicial review (Epstein and Walker 1995, 73; Irons 2006, 107), some scholars describe the Court as capitulating in this case, illustrating "the relative impotence of the federal judiciary during the first decades of the constitutional order" (Graber 1999, 28; see Graber 1998).

---

[2] Quoting David J. Armor, professor at the George Mason University School of Public Policy.

Examples of the Court's impotence extend well past the founding era. In *Worcester v. Georgia* (1831), the Court ruled that Indian tribes were "dependent domestic nations" with rights to lands they had not voluntarily ceded to the United States. President Andrew Jackson defied the ruling and ordered federal troops to expel Creek, Chickasaw, and Cherokee tribes from their lands (Irons 2006, 111). Chief Justice Taney's extremist proslavery decision in *Dred Scott v. Sandford* (1857) is said to have "doomed his cause to ultimate defeat" (Irons 2006, 177). In the decades that followed, the Court was subjected to court-packing, court-shrinking, and jurisdiction-stripping as the Radical Republicans worked to keep the justices in line (Irons 2006, 183; *Ex Parte McCardle* 1869).

These extreme tactics foreshadowed the famous showdown between the Court and President Franklin Roosevelt over New Deal economic policy. After the Court invalidated many of Roosevelt's most ambitious legislative enactments, the New Deal Democrats began to contemplate various methods of reversing the Court. The most popular proposal was a plan to "pack the Court" by allowing President Roosevelt to appoint a new justice for every sitting member over seventy and one-half years of age. The plan would have allowed Roosevelt to appoint as many as six new justices; however, the proposal never came to fruition. Once again, the Court retreated, reversing its previous rulings, yielding to the elected branches, and initiating a so-called "Constitutional Revolution" (Irons 2006, 316; *West Coast Hotel v. Parrish* 1937; *National Labor Relations Board v. Jones & Laughlin Steel Corp.* 1937).

Each of these events from the Court's history involves distinct institutional dynamics: in *Marbury*, the Court strategically ducked a controversial issue; in *Worcester*, the Court failed to implement its ruling; in *Scott* and *Lochner*, the Court was overwhelmed by political backlash. Yet, despite the differences between these cases, each one suggests the Court's underlying lack of power. In classrooms and textbooks, these episodes are frequently explained as evidence that Hamilton was correct: The courts control neither the "sword" nor the "purse."

In contrast, some scholars argue that the courts have been particularly influential during specific periods of American history. For example, Steven Skowronek describes the period between the end of Reconstruction and the beginning of the New Deal as an era of "courts and parties," during which judges played a major role in shaping public policy, especially economic regulation (Skowronek 1982). During the so-called *Lochner* Era at the beginning of the twentieth century, the Supreme Court struck down a wide range of state and federal laws aimed at regulating labor conditions and expanding the role of the government. Although the New Deal eventually reversed most of these policy choices, reformers were not successful at overcoming judicial will for almost half a century. This long period of judicial activism may indicate that the Court is only effective at postponing policy change, but even the act of delaying may shape the form a policy will eventually take. For example, by striking down the programs enacted during Roosevelt's first one hundred days, the Court radically altered the economic policies that eventually emerged during the 1930s (Gillman 1993).

Scholars also frequently depict the 1950s, 60s, and 70s as a period during which the Supreme Court had an unusually strong influence over policy creation. The Warren and Burger Courts issued numerous groundbreaking opinions in a broad range of policy areas, purportedly altering public policy regarding race relations, civil liberties, criminal law, prison administration, political representation, environmental regulation, privacy, and the role of religion in public life. More recently, the Rehnquist Court has made significant changes in the structure of American politics through its revival of federalism. By breathing new life into the Tenth and Eleventh Amendments and reducing the scope of the previously all-encompassing Commerce Clause, the Court has fundamentally altered the role of state governments and limited the ability of the federal government to impose its will in several policy domains (see *United States v. Lopez* 1995; *Seminole Tribe v. Florida* 1996; *Alden v. Maine* 1999; *United States v. Morrison* 2000).

Many of these decisions have been extremely controversial, often provoking strong public reaction and raising objections that the Court is undermining democratic self-government (Waldron 1999, 332; Tushnet 1999; Kramer 2004). The classic articulation of these concerns is Alexander Bickel's "counter-majoritarian difficulty." According to Bickel, the fundamental difficulty with the role of courts in the American political system is the concern that judicial review "thwarts the will of representatives of the actual people of the here and now; it exercises control, not in behalf of the prevailing majority, but against it. That, without mystic overtones, is what actually happens ... it is the reason the charge can be made that judicial review is undemocratic" (Bickel [1962] 1986, 16–7). If Court rulings always prevail over majority will, then Bickel's difficulty undoubtedly poses a serious dilemma for those hoping to reconcile judicial review with democratic principles; if, however, the Court is effectively powerless, then Bickel's difficulty is little more than a hypothetical concern.

It is unlikely that either of these perspectives accurately depicts the Supreme Court's power. Surely the Court's rulings have significant consequences at least occasionally; otherwise lawyers and interest groups would not invest so much time, money, and energy into bringing cases before the Court and trying to win them. However, in a system of government designed to balance political power among separate branches, it would be surprising if the Court were always totally successful at altering policy. The true nature of the Court's power most likely lies somewhere between these extremes. The question then becomes, when is the Supreme Court powerful and when is it not? What factors distinguish those situations in which the Court is resisted, undermined, or simply ignored from those in which the Court initiates sweeping political and social change?

I will argue that the Supreme Court's ability to alter the behavior of state and private actors is dependent on two factors: the institutional context of the

Court's ruling and the popularity of the ruling. The probability of the Court successfully exercising power increases when:

(1) its ruling can be directly implemented by lower state or federal courts; or
(2) its ruling cannot be directly implemented by lower courts, but public opinion is not opposed to the ruling.

However, the probability of the Court successfully exercising power decreases when:

(3) its ruling cannot be directly implemented by lower courts and public opinion is opposed to the ruling.

The distinction between Supreme Court rulings that can and cannot be implemented by lower courts is a critical point that has gone unnoticed by other scholars of judicial politics. In contrast with most prominent empirical studies of judicial power, I find that the Supreme Court has extensive power to alter the behavior of state and private actors in a wide range of politically salient issue areas.

My study is limited to an examination of the Supreme Court's power to alter behavior when it attempts to do so. My goal is not to advance a normative argument regarding this power. Undoubtedly, my empirical argument has normative implications; my findings may inspire and embolden those who support judicial activism in order to promote particular political agendas, while simultaneously disheartening proponents of judicial restraint who decry the antidemocratic nature of the Court's power. However, my primary objective is to set the stage for this debate by asking how powerful the Court is and, more importantly, under what conditions it is more or less powerful.

My examination of Supreme Court power proceeds as follows: In Chapter 2, I explore competing theories of Court power and present a new theory of the conditions that determine whether the Court can successfully exercise power. In Chapter 3, I discuss the methodological issues involved in measuring judicial power and selecting cases for examination. I then apply the methods developed in Chapter 3 to test my theory on four types of Supreme Court rulings: those rulings that face little popular opposition and can be directly implemented by lower courts (Chapter 4), those rulings that face strong popular opposition and can be directly implemented by lower courts (Chapter 5), those rulings that face little popular opposition and cannot be implemented by lower courts (Chapter 6), and those rulings that face strong opposition and cannot be implemented by lower courts (Chapter 7). In Chapter 8, I summarize my findings and consider their implications for the future study of the Supreme Court and its role in American politics.

2

When Courts Command

Armed with the power of determining the laws to be unconstitutional, the American magistrate perpetually interferes in political affairs ... Scarcely any political question arises in the United States that is not resolved, sooner or later, into a judicial question.

Alexis De Tocqueville[1]

By itself, the [Supreme] Court is almost powerless to affect the course of national policy.

Robert Dahl[2]

In this chapter, I begin by developing a working definition of judicial power. I then consider several competing theories of Supreme Court power and the expectations these theories offer about the Court's ability to influence other actors. Most empirical studies of Court power find that the Court is a relatively weak political institution, but numerous positive theorists insist that it should be capable of altering behavior, at least in certain limited circumstances. Next, I suggest several factors that may influence whether the Court is successful at exercising power based on well-established findings from the judicial politics and electoral politics literatures. Specifically, I will argue that the probability of the Court exercising power depends on the institutional context and popularity of its rulings. Finally, based on these factors, I present a new theory of Supreme Court power.

DEFINING JUDICIAL POWER

Understanding when the Supreme Court is capable of exercising power requires a clear definition of judicial power. I base my definition on Jack Nagel's conception of power in his seminal work on the subject: "A power relation, actual

---

[1] Tocqueville (1945, 279–80).
[2] Dahl (1957, 293).

6

or potential, is an actual or potential causal relation between the preferences of an actor regarding an outcome and the outcome itself" (1975, 29). Adapting this definition to the judiciary, I define judicial power as an actual or potential causal relation between the preferences of a judge regarding the outcome of a case and the outcome itself. I take as assumed, as is common in the judicial politics literature, that Supreme Court justices are political actors with policy preferences – that is, preferences regarding policy outcomes – and Court decisions are reflections of those preferences (Segal and Spaeth 2002).[3] Therefore, the Supreme Court is powerful if there is an actual or potential causal relation between the Court's rulings and the outcome of those rulings. Evaluating the Court's power in a particular ruling requires an understanding of the preferences expressed by the Court in the ruling and the outcomes of that ruling.

In this study, I examine the behavior outcomes of Supreme Court rulings. Behavior outcomes are the behaviors of state and private actors that the Court intends to alter through its rulings. Other authors have referred to these outcomes as "behavior responses" (Canon and Johnson 1999, 25). As previous studies have noted, "for a judicial policy to have general effect in the political system, the behavior of many individuals must be affected" (Johnson 1967, 171). However, identifying what behavior outcomes the Court intended to alter in a particular ruling is not always a simple matter. Often the Court demands a specific change in behavior, but also intends other behavior changes as indirect consequences of its decision. In other situations, the Court may be indifferent or even completely opposed to the possible indirect consequences of its rulings.

To illustrate this point, consider the Court's intentions in issuing rulings in the following three cases: *Mapp v. Ohio* (1961), *Roe v. Wade* (1973), and *United States v. Lopez* (1995). In *Mapp*, the Court ruled that illegally obtained evidence must be excluded from a criminal trial. In *Roe*, the Court held that women have a constitutionally protected right to obtain an abortion. In *Lopez*, the Court invalidated the Gun-Free School Zones Act, which made it a crime to carry a gun near a school. In each of these cases, the Court's ruling could be directly implemented by lower courts; in order to conform to the Court's preferences in these rulings, lower court judges need merely refrain from admitting illegally obtained evidence, convicting defendants under abortion statutes, and convicting defendants under the Gun-Free School Zones Act. However, the language of the Court's opinions in these cases, as well as simple common sense, suggests that the Court held very different preferences regarding the indirect consequences of these rulings.

---

[3] A large and growing literature on judicial decision making argues that Supreme Court justices may act strategically in certain situations in order to achieve their policy preferences (i.e., Epstein and Knight 1998). Consequently, the Court's decisions may reflect their choice in a strategic game rather than their genuine policy preferences. For example, the Court may temper its rulings to avoid provoking a reaction from a hostile Congress. Regardless, when the Court does strike down a law, the ruling undoubtedly reflects the justices' preference relative to the status quo.

In *Mapp*, the majority specifically stated that "the purpose of the exclusionary rule 'is to deter – to compel respect for the constitutional guarantee in the only effective available way – by removing the incentive to disregard it'" (*Mapp v. Ohio* 1961, 656). In other words, the Court intended for the exclusion of illegally obtained evidence to deter the police from conducting illegal searches in the first place. In this case, the Court not only intended for its ruling to have indirect effects, the realization of these indirect effects was the primary goal of the decision.

In *Roe*, the Court clearly intended to grant women increased access to legal abortions; however, the Court did not necessarily intend to increase the number of abortions in the same way that it intended to stop illegal searches. One might expect the frequency of legal abortions to increase after *Roe*, but this was not necessarily the Court's intent. Nor is there any reason to believe the Court intended its ruling to have other indirect consequences that have been attributed to it, such as changes in adoption and crime patterns. In this case, the Court was not primarily interested in, and was possibly apathetic toward, the indirect consequences of its ruling.

The possible consequences of the Court's ruling in *Lopez* include the increased presence of guns near schools, as well as an increase in gun-related violence near schools; however, it goes without saying that the justices did not intend to increase gun violence. In this case, the Court obviously hoped that the possible indirect effects of its ruling would be mitigated by other factors, such as the deterrent effects of state and local gun laws.

In order to evaluate the Supreme Court's power, I will consider both the direct and indirect effects of its decisions. I will pay special attention to indirect effects when it is clear that the Court intended to alter behavior through the indirect consequences of its rulings. I will pay little or no attention to the unintended consequences of the Court's rulings, because a proper test of judicial power evaluates the causal relationship between the preferences of judges and the outcomes of their decisions; expecting the Supreme Court's rulings to also have unintended consequences would be a perverse test of its power.

Although I will assess both the direct and indirect effects of the Court's rulings, the reader should carefully consider what standards are appropriate for evaluating the Court's power in each issue area. Consider, for example, the Supreme Court's reapportionment rulings. In *Baker v. Carr* (1962), the Court decided that the constitutionality of legislative apportionment schemes could be challenged in federal court. Two years later, in *Reynolds v. Sims*, the Court ruled that "the Equal Protection Clause requires that a State make an honest and good faith effort to construct districts, in both houses of its legislature, as nearly of equal population as is practicable" (1964, 577). The *Reynolds* decision was an expression of the Court's preferences regarding the apportionment of state legislative districts; the Court preferred that the legislatures of the fifty states create legislative districts with as nearly equal population as practicable. The most direct behavior outcome expected in the *Reynolds* decision is the equal apportionment of legislative districts after the ruling. If there was an actual causal relationship between the *Reynolds* decision and equal reapportionment of state legislative districts, then the Supreme Court successfully exercised power over this behavior outcome.

However, focusing on the most direct behavior outcomes of a ruling may severely limit our understanding of Supreme Court power. First, such a focus might set the bar too low when evaluating whether the Court has exercised power by ignoring its failure to indirectly alter behavior patterns through its rulings. Second, limiting my examination to the direct effects of the Court's rulings may obscure the full extent of the Court's power. For example, some scholars claim that supporters of the *Baker* and *Reynolds* decisions were hoping that "[r]eapportionment would lead the way to liberal social legislation" (Rosenberg 2008, 293). One could argue that causing the reapportionment of legislative districts is not the critical test of the Court's power in these rulings. Instead, one must examine whether or not the reapportionment of state legislatures caused future legislatures to enact different types of legislation. If many advocates of reapportionment – and possibly the justices themselves – intended to indirectly alter the behavior of future state legislatures, then the behavior of these future legislatures may be a more relevant and interesting behavior outcome to examine.

On the other hand, placing too much emphasis on indirect consequences may set the bar too high for evaluating Supreme Court power. Just because some proponents of a ruling hoped it would produce particular downstream consequences does not mean that the Court's power depends on the manifestation of those consequences. As it turns out, the *Baker* and *Reynolds* decisions did cause the reapportionment of legislative districts, and this reapportionment appears to have produced substantially different legislation in state legislatures, but it may not have been the "liberal social legislation" for which some had hoped.[4] This finding does not indicate that the Court failed to implement its preferences; it suggests that those who supported the reapportionment rulings in hopes of such legislation miscalculated the likely behavior of the new legislators.

Behavior outcomes should not be confused with attitude outcomes. Attitude outcomes are the attitudes in the general public or among specific subsets of the population regarding the topic of a Supreme Court ruling. The Supreme Court may have the power to alter these attitudes in various ways. This role for the Court is sometimes described as education (Bickel [1962] 1986, 26; Funston 1975, 810; Rostow 1952, 208), legitimation (Black 1960; Dahl 1957, 293; Wasby 1970, 14), persuasion (Feeley 1973), or "appealing to men's better nature" (Bickel [1962] 1986, 26). Other scholars have subdivided the concept of attitude outcomes into "acceptance decisions," changes in "intensity of a person's attitude," and changes in "people's regard for the court making the decision" (Canon and Johnson 1999, 24), but at its core this function

---

[4] See *infra* Chapter 6, Reapportionment section.

involves the Court causing a change in attitudes as a result of its ruling (Wasby 1970, 15).

For example, much of the Court's opinion in *Reynolds* reads like a persuasive essay on the merits of equal apportionment designed to persuade readers without enlisting legal principles. In his opinion for the Court, Chief Justice Warren appeals to history, fairness, and common sense as much as precedent, text, and original intent:

> A citizen, a qualified voter, is no more nor no less so because he lives in the city or on the farm. This is the clear and strong command of our Constitution's Equal Protection Clause. This is an essential part of the concept of a government of laws, and not men. This is at the heart of Lincoln's vision of 'government of the people, by the people, [and] for the people.' The Equal Protection Clause demands no less than substantially equal state legislative representation for all citizens, of all places as well as of all races. (*Reynolds v. Sims* 1964, 568)

It is at least plausible that the Court may intend to alter public attitudes as well as behavior through rulings such as this one; if it is successful at doing so, then its rulings may have indirect effects on behavior as these changed attitudes begin to alter policy through the normal political process.

A reliable examination of the effects of Supreme Court rulings on attitude outcomes would face numerous methodological problems. Such a study would require survey data on topics directly related to Court rulings in each issue area under consideration. Because these rulings may have different effects on different demographic, geographic, or ideological groups, these surveys would need to be sensitive to "the structure of opinion regarding a ruling" among these different groups (Franklin and Kosaki 1989, 753). Moreover, given the complexity of public opinion toward the Supreme Court and its rulings, persuasive opinion data would need to describe enduring levels of "diffuse support" for the Court itself, "specific support" for actions taken by the Court, and the relative intensity of support (see Caldeira and Gibson 1992; Hoekstra 2000; Marshall 1989; Mondak 1992). The issue of intensity is particularly important when investigating Court rulings, because the Court probably exercises its power over attitude outcomes by employing its diffuse support to enlist specific support or by discouraging opposition to a law by conferring legitimacy on it. An evaluation of whether these dynamics occur would require a measure of public opinion sensitive enough to distinguish between a respondent's agreement with a ruling, support for a ruling, and acceptance of a ruling. Finally, because attitude outcomes inherently involve attitude change, such a study would require time series surveys with all of these components.[5]

By pointing out the difficulties involved in measuring the effects of Court rulings on attitude outcomes, I do not mean to imply that such an investigation would be impossible. In fact, many studies persuasively argue that the Court does possess the power to alter attitude outcomes (see Hoekstra 2000;

---

[5] I am indebted to Professor Paul Brace for his thoughtful analysis of the many methodological issues involved in studying attitude outcomes.

Mondak 1990; 1991; 1992). I only wish to emphasize that the many complications involved in such a study would require different methodological strategies than those required for a study of behavior outcomes.

Perhaps more importantly, there is no theoretical reason to believe that the Court's power over attitude outcomes would operate in the same (or even a similar) manner as its power over behavior outcomes. The Court may have different levels of power over these two types of outcomes in different situations, and the factors influencing whether the Court is able to exercise power in a particular case may be different depending on which type of outcome is considered. Although an examination of the Court's power to alter attitude outcomes would be an interesting and valuable project, the dynamics governing this type of power are probably fundamentally different than those governing the Court's power to alter behavior outcomes; therefore, such an examination would best be conducted in a separate study. For these reasons, I will explore only those factors that influence whether the Supreme Court is successful at altering behavior outcomes.

COMPETING THEORIES OF SUPREME COURT POWER

Despite a broad consensus among legal experts, politicians, the media, and the public that the Supreme Court is extremely powerful, most political scientists who study the Court's capacity to implement policy change emphasize its relative limitations. If the Court were a relatively weak institution, incapable of exerting its will against the elected branches of government, it would not be especially surprising. As Robert Dahl argued in his seminal article on the Court, "if the Court did in fact uphold minorities against national majorities, as both its supporters and critics often seem to believe, it would be an extremely anomalous institution from a democratic point of view" (Dahl 1957, 291). Why would the legislative and executive branches tolerate a countermajoritarian institution overruling their decisions? It seems much more likely that the elected branches would use the Court as an instrument of their own power by staffing it with political allies, reaping the benefits of enhanced legitimacy when the Court is in agreement, and simply ignoring or subverting the Court when it is not. Dahl's view of the Court suggests two expectations for Court behavior: The Court will rarely disagree with the elected branches, and, when it does, it will be incapable of implementing its own preferences.

Dahl describes the first expectation as a natural by-product of the judicial appointment process. Because Supreme Court justices have what Dahl describes as a high turnover rate and must be appointed by the president and confirmed by the Senate, "the policy views dominant on the Court are never for long out of line with the policy views dominant among the lawmaking majorities of the United States" (Dahl 1957, 285). Although the Court may resist change when its policy preferences lag behind those of the lawmaking majority, as was the case in the New Deal, the Court will eventually be the loser in these confrontations (Funston 1975). In addition, the legislative and executive branches can constrain judicial power by overriding judicial interpretation of statutory law, threatening to "pack the Court," removing federal court jurisdiction, or influencing the Court through the solicitor general (Rosenberg 2008, 14). These factors led Robert McCloskey and Gerald Rosenberg, writing three decades apart, to agree: "Supreme Court decisions, historically, have seldom strayed far from what was politically acceptable" (McCloskey 1960, 224; Rosenberg 2008, 13). Consequently, judicial power is usually used to legitimize the "lawmaking majority" and enforce a national consensus against policy outliers (Dahl 1957, 294–5; Funston 1975, 810; Whittington 2007, 105, 152).

Despite the many tools at the disposal of Congress and the president to influence the Court, once in a while the justices will disagree with the "lawmaking majority." When this occurs, Dahl's second expectation suggests that elected officials will simply ignore or undermine the Court's ruling. Because, according to this view, the legislative and executive branches hold all true power (both "the purse" and "the sword"), their policy choices will ultimately prevail. After reviewing situations in which the Court has invalidated legislation less than four years after it was enacted, Dahl concludes that Congress and the president are almost always successful at overruling the Court's decisions. Fears that judicial review contradicts principles of democratic self-government are irrelevant because "lawmaking majorities generally have had their way" (Dahl 1957, 291).

This view, sometimes called the "Constrained Court" view, is joined by a chorus of other judicial scholars. Stuart Scheingold argues that "direct deployment of legal rights in the implementation of public policy will not work very well, given any significant opposition" (1974, 117). Courts can "be of some use in implementing policies that apply principally to government agencies"; however, "[w]ithout the support of the real power holders ... litigation is ineffectual and at times counterproductive. With that support, litigation is unnecessary" (Scheingold 1974, 130). Although Robert McCloskey believes that the Supreme Court can have a significant impact on policy change, he cautions that "[t]he Court's greatest successes have been achieved when it has operated near the margins rather than in the center of political controversy, when it has nudged and gently tugged the nation rather than trying to rule it" (McCloskey 1960, 229). Others doubt the Court's ability to produce substantial changes without support from non-judicial actors when issuing decisions regarding federalism (Nagel 2001) and religious expression in public schools (Abel and Hacker 2006).

Gerald Rosenberg echoes the view of a "Constrained Court" in his book, *The Hollow Hope*. Studying the outcomes of the Supreme Court's decisions in *Brown v. Board of Education* and *Roe v. Wade*, Rosenberg finds that "U.S. courts can almost never be effective producers of significant social reform. At best, they can second the social reform acts of the other branches of government" (Rosenberg 2008, 422). Instead, courts tend to "act as 'fly-paper,'" drawing resources away from direct political action, while "providing only an illusion of change" (Rosenberg 2008, 427). Like Dahl, Rosenberg identifies two major constraints that limit the ability of courts to influence social policy: a lack of judicial independence and the judiciary's "lack of implementation powers" (Rosenberg 2008, 420).[6]

Similarly, Donald Horowitz notes "the impotence of the courts" and contends that the Court is ill-advised to attempt social policy engineering because "[t]he new burdens assumed by the courts seem to raise questions of capacity whatever the issue area or the target environment, or at least they raise these questions in ways that crosscut issue areas and target environments" (Horowitz 1977, 264, 273). In a review of the Supreme Court's influence on policy and social change, Lawrence Baum summarizes the literature as follows: "Implementation of the Court's policies is far from perfect; judges and administrators often balk at carrying out its rulings. The available evidence also indicates that the Court is quite constrained in its ability to secure social change" (Baum 2003, 177).

Not all scholars depict the Supreme Court as powerless to alter social outcomes, and some have fervently attacked this view (see Schultz 1998).[7] Many judicial politics scholars claim that the Court is a powerful institution, capable of producing significant social and political reform. Although these studies offer valuable insights into the nature and scope of judicial power, none of them attempt a comprehensive, scientific examination of the Court's ability to influence behavior. For example, Jonathan Casper (1976) simply extends Dahl's analysis of the number of federal laws declared unconstitutional by the Court, and Roger Handberg and Harold Hill (1980) build on this study by incorporating statistics on the Court's use of statutory interpretation. Michael McCann (1999) and William Lasser (1988) both utilize theory building and interpretive historical analysis to support their arguments, but they do not conduct rigorous empirical analyses of particular cases.[8] In his book, *Rights at Work*, McCann (1994) offers a persuasive empirical examination of judicial power, but he limits his study to judicial action in pay equity cases. Similarly, Douglas Reed (2001) describes the significant effects of judicial action on financing public education and Thomas Keck (2009) provides a persuasive rejoinder to Rosenberg's account of same-sex marriage lawsuits, but these studies are limited to these particular issue areas.

---

[6] Rosenberg originally suggests three potential constraints on judicial power: the limited nature of constitutional rights, the lack of judicial independence, and the judiciary's lack of implementation powers. However, after conducting his case studies, Rosenberg concludes that the first constraint, "the lack of established legal precedents, was weak" (Rosenberg 2008, 337).

[7] Rosenberg has created a Web site with an extensive list of reviews of *The Hollow Hope*, as well as a thoughtful response to the most common criticisms of his work. http://www.press.uchicago.edu/books/rosenberg/. Although my work is in large part an attack on his central thesis, I agree with several of his points in this response.

[8] Even McCann is willing to "concede the central insight ... that federal courts alone rarely 'cause' significant social change in predetermined directions" (1999, 67).

Most observers of the Supreme Court either implicitly assume or explicitly state that the institution is either very powerful or very weak. This dichotomy is problematic for several reasons. First, any absolute claim about the Court's power – that it is omnipotent or impotent – is undoubtedly inaccurate. Second, any relative statement about the Court's power – that it is more or less powerful than previously thought – depends on a consensus of conventional thought, and, as I discussed in Chapter 1, no such consensus exists. Conflicting claims about judicial power extend back to the Founding; therefore, almost any description of the Court's power could be portrayed as surprisingly strong or surprisingly weak when compared to one of these conflicting claims. Third, most studies of judicial power ignore the difference between failures in judicial implementation and failures in implementation in general (Baum 2003, 176). Consequently, some deficiencies in the Court's power may be unrelated to the nature of judicial politics. Fourth, emphasizing a black-and-white depiction of the Court as either dynamic or constrained obscures more interesting and practical puzzles of judicial power. Once the extreme claims have been eliminated from consideration, the critical question is not "How powerful is the Court?" but rather, "Under what conditions is the Court powerful?"

An extensive literature on judicial implementation and impact addresses this question, but these studies have failed to generate a consensus on factors related to the successful exercise of Court power. For example, Stephen Wasby's seminal work, *The Impact of the United States Supreme Court: Some Perspectives*, concludes that "We are not ready, it seems, for a broad 'theory of impact.' We can only move *toward* such a theory" (1970, 245–6). Wasby then lists 136 hypotheses related to the impact of court rulings, including compliance, political reaction, public opinion, interest group actions, and subsequent judicial, legislative, and executive behavior.

Despite a lack of consensus, this literature proposes several factors that might affect whether Supreme Court rulings successfully alter behavior. Frequently suggested factors include the closeness of the vote on the Court (Wasby 1970, 245), the clarity or ambiguity of the Court's opinion (Bradley 1993; Canon and Johnson 1999, 72–4; Wasby 1970, 245), and the attitudes of society, local communities, or particular officials toward the policy or the Court (Birkby 1966; Canon and Johnson 1999, 75–8, 83–6; Nagel 2001; Reich 1968; Skolnick 1966, 227; Wasby 1976, 217–8). Others claim that the Court exercises power by exploiting gridlock in the legislative process in order to impose its own policy preferences when its political opposition lacks the power to overturn its decisions (Eskridge 1991a; 1991b; Eskridge and Ferejohn 1992; Ferejohn 2002). Although these studies certainly do not claim that Court rulings are always implemented, they generally suggest that the Court can successfully alter behavior under certain circumstances (see Johnson 1967).

Many recent studies of judicial power have refined Dahl's depiction of a weak Court by claiming that judicial power – and specifically judicial review – is politically constructed (Clayton and Pickerill 2006; Frymer 2003; Gillman 2002; Graber 1993; 2005; Lovell 2003; McMahon 2004; Peretti 1999;

Pickerill and Clayton 2004; Whittington 2007; see Keck 2007). Following Dahl, these studies argue that "the Supreme Court is integral to, rather than distinct from, the national political regime" (Pickerill and Clayton 2004, 236). Therefore, "when a justice decides in accordance with her personal values, she is vindicating those values deliberately 'planted' on the Court by a recently elected president and Senate" (Peretti 1999, 5). These studies claim that law-makers often invite courts to create policy in situations when judicial action will advance the interests of the governing regime. As a result, some judicial rulings may be implemented because the governing regime supports the Court's policy.

Specifically, elected officials may welcome the exercise of judicial power in five situations: (1) "regime enforcement," in which the Court brings outlier states into line with a national consensus (Graber 1993, 39; 2005; Whittington 2005, 586; 2007, 105–20; see Funston 1975; Klarman 1996; Rosen 2006); (2) "division of labor," in which the Court addresses issues unworthy of attention from Congress or the president (Whittington 2007, 121; see Dahl 1957; Johnson and Canon 1984); (3) "overcoming gridlock," in which the Court resolves issues about which the other branches cannot agree (Eskridge 1991a; 1991b; Eskridge and Ferejohn 1992; Ferejohn 2002; McCloskey 1960; Whittington 2007, 124–34); (4) "blame avoidance," in which the Court orders a policy that elected officials want but cannot endorse without losing popular support (Graber 1993, 43; Lovell 2003; Whittington 2007, 136–7); and (5) "legitimation," in which the Court lends its institutional legitimacy to policies enacted by other government actors (Dahl 1957, 294; Murphy 1964, 17; Whittington 2007, 152–7; see Black 1960; Funston 1975; Miller 1968).

Taken together, the last half-century of scholarship on judicial power suggests that the Court is highly constrained. Based on this work, the Supreme Court appears incapable of exercising power over behavior outcomes in most situations (Dahl 1957; Horowitz 1977; Nagel 2001; Rosenberg 2008; Scheingold 1974). The exceptions to this finding generally fall into one of the five categories summarized in the previous paragraph. Only a few studies argue for a more expansive view of judicial power, and these have been limited in scope or empirical rigor. A tougher test of Supreme Court power would consciously avoid those circumstances in which the Court might wield marginal influence, and instead evaluate the Court's power on a broader scale.

FORMING A NEW THEORY OF SUPREME COURT POWER

I base my theory of Supreme Court power on the rather modest suggestion that the Court is an *implementer-dependent* institution. By that, I mean that the Court, like most political authorities, must rely on other political actors to implement its decisions. In addition, also like other authorities, the likelihood of its decisions being implemented will depend on the institutional and social context of the decision. In some contexts the relevant political actors charged with implementation will tend to follow the Court's instructions; in other contexts they will not. The same could be said of Congress and the president. For example, presidential decisions that must be implemented by military actors will almost always be followed, whereas those decisions that require the cooperation of Congress or independent agencies tend to face more resistance. In this section, I consider well-established findings related to the behavior of judges and elected officials in order to identify institutional and social conditions under which the relevant political actors tend to implement the Court's decisions.

Despite the paucity of comprehensive studies of judicial power, there have been numerous studies of lower-court compliance with Supreme Court rulings. The dominant view in this literature contends that federal district courts and courts of appeals are highly responsive to Supreme Court rulings (Gruhl 1980; Johnson 1987; Songer 1987; Songer et al. 1994; Songer and Sheehan 1990; Spriggs 1997), as are state courts (Benesh and Reddick 2002; Hoekstra 2005; Songer 1988). These findings are consistent with common understandings of a lower-court judge's motivations. Such judges do not like to see their rulings overturned, hope to be promoted to a higher court, have been socialized into the legal culture, and are under strong pressure from their professional community to adhere to the judicial hierarchy.

The finding that lower courts are highly responsive to Supreme Court rulings suggests that the Court may be especially successful at implementing policy changes through these courts. Consequently, the probability of the Court exercising judicial power should be greater in issue areas in which lower courts can directly implement policy change. Issue areas in which lower courts control policy implementation constitute a significant portion of the Court's work. These issue areas are distinct because the Supreme Court's orders can be implemented by political actors located directly below the Court in the judicial hierarchy; therefore, I will call issue areas in which lower courts can implement policy change *vertical issues*.

Vertical issues usually involve the Court identifying a group of potential criminal defendants as constitutionally immune from criminal prosecution. For example, the Court has declared that abortionists and online pornographers cannot be convicted in lower courts.[9] The lower courts can directly implement this ruling by simply not convicting defendants charged with these crimes. In addition, the Court may rule that all criminal defendants are immune from a certain type of criminal prosecution. For example, the Court ruled at one point that no person could be sentenced to the death penalty.[10] Or the Court may combine these methods by, for example, ruling that no minor can be sentenced to the death penalty.[11] Vertical issues also include cases in which the Court announces new rules regarding civil law or the administration of lower courts. For example, in *Plaut v. Spendthrift Farm, Inc.* (1995), the Court struck down

[9] *Roe v. Wade* (1973), *Ashcroft v. ACLU* (2004).
[10] *Furman v. Georgia* (1973).
[11] *Roper v. Simmons* (2005).

part of the Securities and Exchange Act that required lower courts to reopen federal civil actions.

The critical commonality among these cases is that the Court's direct instructions can be implemented by lower-court judges without the aid of non-court actors. This distinction may be difficult to see in some cases, but it is vital for understanding the implementation of Supreme Court decisions. Consider *Miranda v. Arizona* (1966; hereafter *Miranda*), in which the Court ruled that statements arising from custodial interrogation of a criminal defendant could not be admitted into evidence unless the police had informed the defendant of his constitutional rights. Although some might interpret this ruling as a directive to the police, it was not. Instead, it was an order for lower-court judges to exclude any statements from the defendant obtained by the police unless the police first read the warnings. Undoubtedly, the Court hoped and anticipated that as an indirect consequence of the ruling the police would start reading Miranda warnings. The justices did not need the willing cooperation of police officers in order to implement the decision; they only needed the cooperation of lower-court judges. The police, in an effort to obtain more convictions, would then respond to this new situation and start reading the warnings. As long as rulings in vertical issues are implemented by the lower courts, their impact should extend well outside the courtroom.

On the other hand, in numerous Supreme Court cases implementation is controlled by non-court government actors, such as lawmakers, administrative agencies, individual bureaucrats, city councils, school boards, and law enforcement officials.[12] Because policy changes in these issue areas must be implemented by officials outside the judicial hierarchy, I call these issue areas *lateral issues*. It is important to emphasize that lateral issues do not merely refer to cases in which Congress or the president must implement policy. Usually, these instructions are directed to state or federal agencies, such as the Social Security Administration and the U.S. Postal Service, or local officials, such as public school boards and school administrators.[13] However, sometimes the orders are aimed directly at the president, Congress, and state legislators.[14] The critical commonality among these cases is that in each of these rulings the Supreme Court is dependent on non-court actors to implement policy change.

---

[12] I divide all Supreme Court rulings into orders directed at lower courts and orders directed at other non-court, government actors. One might claim that the Court also issues orders to non-government, private actors. For example, the Court might order a business monopoly to break up, certain defendants to go to jail, or black and white school children to go to school together. However, for each order the Court issues, it relies on a government actor to implement the decision: The police and administrative agencies must oversee and enforce the monopoly breakup; the lower court must sentence the defendant to jail; the school officials must assign black and white children to the same school. Therefore, as I divide the universe of Supreme Court cases, every case falls into one of these two categories.

[13] See *Lamont v. Postmaster General* (1965), *Califano v. Westcott* (1972), *Brown v. Board of Education* (1954), and *Engel v. Vitale* (1962).

[14] See *Baker v. Carr* (1962), *Immigration and Naturalization Service v. Chadha* (1983), and *Clinton v. New York* (1998).

Sometimes the Court will attempt to utilize lower courts to implement rulings in lateral issue areas; for example, the Court used federal district judges to supervise the desegregation of schools in the South following its ruling in *Brown v. Board of Education*. Ultimately, however, the Court was dependent on the school officials to implement the ruling because the schools did not rely on the lower courts for action the way a prosecutor does.

Non-court government officials are relatively insulated from the Court's influence and may not share the same professional norms that judges do. Consequently, they may be in a position to pursue their own policy preferences (Johnson and Canon 1984, 83). These other government actors may also be under strong political pressure from superiors or electoral constituents to ignore the Court (Johnson and Canon 1984, 89–92). If elected officials are primarily concerned with reelection, they will probably defy the Court in these situations (Mayhew 2004). In addition, attacking the Court as an anti-democratic institution may, in and of itself, offer electoral benefits (Engel 2009). Finally, if there were a total consensus against the Court's ruling, there may simply be no one to bring a complaint to court protesting violation of the Supreme Court's ruling. These factors suggest that the Court may face more difficult obstacles when issuing orders to non-court actors.

These factors also imply that elected officials may be unwilling or unable to resist the Court when it is supported by strong public opinion. If the ruling is popular, there may be numerous sympathetic officials eager to implement the decision regardless of how isolated they are from the Court's influence; if the ruling is supported by public opinion, there will be little political cost to comply and little electoral incentive to resist.

These generalizations about the nature of judicial power and electoral incentives suggest that whether the Supreme Court is successful at exercising power is influenced by the institutional context of the issue at stake and the popularity of the Court's ruling. The probability of the Court altering behavior outcomes increases when the Court issues a ruling in a vertical issue area or when the Court issues a ruling that does not face strong public opposition in a lateral issue area. Conversely, the probability of the Court altering behavior outcomes decreases when the Court issues a ruling that does face strong public opposition in a lateral issue area. In the next chapter, I develop methodologies to evaluate this theory.

3

Judging the Court

Does anybody know ... where we can go to find light on what the practical consequences of these decisions have been? ... I don't know to what extent these things can be ascertained. I do know that, to the extent that they may be relevant in deciding cases, they ought not to be left to the blind guessing of myself and others only a little less informed than I am.

Justice Felix Frankfurter[1]

In this chapter, I develop methodologies for evaluating Supreme Court power. First, I consider the complicated issue of strategic Court action and problems it poses for my examination of Court power. Second, I identify principles that will guide my case selection process in order to make reliable causal inferences about the relationship between Court rulings and outcomes. Next, I borrow methodology developed by David Mayhew in order to identify "important" Supreme Court rulings, which will be a critical component of my case selection process. Then, I explain how I will measure the dependent variable (behavior outcomes) and independent variables (the institutional context of the issue and political opposition to the Court's rulings). Finally, I present a summary of the hypothesis I will test regarding Supreme Court power.

THE PROBLEM OF STRATEGIC COURT ACTION

To this point, I have defined judicial power as an actual or potential causal relation between the preferences of a judge or judges regarding the outcome of a court ruling and the outcome itself. However, proving the existence of a *potential* causal relationship in the context of Supreme Court rulings is extremely difficult. If the Court does not act, it is impossible to determine with any degree of certainty what might have happened if it had. The Court's power can be measured when it chooses to issue a ruling, but we cannot assume that its

[1] Frankfurter (1954) as quoted in Miller and Scheflin (1967).

power would operate in the same manner had it issued rulings in those situations when it did not.

This concern is especially problematic for my study because Supreme Court rulings are not randomly assigned; the justices very carefully choose which cases they want to hear. They may strategically choose to take action only in circumstances in which they know they will be successful. If so, the Court may be substantially more successful at altering behavior outcomes when it chooses to act than it would be in situations when it does not. If the Court does act strategically in this manner, we should observe a high degree of success when the Court issues a ruling; any observed Court failures would indicate that the justices either miscalculated their odds of success or decided the strategic interest was overridden by other concerns. This high degree of observed success would greatly exaggerate the Court's potential power because we would not observe the many instances in which the justices wanted to act but knew they would fail. Consequently, the possibility of strategic action by the Court poses a significant threat to the validity of my findings.

To some degree, the possibility of strategic action by the Court is an unavoidable problem. There is simply no way to know for certain how successful the Court would have been in situations when it did not act, nor is it possible to convincingly establish which cases might be examples of strategic avoidance by the Court. This problem is so pervasive that most empirical studies of judicial power have failed to address the strategic issue at all. In fact, measuring political power by examining those cases in which actors attempt to change policy is a common practice in political science; for example, numerous scholars measure the ability of presidents to pass their legislative proposals without considering the infinite universe of policies that presidents could have proposed but did not (see Edwards 1980, Ch. 1; 1985, 667–85; Wayne 1978, 168–72).

From a substantive perspective, the scope of the Court's power is much more interesting in those cases when it chooses to act than in those cases in which it avoids an issue. Understanding why the Court succeeds or fails when it attempts to change policy has more direct implications for explaining policy outcomes than does an explanation of what the Court might have done. In addition, there is reason to doubt that the Court acts strategically. As my study will show, there are numerous cases in which the Court fails to implement policy change. This means that if the Court's strategic goal is to issue only those orders the justices believe will be implemented, they are either not very good at this task or this interest frequently gives way to other concerns.

Most importantly, the potential threat of strategic Court action biasing my findings is mitigated by the nature of my research question. Were I trying to establish how powerful the Court is on some absolute or relative scale, strategic action by the Court might make it appear as if the Court were more powerful than it really is; however, establishing the degree of the Court's power is not my primary goal. Instead, my goal is to identify factors that influence the probability of the Supreme Court successfully exercising power. If strategic action by the Court inflates my estimation of the Court's power, it should not bias the results of my study unless the Court's strategic action is correlated with the factors I identify as influencing the Court's power.

For example, suppose I find that the Court is more successful when issuing rulings in vertical issues than in lateral issues. Based on this finding, I will conclude that this institutional factor increases the probability of the Court successfully altering behavior. The skeptical reader might disbelieve my claim because I have not established that this factor would influence the probability of the Court altering behavior in those cases when it chose not to act. However, in order to doubt my findings based on this concern, the reader must make two assumptions: first, that the Court does in fact act strategically in this manner and, second, that the Court's strategic action is correlated with this institutional factor. In order for strategic Court action to bias my findings, there must be some plausible reason why the Court's strategic action inflates the observed success rate in vertical issues but not in lateral issues. In other words, the reader must believe that the Court is better able to predict when it will be successful in vertical issues than in lateral issues or that the Court cares more about the strategic interest in vertical issues than it does in lateral issues. I cannot claim that these alternate explanations are totally implausible; instead, I simply argue that these explanations are less convincing than my explanation: that the Court actually is more powerful in vertical issues.

Although there are several reasons to discount the threat posed by the possibility of strategic Court action, any conclusions about the Court's power in situations when it chooses to act cannot be confidently applied to situations when it does not. At best, understanding the nature of the Court's actual power only allows us to make educated guesses about the nature of the Court's potential power. Accordingly, this study will only test the power of the Supreme Court to alter behavior when it attempts to do so; stated another way, I will only measure the *actual* causal relation between the justices' expressed preferences and behavior outcomes.

EVALUATING SUPREME COURT POWER

A critical element in establishing the existence of Supreme Court power in a particular case is verifying that any relationship between the Court's ruling and a behavior outcome is causal. In the preceding chapter, I identified five limited functions often attributed to the Court: regime enforcement, division of labor, overcoming gridlock, blame avoidance, and legitimation. Each of these functions suggests a reason why Supreme Court rulings and behavior outcomes might be correlated and yet lack a causal connection. For example, if the Court is enforcing the policy preferences of the dominant regime against a policy outlier, the Court's decision and the behavior outcome will be correlated, but the Court's decision did not cause the behavior outcome. Instead, it was the dominant political regime, through action or the threat of action, that actually exercised power against the policy outlier. Consequently, merely proving a correlation between the Court's decision and a behavior outcome in such a case will not provide a definitive measure of Supreme Court power.

To avoid this problem, I have taken the following steps:

(1) In order to avoid cases in which the Court is simply legitimizing the dominant political regime, I examine only those cases in which the Court invalidates a law or practice;

(2) In order to avoid cases of "regime enforcement" against outlier states, I examine only cases in which the Court invalidates a federal law or a state law common to a significant number of states. In addition, I examine only cases in which the court invalidates a policy on constitutional grounds. This criterion eliminates cases in which the Court invalidates state laws on the basis of federal statutes;

(3) In order to avoid "division of labor" cases, in which the Court deals with issues unworthy of attention in the legislative branch, I examine only especially important Supreme Court rulings.[2]

Avoiding cases of "blame avoidance" and "overcoming gridlock" is a more complicated task. Whittington's (2005; 2007) descriptions of both situations are very similar. In a blame avoidance case, the Court issues a ruling that elected officials want but cannot support without losing popular support. In a gridlock case, the Court issues a ruling that is "consistent with regime commitments," that is, a ruling that elected officials want but cannot accomplish due to institutional barriers. Whittington places some of the most famous cases of the last half-century into these two categories, including *Brown v. Board of Education, Baker v. Carr, Roe v. Wade, Texas v. Johnson,* and *United States v. Lopez.*

Unfortunately, cases in either of these categories are nearly impossible to identify with any certainty. Establishing that a case was an example of blame avoidance requires proving that legislators held undisclosed policy preferences at odds with those of their constituents. Of course, if the elected officials were unwilling to reveal their true preferences to their own constituents for fear of electoral reprisal, it is unlikely that social scientists will be able to reliably measure these true preferences. Ultimately, the question may be unanswerable and largely irrelevant. Whether or not elected officials wanted the policy, they were either unwilling or unable to implement it on their own.

Verifying that the Court was achieving results consistent with the commitments of the dominant political regime is also extremely complicated. First of all, Whittington's conception of which political coalition is dominant at any particular time, which he borrows from Stephen Skowronek (1997), is intricate and controversial. Second, even if everyone could agree that dominant political regimes existed at particular times, establishing what exactly its "regime commitments" were is no simple task. Was the New Deal regime still dominant during the 1970s? If so, was the pro-choice agenda consistent with New Deal regime commitments? These are complicated questions with no definitive

---

[2] See Appendix I for a more detailed discussion of my case selection process.

answers; and even if these claims could be confidently verified in a particular case, the dominant regime's failure to implement one of its own policy commitments would raise serious doubts about either the coalition's dominance or the importance of the policy commitment.

William Eskridge (1991b) offers a different conception of overcoming gridlock. In his view, the Court exploits gridlock to impose its own policy preferences, independent of the dominant political regime. According to this view, the Court is only able to exercise power when policy questions arise in the "gridlock interval," meaning that neither supporters nor opponents of a particular policy command large enough super-majorities to reverse the Court. Although he focuses on the Court's power to exploit gridlock through statutory interpretation, the same logic could be applied to invalidations on constitutional grounds. In fact, when the Court invalidates a law as unconstitutional, it can only be reversed by passing a constitutional amendment. Due to the difficulty of amending the Constitution, the gridlock interval and hence the Court's power, is even larger for constitutional issues than for statutory interpretations. These instances are easier to identify, but because this view attributes a causal role to the Court, there is no need to avoid these cases in my analysis. In fact, by definition, every time the Court invalidates a law on constitutional grounds, it is overcoming gridlock in the sense that the law's opponents lacked the political strength to stop the passage of the law, and the law's proponents lack the political strength to overturn the Court's decision through constitutional amendment. In the few cases when the latter succeed in doing so, the Court quickly concedes the dispute. This understanding of "overcoming gridlock" is exactly the type of power I wish to evaluate. Consequently, I do not eliminate these cases from my study.

My final case list includes fifty-nine Supreme Court cases.[3] I then group these cases into twenty-seven issue areas for investigation. For each issue area, I code two independent variables and one dependent variable. The case identified by my case selection process are listed in Table 3.1, grouped by issue area and the coding of the independent variable.

The first independent variable is the institutional context of the issue at stake, coded as either vertical or lateral. Vertical issues are those in which the Court can directly implement policy through lower-court judges. All other cases are coded as lateral issues. Cases are only coded as vertical issues if lower courts are an inherent part of the process that the Supreme Court intends to reform. These cases usually involve the Court protecting a particular class of defendants from criminal prosecution. For example, the abortion rulings are coded as a vertical issue because lower courts are inherently involved in convicting defendants under abortion statutes. On the other hand, school desegregation is coded as a lateral issue because the operation of segregated schools does not inherently involve lower courts. Lower courts may attempt to inject themselves into this policy area by issuing injunctions or, in extreme

---

[3] See Appendix I.

cases, holding school officials in contempt; however, lower courts are not normally involved in the assignment of students to public schools.

The second independent variable in my model is the strength of the Court's political opposition. Measuring the Court's opposition is a difficult task because so many different political actors may be in a position to thwart the Court's will depending on the issue area. Opposition from local school boards might hinder implementation of *Brown* but be irrelevant for the implementation of *Baker v. Carr*. In addition, even for a specific ruling, it is not always clear which political actors may be critical for implementation, and successful Court action may depend on support from several different actors.

In order to avoid these measurement problems, I rely on the broadest possible measure of political opposition: public opinion surveys. Using surveys from a variety of sources, I classify individual Court rulings as popular, mixed, or unpopular. For those issues involving policy traditionally managed at the state or local level, I also investigate public opinion at the regional level. In several issue areas (abortion, school desegregation, and school prayer), although the Court's decisions were supported by a narrow majority in national polls, they faced strong opposition in a number of southern states. Because my theory predicts different results for popular and unpopular rulings in lateral issues, for these issue areas I consider variation in the Court's efficacy in different regions.

The dependent variable for my study is the successful exercise of Supreme Court power. As described previously, I define the Court as powerful if there is an actual causal relation between the Court's ruling and the outcome of that ruling. For each issue area identified through my case selection process, I conduct a brief case study to determine whether or not the Court successfully exercised judicial power through its rulings in that area. For each of these studies, I employ a longitudinal design strategy to evaluate the causal relationship between the Court's ruling and a change in a quantitative measure of a behavior outcome.

A longitudinal study measures trends in a particular variable over time. For each case category, I identify a behavior outcome and collect as many measures of that variable as possible both before and after the Supreme Court's ruling. In some cases, only a single measurement of the behavior outcome before and after the Court ruled is available; in other cases, measurements are available for many years before and after the ruling. For each issue area, I evaluate whether the Court's ruling caused a sudden change in the expected trend of the behavior outcome. I measure this change by estimating *behavior conformity* in each issue area; the estimate of behavior conformity is an estimate of the Court's causal effect on the most relevant behavior outcome in that issue area. The higher the conformity, the more powerful the Court was in that issue area; 100 percent conformity implies that the Court's ruling caused the behavior outcome of interest to conform perfectly to the Court's preferences.

In some contexts, the estimate of conformity reflects compliance with the court's ruling by government actors. For example, in the school prayer issue

TABLE 3.1. *Supreme Court Cases by Issue Area*

Chapter 4: Popular Vertical Issues

1. Religious Freedom Restoration Act
   City of Boerne v. Flores
2. The Pentagon Papers Case
   New York Times v. United States

Chapter 5: Unpopular Vertical Issues

1. Abortion
   Roe v. Wade
   Hodgson v. Minnesota
   Planned Parenthood v. Casey
   Sternberg v. Carhart
2. Flag Desecration
   Texas v. Johnson
   United States v. Eichman
3. Obscenity
   Redrup v. New York
   Jenkins v. Georgia
   Denver Area Consortium v. F.C.C.
   Reno v. A.C.L.U.
   Ashcroft v. A.C.L.U.
4. The Exclusionary Rule
   Rios v. United States
   Mapp v. Ohio
   Chimel v. California
5. Miranda Warnings
   Miranda v. Arizona
   Dickerson v. United States
6. Warrantless Eavesdropping
   Berger v. New York
   United States v. U.S. District Court
7. Right to Counsel
   Gideon v. Wainwright
   United States v. Wade
8. Capital Punishment
   Furman v. Georgia
   Booth v. Maryland
   Atkins v. Virginia
   Ring v. Arizona
   Roper v. Simmons
9. Free Press in the Courtroom
   Nebraska Press Association v. Stuart
   Richmond Newspapers v. Virginia
10. Sovereign Immunity
    Seminole Tribe v. Florida
    Alden v. Maine
11. The Gun-Free School Zones Act
    United States v. Lopez

Chapter 6: Popular Lateral Issues

1. Reapportionment
   Baker v. Carr
   Reynolds v. Sims
   Wesberry v. Sanders
   Avery v. Midland County
2. Majority-Minority Legislative Districts
   Miller v. Johnson
   Bush v. Vera
   Shaw v. Hunt
3. The Legislative Veto
   INS v. Chadha
4. Public Aid to Religious Schools
   Lemon v. Kurtzman
   Aguilar v. Felton
   Grand Rapids v. Ball
5. Affirmative Action in College Admissions
   Regents v. Bakke
   Gratz v. Bollinger
6. Religious Publications at Public Universities
   Rosenberger v. Virginia
7. Minimum Wage for State Employees
   National League of Cities v. Usery
8. *Bush v. Gore*
   Bush v. Gore

Chapter 7: Unpopular Lateral Issues

1. School Desegregation
   Brown v. Board of Education I
   Bolling v. Sharpe
   Brown v. Board of Education II
   Green v. County School Board
2. School Prayer
   Engel v. Vitale
   Wallace v. Jaffree
   Lee v. Weisman
   Santa Fe Ind. School Dist. v. Doe
3. Censorship in Public Education
   Board of Education v. Pico
   Tinker v. Des Moines Ind. Sch. Dist.
4. Minority Set-Aside Programs
   Adarand Constructors v. Pena
5. Congressional Exclusion
   Powell v. McCormack
6. The Brady Bill
   Printz v. United States

area, I measure the frequency of school prayer in public schools before and after the Court's ruling in *Engel v. Vitale*. The estimate of behavior conformity in the school prayer issue area is the degree to which school teachers complied with the Court's ban on school prayer in public schools. One hundred percent conformity in this issue area would indicate that 100 percent of school teachers stopped conducting school prayer in public schools after the ruling.

In other contexts, the estimate of behavior conformity reflects the behavior of private actors conforming to the behavior one would expect once they enjoy the effective exercise of rights granted by the Court. For example, in the abortion issue area I measure the difference in the frequency of abortion in states where abortion was legal before *Roe v. Wade* and in states where abortion was illegal before *Roe v. Wade*. The estimate of behavior conformity in the abortion issue area is the degree to which the behavior of women seeking abortions in the former group of states conformed to the behavior of women in the latter groups of states. One hundred percent conformity in this issue area would indicate that after *Roe v. Wade*, women sought abortions at the same rate in these two groups of states.

Because selecting the most relevant behavior outcome in each issue area is a somewhat subjective process, I make two estimates of behavior conformity in each issue area: a conservative estimate and a generous estimate. When making a conservative estimate of conformity, I use the behavior outcome that is least advantageous for my theory of judicial power. When making a generous estimate of conformity, I use the behavior outcome that is most advantageous for my theory. In most cases, this means that the higher possible estimate will be coded as the generous estimate of behavior conformity; however, because I predict low conformity when the Court issues unpopular lateral rulings, the lower estimate will be coded as the generous estimate in these issue areas.

As an example, when the Court ruled in *Baker v. Carr* (a popular ruling in a lateral issue area), it ordered state legislatures to apportion their state and congressional legislative districts as equally as possible. Consequently, if this ruling had a causal effect on the behavior of these legislatures, then we should observe a sudden drop in the malapportionment of state and congressional legislative districts following the Court's ruling. If no change in inequality between districts occurred after the Court's ruling, I would code the behavior conformity as 0 percent. If the inequality is completely eradicated, I would code the conformity as 100 percent. If there are two ways to measure the change in inequality, I would code the larger estimate as the generous behavior conformity and the smaller estimate as the conservative behavior conformity.

SUMMARY OF HYPOTHESES

I can now state my theory of Supreme Court power using the terminology I have developed in this chapter: The probability of the Court achieving high behavior conformity when it issues a ruling will increase when one of the following conditions has been met:

(1) The Court issues a ruling in a vertical issue area, or

(2) The Court issues a popular ruling in a lateral issue area.

However, the probability of the Court achieving high behavior conformity will decrease when:

(3) the Court issues an unpopular ruling in a lateral issue area.

In Chapters 4, 5, 6, and 7, I test this theory by conducting longitudinal studies in a variety of issue areas in order to evaluate the power of the U.S. Supreme Court.[4]

---

[4] This hypothesis can be formally stated as $\mu_i = \alpha + \beta_1 \, vertical + \beta_2 \, lateral \times popularity + \varepsilon$, where μ is the average behavior conformity, α is a constant, *vertical* is an indicator variable for vertical issues, and *lateral* $\times$ *popularity* is an interaction term between an indicator variable for lateral issues and a popularity variable, β_1 and β_2 are coefficients for the effects of these three variables, and ε is the unobserved disturbance. The popularity variable is a trichotomous indicator variable, taking on the value 1 if less than 30% of respondents in national public opinion polls oppose the Court's ruling, the value 0 if more than 70% of respondents oppose the Court's ruling, and the value 0.5 otherwise. The results of my regression analyses are reported in Appendix VI.

4

Popular Vertical Issues

> At the foundation of our civil liberties lies the principle that denies to government officials an exceptional position before the law and which subjects them to the same rules of conduct that are commands to the citizen.
>
> Justice Louis D. Brandeis[1]

In this chapter, I examine popular vertical issues – cases in which the Supreme Court issued a popular ruling that could be implemented by lower-court judges. Because these rulings faced little public opposition and could be directly implemented by judicial actors, few scholars would be surprised to find that these rulings had a strong effect on the behavior of state and private actors. My case selection process identifies only two cases that meet these criteria. In each of these cases, I find that the Court's rulings successfully altered the behavior of the relevant actors.

THE RELIGIOUS FREEDOM RESTORATION ACT

Although some Supreme Court rulings involve a few isolated events crammed into a relatively short time period, other legal issues span centuries of interrelated political conflict. A prime example of such a sprawling legal issue is the Religious Freedom Restoration Act of 1993 (RFRA). The explanation of why Congress passed RFRA must begin more than a century earlier with the passage of the Fourteenth Amendment to the U.S. Constitution. Following the end of the Civil War in 1865, Congress quickly approved and the states ratified the Thirteenth Amendment prohibiting the practice of slavery. Although President Andrew Johnson believed this step was sufficient to resolve the political questions following the five-year armed struggle, Radical Republicans in Congress disagreed. In the 1866 midterm elections, these Radical Republicans promised to enact a fourteenth amendment that would define national citizenship and protect the rights of the newly freed slaves. The Radical Republicans won

---

[1] *Burdeau v. McDowell* (1921).

landslide victories in 1866 and approved the proposed amendment, which was ratified in 1868.

Section 1 of the Fourteenth Amendment defined national citizenship and placed several restrictions on state governments. Section 1 prohibited the states from "abridg[ing] the privileges or immunities of citizens of the United States ... depriv[ing] any person of life, liberty, or property, without due process of law ... [or] deny[ing] to any person within its jurisdiction the equal protection of the laws" (U.S. Constitution, amend. XIV). These three requirements have come to be known respectively as the Privileges and Immunities Clause, the Due Process Clause, and the Equal Protection Clause. Sections 2, 3, and 4 dealt with unrelated matters; however, thanks in part to their mistrust of southern state governments, the Radical Republicans included in the amendment a Section 5, which provided that "[t]he Congress shall have power to enforce, by appropriate legislation, the provisions of this article" (U.S. Constitution, amend. XIV). This passage is called the Enforcement Clause of the Fourteenth Amendment. Two years later the Fifteenth Amendment was ratified, which prohibited states from denying the right to vote based on race, color, or previous condition of servitude. This amendment included a similar Enforcement Clause.

Less than a decade after the ratification of the Fourteenth Amendment, Congress passed the Civil Rights Act of 1875, which created criminal penalties for denying "the full enjoyment" of public accommodations and conveyances to any person. The law was designed to criminalize the common practice of racial segregation in hotels, trains, and buses in the states of the former Confederacy. Congress based its authority for passing such a law on the Fourteenth Amendment Enforcement Clause; however, in the *Civil Rights Cases* (1883), the Supreme Court invalidated the act as exceeding Congress's authority. The Court ruled that the Enforcement Clause in Section 5 did not authorize Congress to pass "general legislation upon the rights of the citizen, but corrective legislation, that is, such as may be necessary and proper for counteracting such laws as the States may adopt or enforce, and which, by the amendment, they are prohibited from making or enforcing ..." (*Civil Rights Cases* 1883, 13–4).

In spite of this very limited interpretation of Section 5, later Courts acknowledged that the Enforcement Clause is "a positive grant of legislative power" to Congress (*Katzenbach v. Morgan* 1966) that may intrude into "legislative spheres of autonomy previously reserved to the states" (*Fitzpatrick v. Bitzer* 1976, 445). In fact, the Supreme Court has upheld numerous prohibitions on literacy tests and other voting restrictions based on the Fifteenth Amendment Enforcement Clause (*South Carolina v. Katzenbach* 1966; *Katzenbach v. Morgan* 1966).

Although the Fourteenth Amendment was originally designed to protect the rights of newly freed slaves, during the twentieth century its role in constitutional law was expanded into many other issue areas. Until the 1920s, the many restrictions in the Bill of Rights were only applicable to the federal government. For example, the First Amendment states that "Congress shall make no law" abridging the freedoms of religion, speech, assembly, or the press. This passage had always been interpreted as limiting only the federal government, not the state governments. Accordingly, the federal Constitution did not prohibit the states from abridging these freedoms, nor any others protected in the Bill of Rights.

This situation changed in a series of cases between the 1920s and 1960s. In these cases, the Supreme Court ruled that most provisions in the Bill of Rights were among the "fundamental personal rights and 'liberties' protected by the Due Process Clause of the Fourteenth Amendment from impairment by the States" (*Gitlow v. New York* 1925, 666; see *Near v. Minnesota* 1931; *Palko v. Connecticut* 1937; *Cantwell v. Connecticut* 1940; *Mapp v. Ohio* 1961; *Gideon v. Wainwright* 1963; *Malloy v. Hogan* 1964; *Benton v. Maryland* 1969). In other words, the Due Process Clause "incorporated" the Bill of Rights and made its restrictions applicable to state governments, as well as the federal government. Therefore, if a state passed a law abridging one of the provisions in the Bill of Rights, the law could be attacked as violating that provision as made applicable to the states through the Due Process Clause of the Fourteenth Amendment. The theory of incorporation has greatly expanded the role of the federal courts and has prompted some of the most controversial decisions of the last century. In fact, many of the cases studied in this project – the Eighth Amendment's prohibition on capital punishment, the Fourth Amendment's requirement of the exclusionary rule, and the First Amendment's protection of flag desecration – are technically Fourteenth Amendment cases because they involve state laws instead of federal laws.

The Court "incorporated" the Free Exercise Clause in the 1940 case *Cantwell v. Connecticut*. In that case, the Court ruled that the "fundamental concept of liberty embodied in [the Fourteenth] Amendment embraces the liberties guaranteed by the First Amendment" (303), including the free exercise of religion. Five years later the Court emphasized, in no uncertain terms, that the liberties protected by the First Amendment enjoy "a sanctity and a sanction not permitting dubious intrusions ... Only the gravest abuses, endangering paramount interests, give occasion for permissible limitation" (*Thomas v. Collins* 1945, 530). Although this high standard made it difficult for the government to regulate religious activity, such regulation could be "justified by clear public interest, threatened not doubtfully or remotely, but by clear and present danger" (*Thomas v. Collins* 1945, 530).

The Court clarified the requirements of the Free Exercise Clause in *Sherbert v. Verner* (1963, hereafter *Sherbert*). Adell Sherbert, a member of the Seventh-Day Adventist Church, was fired from her job in a textile mill because her religion precluded her from working on Saturdays. When she applied for unemployment compensation, her claim was denied because she had refused to accept "suitable work when offered by the employment office or the employer" (*Sherbert* 1963, 401). In evaluating her claim, the Court held that the regulation of religious conduct could only be justified if it "represents no infringement by the State of her constitutional rights of free exercise, or [if] any incidental burden on the free exercise of appellant's religion may be justified by a 'compelling state interest in the regulation of a subject within the State's constitutional power to regulate'" (*Sherbert* 1963, 403). Based on this standard of interpretation, the Court in *Sherbert* ruled that the Employment Security Commission's rejection of Sherbert's claim was unconstitutional and ordered it to pay her unemployment benefits.

For the next twenty-seven years, the Court used the test announced in *Sherbert* to evaluate most claims made under the Free Exercise Clause, but this practice was brought to an abrupt halt in *Employment Division v. Smith* (1990, hereafter *Smith*). The facts in *Smith* were remarkably similar to those in *Sherbert*. Alfred Smith and Galen Black were members of the Native American Church and employees at a drug rehabilitation clinic. They were fired for ingesting peyote, a powerful hallucinogen, as required by their religious beliefs. When they applied for unemployment compensation, their request was denied because the reason for their dismissal was considered work-related misconduct. They challenged the denial of their benefits as restricting the free exercise of their religious beliefs. In evaluating their claims, the Court declined to employ the *Sherbert* test and instead ruled that "the right of free exercise does not relieve an individual of the obligation to comply with a 'valid and neutral law of general applicability on the ground that the law proscribes (or prescribes) conduct that his religion prescribes (or proscribes)'" (*Smith* 1990, 879 quoting *United States v. Lee* 1982, 263). Based on this new standard, the Court found that the First Amendment did not "require exemptions from a generally applicable criminal law" (*Smith* 1990, 884) and, therefore, did not prohibit the state from denying unemployment benefits to Smith and Black.

In response to the *Smith* ruling, Congress passed the Religious Freedom Restoration Act. The purpose of the act was "to restore the compelling interest test as set forth in *Sherbert v. Verner* ... [and] to provide a claim or defense to persons whose religious exercise is substantially burdened by government" (*City of Boerne v. Flores* 1997, 515; hereafter, *Boerne*). RFRA prohibited any federal or state government actor from "substantially burden[ing]" a person's free exercise of religion, even if the burden resulted from a rule of general applicability, unless the government could demonstrate that the burden "(1) is in furtherance of a compelling governmental interest; and (2) is the least restrictive means of furthering that compelling governmental interest" (*Boerne* 1997, 515). Because the Free Exercise Clause was incorporated through the Fourteenth Amendment, Congress relied on its Fourteenth Amendment enforcement power to enact the law.

The first test of RFRA's constitutionality involved a dispute over the expansion of the St. Peter Catholic Church in Boerne, Texas. Because the church was too small to accommodate the size of the congregation, the Archbishop of San Antonio, P. F. Flores, gave permission for the building to be expanded. A few months later, the Boerne City Council authorized the creation of a historic preservation district. Under the ordinance, the city's Historic Landmark Commission must approve any construction plans affecting historic landmarks or buildings in the district (*Boerne* 1997, 512). When the Archbishop applied for a building permit to begin construction, the city denied the application, claiming that the church was part of the historic district. The Archbishop filed suit in federal court, relying in part on RFRA as one basis for relief from the city's denial of the building permit. After winning in the district court and losing in the Fifth Circuit Court of Appeals, the city appealed the case to the U.S. Supreme Court. The Court ruled in favor of the city, holding RFRA unconstitutional because it exceeded Congress's power under the Enforcement Clause and "contradict[ed] vital principles necessary to maintain separation of powers and the federal balance" (*Boerne* 1997, 536).

No national polls have directly asked respondents about the Religious Freedom Restoration Act or the Supreme Court's invalidation of the Act; however, just a month after the Court's ruling in *Boerne*, two polls were conducted asking respondents if Americans have too much, too little, or the right amount of religious freedom. Both polls indicated that the vast majority of respondents believed that the amount of religious freedom Americans have is "about right"; only 21 percent of respondents said that Americans had "too little" religious freedom.[2] These polls suggest that, at the very least, there was no strong public outcry against the Court's invalidation of RFRA after its ruling. However, because the ruling could be directly implemented by lower courts, I expect it to have had a strong effect on behavior outcomes irrespective of public opinion.

The Court's ruling in *Smith* established a more stringent test for applying the Free Exercise Clause, which would presumably make it more difficult for claimants in free exercise cases to win in the lower courts. Congress's passage of the Religious Freedom Restoration Act was undoubtedly intended to return the lower courts to the pre-*Smith* status quo. In *Boerne*, the Court expressed a preference for lower courts to return to the *Smith* standard. If each of these actions had the intended consequence on lower-court behavior and if the quality of free exercise claims filed during this time period remained constant, we should observe a shift in the behavior of lower-court judges corresponding to the preferences of the most recent change in policy.

The most extensive research done on the response to these decisions in the U.S. Courts of Appeals was conducted by James Brent (1999; 2003).[3] In two separate studies, Brent examined 392 free exercise cases decided by the courts of appeals between 1987 and 2000 and coded the decisions as either favorable or unfavorable to free exercise claimants. Brent's findings from these two studies are combined and reported in Table 4.1. In the three years prior to the *Smith* decision, about 32 percent of claimants in free exercise cases won favorable rulings in the courts of appeals. After *Smith*, that

---

[2] See Appendix II for survey information and citations.
[3] See Adamczyk et al. (2004) for an analysis of federal district court responses to the *Smith* decision and RFRA. Adamczyk et al. demonstrate that the pattern of free exercise claimant success in the district courts after these events mirrored the pattern in the U.S. Courts of Appeals, but the authors do not examine federal district court response to the *Boerne* decision.

TABLE 4.1. *Success of Free Exercise Claimants, 1987–2000*

	Three Years Prior to *Smith*	Between *Smith* and RFRA	Between RFRA and *Boerne*	Three Years after *Boerne*
% Won	31.8	20.0	32.4	20.6
(# Won)	(27)	(21)	(23)	(27)
% Lost	68.2	80.0	67.6	79.4
(# Lost)	(58)	(84)	(48)	(104)

Note: Data based on survey of 392 free exercise cases in U.S. Courts of Appeal between 1987 and 2000, as reported in Brent (1999; 2003).

percentage dropped to 20 percent. Following Congress's passage of RFRA in 1993, the percent of successful free exercise claimants increased to 32.4 percent, almost the exact same rate as before *Smith*. Assuming that the Court's intention in issuing the *Boerne* ruling was to reverse the effect of RFRA and return to the post-*Smith*, pre-RFRA status quo, perfect behavior conformity would mean that the success rate for free exercise claimants would return to approximately 20 percent. This is exactly what occurred after *Boerne*; only 20.6 percent of post-*Boerne* claimants were successful.[4] Consequently, the conservative estimate of behavior conformity to the *Boerne* ruling is 95.2 percent $[(32.4 - 20.6)/(32.4 - 20) = 0.952]$.

Another way to examine lower-court compliance with the *Boerne* decision is to simply identify cases in which the courts of appeals ruled in favor of a claim under RFRA after *Boerne*. Brent identifies two such instances (2003, 563).[5] Both of these cases involved issues of federal rather than state law. Because the Enforcement Clause involves Congress's power to alter state laws, these courts held that the Supreme Court had declared RFRA unconstitutional as it related to state laws but not federal laws. Assuming these cases constitute noncompliance, which is a dubious claim (see Blatnik 1998), the courts of appeals complied with the *Boerne* ruling in 129 of the 131 post-*Boerne* free exercise cases. Therefore, the generous estimate of behavior conformity to the *Boerne* ruling is 98.5 percent (129/131 = 0.985).

Each of these studies relies on the assumption that the merits of free exercise claims are constant over time. However, if potential claimants respond to actions taken by the Court or Congress by filing claims they would have otherwise not filed or failing to file claims they would have otherwise filed, this assumption is inaccurate. For example, "qualitative research suggests that following the *Smith* decision and prior to RFRA (May 1990 – November 1993),

[4] Brent conducted a logit regression analysis of free exercise claimant success on an indicator variable for post-*Boerne* cases and several other control variables (2003, 566). The effect of the Boerne decision fell just short of conventional levels of statistical significance (p = 0.062).

[5] *Sutton v. Providence St. Joseph Medical Center* (1999) and *Christians v. Crystal Evangelical Free Church* (1998).

minority religions were less likely to turn to the courts for protection and that the most marginal and frivolous cases were not brought before the court" (Adamczyk et al. 2004, 242; see Richardson 1995, 254). Adamczyk et al. find that "the rate of free exercise cases initiated by religious groups dropped by over 50 percent immediately after *Smith*" (2004, 242). If potential free exercise claimants responded to the *Boerne* ruling by filing fewer claims, then the decline in successful claimants would be counterbalanced by a decline in total claims. The rate of success would then remain fairly constant, suggesting that the effect of the ruling was negligible, when in fact the Court had significantly affected both case outcomes and the behavior of potential claimants. In other words, to the degree that these potential claimants are anticipating changes in lower-court action, my findings actually underestimate the effect of the Court's ruling in *Boerne*.

The Court in *Boerne* added another chapter to a long and complicated history of conflict over the rights of the individual versus the state, the power of the federal government versus state governments, and the authority of Congress to define the meaning of constitutional rights versus that of the Court itself. The ruling had swift and significant effects on the resolution of free exercise claims in the United States and probably had sweeping indirect effects on numerous other areas of legal conflict that involve the Enforcement Clause, not all of which have yet been realized. By altering the behavior of lower courts in this issue area, the Supreme Court was able to successfully exercise power by causing relevant actors to comply with its preferences.

THE PENTAGON PAPERS CASE

The *Boerne* ruling dealt a serious blow to congressional authority; three decades earlier, the Court issued a challenge to executive power in the infamous Pentagon Papers case. The creation of the Pentagon Papers was ordered by Secretary of Defense Robert McNamara. By April of 1967, McNamara had become thoroughly convinced that the American strategy in Vietnam was doomed to failure. He began advocating a new strategy of negotiation with the North Vietnamese, but his ideas found little sympathy within the Johnson administration, and McNamara began to feel increasingly marginalized. Possibly out of his desire to understand how the United States had become entangled in a draining, complicated war on the other side of the world or possibly because he hoped to preserve the record for history's sake, McNamara ordered the creation of an "encyclopedic history of the Vietnam War," written entirely within the Department of Defense (Rudenstine 1996, 19–20).

Officially titled "History of U.S. Decision Making Process on Vietnam Policy," the massive study was eventually bound into forty-seven volumes containing more than 7,000 pages, more than 2.5 million words, and weighing sixty pounds (Rudenstine 1996, 2). The report, informally known as the Pentagon Papers, chronicled the actions of the Truman, Eisenhower, Kennedy, and Johnson administrations that contributed to the United States' involvement in the bloody Vietnam conflict. Among the extensive collection of information, the report contained evidence that administration officials had intentionally escalated hostilities in Vietnam to an extent never revealed to the public. "Only fifteen copies of the completed study were made, and they were classified 'top secret – sensitive'" (Rudenstine 1996, 2).

One of the experts asked to participate in the creation of the Pentagon Papers was a man named Daniel Ellsberg. Ellsberg had served as assistant to John T. McNaughton, McNamara's assistant secretary of defense for international security affairs, and as a special liaison officer for General Edward Lansdale in Vietnam (Rudenstine 1996, 35). After the election of Richard Nixon in 1968, Ellsberg wrote a series of reports for Henry Kissinger and the Nixon adminis- tration detailing policy options in Vietnam (Rudenstine 1996, 39). Following his divorce from his wife, his experience serving in Vietnam, and increased contact with the antiwar movement, Ellsberg became increasingly disillusioned with the military establishment and the American war effort in Vietnam. In an attempt to help end the war, he decided to leak the Pentagon Papers to the public. After first trying to convince several U.S. Senators to release the report on the floor of the Senate, Ellsberg approached Neil Sheehan of the *New York Times* in February 1971 to discuss the possibility of the *Times* publishing the report.

After months of negotiation and consideration, and without specifically informing Ellsberg of its intention to run the story, the *New York Times* pub- lished the first article about the Pentagon Papers on Sunday, June 13, 1971, and a second article the next day. The Nixon administration was shocked by the publication of the papers. Although originally deciding not to take any action against the *Times*, by late Monday evening Nixon changed his mind. On Tuesday, June 15, Nixon brought suit in federal district court to enjoin the *Times* from publishing more stories on the Pentagon Papers. "It was the first time since the adoption of the U.S. Constitution that the federal government had sued the press to stop it from disclosing information because of national security" (Rudenstine 1996, 2). U.S. District Judge Murray I. Gurfein, a Nixon appointee, issued a temporary restraining order against the *Times* and sched- uled a hearing for Friday of that week.

The next day, Ellsberg tried to make the report public through the three major television networks, but they declined to do so. After being turned down by the networks, he arranged for the Pentagon Papers to be published in the *Washington Post* (Rudenstine 1996, 127). On Friday, June 18, the *Post* started to publish parts of the report, and the government brought suit against the paper in the U.S. District Court in Washington, D.C. (Rudenstine 1996, 2).

The same day, Judge Gurfein held his hearing to determine whether or not the *Times* should be permanently enjoined from publishing the classified documents. Although appearing strongly predisposed to support the govern- ment's position, after a frustrating hearing that lasted late into the night, Judge Gurfein ruled that the government had failed to offer any "cogent reasons" to support its request for an injunction (Rudenstine 1996, 3). On Monday, Judge

Gerhard A. Gessell reached the same conclusion in the *Washington Post* case. On appeal, the D.C. Circuit affirmed Gessell's order, but the Second Circuit Court of Appeals ordered Judge Gurfein to conduct more hearings in the *Times* case. Both the government and the *Times* appealed their losses to the Supreme Court. On Friday, June 25, the Court announced it would immediately review both cases. The parties were ordered to file briefs and participate in oral arguments the very next morning. Five days later, the Court ruled against the government in both cases.

The rushed nature of the Court's decision resulted in a deeply fractured Court. The justices wrote ten separate opinions, one per curium opinion for the Court, and a separate opinion for each individual justice. Although the combined opinions occupied almost fifty pages, the opinion of the Court was less than 200 words. The Court ruled that the government had not met the "heavy burden of showing justification" for a "system of prior restraints of expression" but could not agree on a rationale (*New York Times v. United States* 1971, 714). Nonetheless, the majority did agree that the government could not stop the publication of the Pentagon Papers. The public was somewhat uncertain about the Court's decision. A plurality of respondents to one public opinion poll agreed with the decision, but more than a third of respondents were unsure. Less than a fourth of the public disagreed with the ruling.[6]

Reporters and editors at the *Times* and the *Post* were naturally thrilled with the decision. The *Times* held a press conference to mark the occasion. Upon hearing the news of the decision, Eugene Patterson, the managing editor at the *Post*, "jumped on a desk and shouted 'We win, and so does the *New York Times*.' Reporters applauded and paid off bets made while the case was pending" (Rudenstine 1996, 323). Both papers immediately continued publishing the Pentagon Papers reports. The two papers printed a total of nine articles over the next week; within the next year, three different book versions of the Pentagon Papers were published. Clearly, by any standard, the Court achieved 100 percent behavior conformity through this ruling. The case set a striking precedent for the extreme presumption against prior restraint of speech and the press, even during times of war. More importantly, the ruling was a clear victory for the Court and an impressive display of the institution's power.

SUMMARY: POPULAR VERTICAL ISSUES

My study of popular Supreme Court rulings in vertical issues strongly supports my theory of judicial power: When the Court issues popular rulings that can be directly implemented by lower courts, those rulings tend to cause significant behavior changes. In the *Boerne* ruling, the Court altered the resolution of free exercise claims in federal courts and rebuked efforts by Congress to help free exercise claimants. More dramatically, the Court's ruling in the Pentagon

---

[6] See Appendix II for survey information and citations.

Papers case caused the immediate release of a controversial and potentially dangerous report on U.S. war policy to the public. The Court was extraordinarily successful at altering behavior through these rulings, but this is not especially surprising because the rulings faced little public opposition. In the next chapter, I consider a more demanding test of the Court's power.

5

Unpopular Vertical Issues

> The very purpose of a Bill of Rights was to withdraw certain subjects from the vicissitudes of political controversy, to place them beyond the reach of majorities and officials and to establish them as legal principles to be applied by the courts. One's right to life, liberty, and property, to free speech, a free press, freedom of worship and assembly, and other fundamental rights may not be submitted to vote; they depend on the outcome of no elections.
>
> Justice Robert H. Jackson[1]

In this chapter, I examine unpopular vertical issues – cases in which the Supreme Court issued an unpopular ruling that could be implemented by lower-court judges. Each of these rulings faced significant public opposition, and some of them were overwhelmingly disfavored in public opinion polls. Consistent with my theory of judicial power, I find that the Supreme Court successfully exercised power in each of these cases. Accordingly, these cases highlight Bickel's "countermajoritarian difficulty" by demonstrating the Court's ability to flout public opinion and impose its will on public policy when issuing rulings in vertical issues.

ABORTION

On January 22, 1973, the Supreme Court issued its opinion in *Roe v. Wade*. The case involved a single pregnant woman from Texas, Norma Leah McCorvey (dubbed "Jane Roe" to protect her identity), who sought to terminate her pregnancy in violation of a Texas criminal abortion law. The Texas law was similar to laws in most states that prohibited abortion unless the pregnancy seriously threatened the life of the mother. Until the early 1960s, all but a few states had such laws. In the years leading up to the *Roe* decision, "a trend toward liberalization of abortion statutes" resulted in the adoption by many states of the American Law Institute Model Abortion Law, which permitted abortion

---

[1] *West Virginia Board of Education v. Barnette* (1943).

if "continuance of the pregnancy would greatly impair the physical or mental health of the mother, or ... the child would be born with grave physical or mental defect, or ... the pregnancy resulted from rape, incest or other felonious intercourse" (Center for Disease Control 1970; hereafter CDC). The vast majority of abortions in these jurisdictions were attributed to preserving the "mental health" of the mother.

McCorvey ("Roe") challenged the constitutionality of the Texas abortion law as violating her right to privacy protected by the "penumbras" of the Constitution, the Ninth Amendment, and the Fourteenth Amendment. After she won her challenge in federal district court, the State of Texas appealed the decision directly to the Supreme Court. The Court agreed with McCorvey and invalidated the Texas statute and those like it as inconsistent with the Due Process Clause of the Fourteenth Amendment. In doing so, the Court invalidated the laws of forty-six states[2] and issued an order to every state and federal judge in the country to refrain from convicting any person for seeking or performing an abortion during the first trimester.

Classifying the popularity of Court's abortion rulings is a difficult task. When the decision was handed down in 1973, it enjoyed the support of a narrow majority of American citizens; and to this day, consistent majorities support a woman's right to choose.[3] On the other hand, a substantial and determined minority continues to oppose the *Roe* decision. In fact, levels of public opposition have changed very little in the three decades since *Roe* was handed down. As of 2006, a majority of survey respondents supported the pro-choice position in only 36 states. Considering that bicameral and separation-of-powers systems tend to entrench the status quo, without *Roe v. Wade* it is not even certain that pro-choice groups could have secured the liberalization of abortion laws in all of these states. In addition, a majority of survey respondents describe themselves as pro-life in at least nine states, most of them in the South. Beginning in 1972, the General Social Survey reports that narrow majorities oppose a woman's right to get an abortion if she is unmarried or in a low-income group, but overwhelming majorities support the right to obtain an abortion if the mother's health is in danger, there is serious risk of a birth defect, or the pregnancy is due to rape. The first time respondents were asked whether a woman should be allowed to have an abortion for any reason in 1977, a majority were opposed to this right. The General Social Survey also reveals important regional differences for this question; respondents in the South are more likely to oppose abortion rights in any situation in any year.[4]

Most observers of the criminal law would agree that the most significant impact of the law is not reflected by the conviction of violators, but rather by the deterrence of would-be offenders. Focusing only on the decrease in

---

[2] Abortion laws in Alaska, Hawaii, New York, and Washington were basically unaffected by the *Roe* decision because they were already consistent with the ruling.

[3] See Appendix II for survey information and citations.

[4] See Appendix II for survey information and citations.

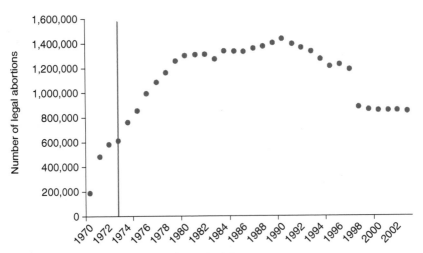

FIGURE 5.1. Legal abortions in the United States, 1970–2002.

convictions may obscure the broader effects of the Court's ruling. I will examine the indirect effects of the *Roe* decision by measuring the change in the actual
number of abortions in the United States in its immediate aftermath. I begin by
replicating Gerald Rosenberg's analysis of abortion after *Roe* in *The Hollow
Hope*. Rosenberg utilized abortion statistics from the Abortion Surveillance
Reports compiled by the Center for Disease Control as part of its Morbidity
and Mortality Summaries (CDC 1969–2003). These reports provide the number of legal abortions, by state and year, between 1969 and the present. The
reports are limited by the fact that some states that permitted abortion before
1973 when the mother's life was not seriously threatened did not report abortion statistics; more recently, several states, including California, have stopped
reporting legal abortions.

I reproduce and update Rosenberg's graph of the number of legal abortions
in the United States, by year, in Figure 5.1. The number of legal abortions
increased steadily from 1969 until around 1980 when it leveled off at around
1.3 million abortions each year. Based on this graph, Rosenberg concludes that
"rather than starting a social revolution, the Supreme Court merely acknowledged one that was already in progress and let it continue" (Rosenberg 2008,
179). The trend in Figure 5.1 appears to confirm this conclusion; the number of
legal abortions was already increasing before the *Roe* decision in 1973, and the
rate of increase did not change significantly after the Court's ruling.[5]

Unfortunately, Rosenberg's analysis obscures the dramatic impact of the
Roe decision on abortion in the United States.[6] Rather than simply blessing

---

[5] Figure 5.1 shows a significant drop in the number of legal abortions in the United States in 1998,
but this is simply due to a lack of reporting for several states during this period, including, most
importantly, California.

[6] Wetstein (1995) conducts a similarly flawed analysis.

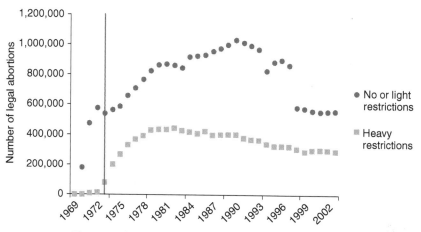

FIGURE 5.2. Abortions by type of pre-*Roe* laws, 1969–2003.

the continuation of an inevitable social trend, the Court in *Roe* ordered the vast majority of states to alter their policy regarding an important and controversial issue. Without *Roe*, it is highly unlikely that every state in the country would have legalized abortion in the last thirty years and even more improbable that the change would have happened in the mid-1970s. The critical error in Rosenberg's analysis is that he examines the abortion rate for the entire country, but the *Roe* decision had different effects in different states, depending on the type of abortion restrictions in place before *Roe*.

A closer look at abortion following the Court's decision in *Roe v. Wade* reveals a very different story of judicial power. Figure 5.2 presents the number of legal abortions in the United States between 1969 and 2002, broken down by the type of abortion restrictions in each state before *Roe*. In states with heavy restrictions on abortion before 1973, the *Roe* decision had a profound impact on the frequency of legal abortion.[7] In just two years, legal abortions in these states increased from fewer than 56,000 the year before *Roe* to more than 270,000 the year after. In states with legalized abortion or only light restrictions before *Roe*, such as the American Law Institute Model Abortion Law, the number of legal abortions actually decreased slightly before continuing the trend of steadily increasing. In fact, the year of the *Roe* decision marked the only decrease in abortions in these states between 1969 and 1981.

The *Roe* decision also had a similar effect on the abortion ratio – the number of abortions per 1,000 women aged 15–44 (see Figure 5.3). After *Roe*, the difference between abortion ratios in states with no or light restrictions and states with heavy restrictions decreased by 54.6 percent; I use this figure as the conservative estimate of behavior conformity to the abortion rulings. However,

---

[7] For a more comprehensive examination of the effects of the *Roe* decision on abortions rates, see Hansen (1980).

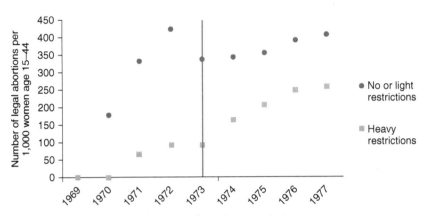

FIGURE 5.3. Abortion rate by type of pre-*Roe* restrictions, 1969–77.

because there is no evidence that anyone was convicted under criminal abortion codes after *Roe*, the remaining difference between these abortion ratios may be due entirely to the different underlying propensities of these populations to obtain abortions. Accordingly, the generous estimate of behavior conformity to the abortion ruling is 100 percent.

The counterintuitive finding that abortions decreased in certain states after *Roe v. Wade* is easily explained by examining the percentage of legal abortions obtained by out-of-state residents presented in Figure 5.4.[8] Because legal restrictions on abortion were so widespread before 1973, a large percentage of legal abortions obtained in those states with few or no restrictions were for out-of-state residents. These women would cross state lines in search of a legal abortion that they could not receive in their own state. In 1972, the last year before *Roe*, 43.8 percent of all legal abortions in the United States were obtained by out-of-state residents. After the *Roe* decision, crossing state lines was no longer necessary to obtain a legal abortion. As a result, just a year after *Roe*, this statistic plummeted to 13.4 percent. To this day, the figure remains steady around 8 percent due largely to the significant number of women who cross state lines in order to obtain an abortion in the District of Columbia, most of whom probably live in nearby suburbs in Maryland or Virginia.

The legalization of abortion undoubtedly had numerous indirect effects, and several scholars have attempted to measure these effects. For example, Marianne Bitler and Madeline Zavodny have found that the legalization of abortion led to a decline in the adoption rate of children born to white women. They conclude that "[r]elative to other states, states that repealed their abortion restrictions before *Roe v. Wade* saw significant declines in adoption rates for children born to white women; these declines were 34–37%, depending on whether adoptions are measured compared to total births or total population"

---

[8] See Wetstein (1995, 615) for a similar analysis of abortions obtained by out-of-state residents.

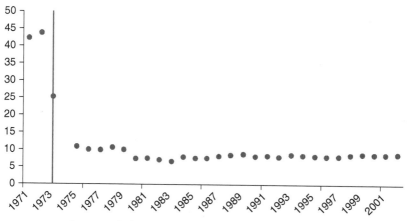

FIGURE 5.4. Percent of abortions obtained by out-of-state residents, 1971–2002.

(Bitler and Zavodny 2002, 29). Although their results are only statistically significant in those states that repealed restrictive abortion laws before *Roe*, the effects of the *Roe* decision nonetheless "suggest a negative effect similar in magnitude to the effects of repeal prior to *Roe*" (Bitler and Zavodny 2002, 29). They hypothesize that the *Roe* effect may lack statistical significance due to women traveling across state lines before *Roe*, thus blurring and diminishing *Roe's* effect.

More famously, John J. Donohue and Steven D. Levitt have argued that the legalization of abortion in the early 1970s contributed significantly to the reduction in the U.S. crime rate during the 1990s. They demonstrate that those states with legalized abortion in 1970 experienced earlier declines in the crime rate than those states affected by *Roe*, and "[s]tates with higher abortion rates in the 1970s and 1980s experienced greater crime reductions in the 1990s" (Donohue and Levitt 2001, 379). The authors conclude that "legalized abortion appears to account for as much as 50 percent of the recent drop in crime" (Donohue and Levitt 2001, 379). They hypothesize that legalized abortion may have affected the crime rate by either reducing the size of the cohort, and thus reducing the number of people who commit crimes, or because "women who have abortions are those most at risk to give birth to children who would engage in criminal activity" (Donohue and Levitt 2001, 381). The Donohue and Levitt study remains both empirically and normatively controversial,[9] but it suggests that the *Roe* decision may have had far-reaching indirect effects on a wide range of social patterns.

---

[9] See Foote and Goetz (2008) for a methodological critique of Donohue and Levitt's empirical claims and Donohue and Levitt (2008) for a response to this critique. See also Joyce (2004) for another empirical critique of Donohue and Levitt. See DiNardo (2007, 990–1) for a brief comment about normative concerns with Donohue and Levitt's project.

After carefully evaluating the evidence of judicial power in abortion-related rulings, it appears clear that the Supreme Court has significantly altered behavior in this issue area. Immediately following the Court's decision in *Roe v. Wade*, the number of legal abortions in states that had previously placed heavy restrictions on the practice increased sharply. At the same time, the number of women traveling across state lines to obtain an abortion decreased significantly. The evidence suggests that the *Roe* decision made it possible for thousands of American women to receive abortions who would otherwise not have been able to do so, and made it more convenient and economical for many others.

FLAG DESECRATION

The Supreme Court has also profoundly impacted American society through several rulings protecting the freedom of speech. Perhaps the most controversial of these rulings is the Court's decision protecting the right to desecrate the American flag. In August of 1984, Gregory Lee Johnson participated in a political protest at the 1984 Republican National Convention in Dallas, Texas. Although several protesters spray painted buildings and overturned potted plants, Johnson took no part in these activities. During the demonstration, a fellow protester handed Johnson an American flag. Once the protest reached the Dallas City Hall, Johnson poured kerosene on the flag and set it on fire. As the flag burned, the protesters chanted, "America, the red, white, and blue, we spit on you." No one was physically injured or threatened with injury as a result of the flag burning, but "several witnesses testified that they had been seriously offended" (*Texas v. Johnson* 1989, 399).

Out of approximately 100 protesters, only Johnson was charged with a crime. He was convicted of "desecrating a venerated object" in violation of a Texas criminal statute, fined $2,000, and sentenced to one year in prison. The Court of Appeals for the Fifth District of Texas at Dallas upheld the conviction, but "the Texas Court of Criminal appeals reversed, holding that the State could not, consistent with the First Amendment, punish Johnson for burning the flag in these circumstances" (*Texas v. Johnson* 1989, 400). The Supreme Court upheld the decision, ruling that flag burning was expressive conduct protected by the First Amendment and that the State's interest in preserving the flag as a symbol of nationhood and national unity could not justify Johnson's conviction.

The Court's ruling in *Texas v. Johnson* was overwhelmingly unpopular. A national public opinion poll conducted shortly after the ruling indicated that 75 percent of respondents disagreed with the Court's decision. Congress responded by promptly passing The Flag Protection Act of 1989, which became effective on October 28, 1989, less than four months after the ruling. The statute threatened anyone who "knowingly mutilates, defaces, physically defiles, burns, maintains on the floor or ground, or tramples upon any flag of the United States" with potential fines and imprisonment (*United States v. Eichman* 1990, 313). After the law took effect, three protestors burned an

American flag on the steps of the U.S. Capitol; a fourth burned a flag in Seattle, Washington, specifically to protest passage of the new law. The Supreme Court reaffirmed the *Johnson* ruling and struck down the federal law as unconstitutional in *United States v. Eichman* (1990).

The Court's rulings in these cases were obviously intended to protect flag burning as expressive conduct under the First Amendment. Therefore, the most direct intended consequence of the Court's ruling would be a decrease in the number of convictions under flag desecration statutes. In an "intensive study of legal, Congressional, newspaper, and other records" Justin Goldstein found only forty-one incidents of flag burning in the United States between 1963 and 1989, twenty-one of which resulted in criminal convictions (1995, 68–75). After the Supreme Court's decision in *Texas v. Johnson*, the only person then imprisoned under the federal Flag Desecration Act of 1968, Carlos Mendoza-Lugo, was released from jail. According to statements from the Citizens Flag Alliance and Lexis Nexis searches, no person has been convicted under a flag discretion statute since the *Eichman* decision. Based on this information, it appears that the very small number of convictions for flag desecration in the United States was reduced to zero after the Court's rulings. Because this is the most generous interpretation of the effect of these rulings, I code the generous estimate of behavior conformity to the flag desecration ruling as 100 percent.

Just as in the case of abortion, the Court in these rulings prohibited the states and the federal government from proscribing a particular type of conduct. Consequently, one could claim that the Court intended to indirectly alter behavior outcomes by encouraging more people to burn American flags. Just as in the abortion issue area, this interpretation of the Court's intentions is questionable at best. In fact, in his concurrence in *Texas v. Johnson*, Justice Kennedy emphasized that "sometimes we must make decisions we do not like ... except in the rare case, we do not pause to express distaste for the result ... This is one of those rare cases" (*Texas v. Johnson* 1989, 421). It is doubtful that the justices in these cases actually hoped more people would burn flags as a result of their decisions; however, in order to obtain the most conservative possible estimate of behavior conformity, I will examine the impact of the decision on instances of flag burning.

The most comprehensive list of flag burning incidents since the *Eichman* ruling is maintained by the Citizens Flag Alliance (CTA), a nonprofit organization dedicated to amending the constitution to prohibit flag burning. The CTA started collecting reports of flag burning in 1994. Between 1994 and 2007, the organization recorded 148 flag burning incidents, for an average of 10.57 incidents per year. By comparison, Goldstein found only 41 flag burning incidents between 1963 and 1989, for an average of 1.52 incidents per year. In other words, the average number of yearly flag burnings increased by almost 600 percent after the Court's ruling. Flag burning incidents are reported in Figure 5.5.

Unfortunately, I am unable to calculate a behavior conformity rate based on these figures in the same manner I did for the abortion rulings. There were only two states, Alaska and Wyoming, without flag desecration laws before

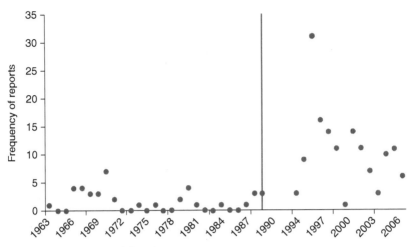

FIGURE 5.5. Reports of flag desecration, 1963–2006.

the *Johnson* ruling, and there is no report of a flag burning incident in either of these states. On the federal level, The Flag Desecration Act of 1968 applied to every state before the *Eichman* ruling. Because there is no baseline for comparison, I have no good measurement of how many flag burnings there would have been if the practice had never been illegal. I can only note the lack of any convictions under flag desecration statutes and the drastic increase in flag burning incidents after the Court's decision. Based on this evidence, I code the conservative estimate of behavior conformity to the flag desecration ruling as 100 percent.

The Court's ruling in the flag desecration case was extremely unpopular; the decision prompted Congress to pass a federal law protecting flags and provoked numerous citizens to form organizations defending the flag. Nonetheless, because the ruling could be directly implemented by lower courts simply refusing to convict defendants under flag desecration laws, the Court was highly successful at altering behavior in this issue area. Following the *Johnson* and *Eichman* rulings, convictions for flag desecration ceased, the only person imprisoned for violation of the federal flag desecration statute was released, and incidents of flag burning increased dramatically.

OBSCENITY

In 1996, Congress passed the Telecommunications Act in order to encourage "the rapid deployment of new telecommunications technologies" (*Reno v. American Civil Liberties Union* 1997, 857; hereafter *Reno*). Title V of this statute, known as the Communications Decency Act of 1996 (CDA), criminalized the "knowing transmission of obscene or indecent messages" or depictions of "sexual or excretory activities or organs" in a manner deemed "patently offensive as measured by contemporary community standards" over the Internet to any recipient under eighteen years of age (*Reno* 1997, 859–60). The statute threatened violators with a fine and up to two years in prison (*Reno* 1997, 859). On February 8, 1996, immediately after President Clinton signed the Telecommunications Act into law, twenty organizations, including the American Civil Liberties Union, filed suit against the Attorney General of the United States challenging the constitutionality of the CDA and requesting that Attorney General Reno be enjoined from enforcing the act. Another twenty-seven organizations later joined the suit. After a three-judge district court ruled that the CDA was unconstitutional, the Attorney General appealed the case directly to the Supreme Court under the CDA's special review provisions.

The Court unanimously affirmed the decision of the three-judge panel in *Reno v. American Civil Liberties Union*, finding that the vagueness of regulation based on the terms "indecent" and "patently offensive" "raises special First Amendment concerns because of its obvious chilling effect on free speech" (1997, 871–2). Although the Court's definition of obscenity as set forth in *Miller v. California* (1973) included a "patently offensive" standard, the *Miller* test included several limitations that were omitted from the CDA. As such, the Court ruled that the CDA was unconstitutional because it violated the Free Speech Clause of the First Amendment.

In response to the Court's decision in *Reno*, Congress once again tried to regulate the transmission of sexually explicit material to minors over the Internet by passing the Child Online Protection Act (COPA) in 1998. In formulating COPA, "Congress gave consideration to [the Court's] earlier decisions on this subject, in particular the decision in *Reno v. American Civil Liberties Union*" (*Ashcroft v. American Civil Liberties Union* 2004, 660; hereafter *Ashcroft*). Accordingly, the critical language in COPA came directly from the Court's three-pronged definition of obscenity in *Miller v. California*. The new statute criminalized the knowing posting of World Wide Web content that is "harmful to minors." Such material was defined as:

> any communication, picture, image, graphic image file, article, recording, writing, or other matter of any kind that is obscene or that –
>
> (A) the average person, applying contemporary community standards, would find, taking the material as a whole and with respect to minors, is designed to appeal to, or is designed to pander to, the prurient interest;
> (B) depicts, describes, or represents, in a manner patently offensive with respect to minors, an actual or simulated sexual act or sexual contact, an actual or simulated normal or perverted sexual act, or a lewd exhibition of the genitals or post-pubescent female breast; and
> (C) taken as a whole, lacks serious literary, artistic, political, or scientific value for minors. (*Ashcroft* 2004, 661–2)

The statute also provided an affirmative defense for defendants who could prove that they took reasonable steps to restrict access to such material by minors.

Once again several organizations, including the American Civil Liberties Union, filed suit in federal district court seeking a preliminary injunction against the enforcement of the statute. The district court agreed, and the Third Circuit Court of Appeals affirmed its decision, finding that because the act used "community standards" to establish which material was harmful to minors, it would prohibit material felt offensive in the most "puritanical" communities from being displayed in more "tolerant" ones (*American Civil Liberties Union v. Reno* 2000). The Supreme Court vacated this decision because COPA's reliance on "community standards" to identify what material is "harmful to minors" did not by itself render the statute overbroad for First Amendment purposes (*Ashcroft v. American Civil Liberties Union* 2002). On remand, the Third Circuit once again affirmed the district court's ruling on the basis that COPA was not the least restrictive means available for the government to protect minors from harmful material on the Internet (*American Civil Liberties Union v. Ashcroft* 2003).

This time the Supreme Court upheld the decision of the Third Circuit in *Ashcroft v. American Civil Liberties Union* (2004), ruling that the government failed to meet its burden of proving that proposed alternatives would not be as effective as the challenged statute. Because blocking and filtering software would be less restrictive on speech, COPA was not the least restrictive means available to Congress to accomplish its goal. Consequently, the Court ruled that COPA also violated the freedom of speech protected by the First Amendment.

No public opinion polls were conducted regarding the Court's decisions in *Reno* or *Ashcroft*, but they were likely very unpopular. A Pew News Interest Index Poll conducted in April of 1997 reported that 77 percent of respondents were familiar with the pending *Reno* case and 83 percent of respondents approved of a "federal law which makes it illegal to send indecent or obscene material to children under 18 through the internet."[10] Although no public opinion polls were conducted after Congress passed COPA, there is no reason to believe public opinion regarding the second version of the law would differ significantly from the first. Because these laws were very popular among the public, the Court's rulings invalidating them were probably very unpopular.

Both the CDA and COPA were challenged by public interest groups seeking injunctions against their enforcement before any prosecutions were initiated under either statute. Because both challenges were supported by the federal district courts that originally heard the cases and were eventually upheld by the Supreme Court, there is no record of any person being indicted or convicted under the CDA or COPA.[11] Because the Court's rulings in *Reno* and

---

[10] See Appendix II for survey information and citations.

[11] Lexis Nexis searches of "U.S. District Court Cases, Combined" containing the phrase "Communications Decency Act" returned 137 cases. All of these cases were either civil actions involving immunity from civil action provided for in a separate part of the CDA, unrelated criminal cases citing the CDA incidentally, or the initial challenges to the CDA discussed previously. Lexis Nexis searches of "U.S. District Court Cases, Combined" containing the phrase "Child Online Protection Act" returned 25 cases. All of these cases were either civil actions, unrelated criminal cases citing COPA incidentally, or the initial challenges to COPA discussed previously.

Ashcroft invalidated these laws before they were ever enforced, there is no reason to expect the Court's rulings in these cases to have any effect on the private behavior of consumers or producers of Internet pornography. The Court was able to completely nullify the effects of both statutes before they were ever implemented in the first place. Consequently, I code both the conservative and generous estimates of behavior conformity to the obscenity rulings as 100 percent.

Because the CDA and COPA were never properly implemented, it is difficult to determine the degree to which the Court altered behavior through its rulings in the obscenity cases. In each of my case studies, I attempt to infer the causal effect of the Court's actions by comparing behavior patterns shortly before a ruling to those shortly after the ruling. In this issue area, a comprehensive evaluation of the Court's causal effect on behavior outcomes would require a comparison between the observed behavior outcomes and those that would have occurred in a hypothetical world in which the CDA or COPA were actually enforced. Such a comparison is, of course, impossible; there is no way to know what the world would have looked like had the CDA and COPA been fully implemented. Consequently, it is impossible to evaluate the significance of the Court's ruling compared to other rulings; however, it is clear that whatever behavioral changes that would have occurred as a result of the CDA and COPA were completely suppressed by the Court's rulings.

THE EXCLUSIONARY RULE

The Supreme Court has also dramatically influenced public policy through a series of rulings during the 1960s extending procedural rights to defendants in criminal trials. The first of these rulings was the Court's decision in *Mapp v. Ohio*. On May 23, 1957, after receiving an anonymous tip that Dollree Mapp and her daughter were harboring a suspected fugitive, the Cleveland police went to her residence and demanded entrance to the house. Mapp called her attorney and, under his advice, refused to allow the police to enter because they did not have a warrant. Several hours later, more police arrived and again attempted to enter the house. When Mapp did not come to the door immediately, the police forced the door open and entered the house. Mapp confronted the officers and demanded to see a search warrant. An officer waived a paper in the air claiming that it was a warrant. Mapp snatched the paper out of the officer's hands and stuffed it down her shirt. The officer struggled with Mapp to recover the piece of paper and then handcuffed her "because she had been 'belligerent' in resisting their official rescue of the 'warrant' from her person" (*Mapp v. Ohio* 1961, 644–5; hereafter *Mapp*). The officer then grabbed her, "twisted her hand" (she "yelled [and] pleaded with him" because "it was hurting"), forced Mapp upstairs, and searched through her belongings, including her bedroom, her child's bedroom, the living room, the kitchen, and the basement (*Mapp* 1961, 645). The search produced obscene materials, and Mapp was ultimately convicted of possessing these materials.

At the trial, no search warrant was produced, nor was the absence of a warrant explained. Nonetheless, the Ohio Supreme Court upheld the conviction on appeal because the evidence was not taken "from the defendant's person by the use of brutal or offensive physical force against the defendant" (*Mapp* 1961, 645). In previous cases, the U.S. Supreme Court had ruled that illegally seized evidence must be excluded from federal criminal trials upon a timely motion to suppress from the defendant (*Boyd v. United States* 1886; *Weeks v. United States* 1914; *Rios v. United States* 1960), but this rule, the "exclusionary rule," did not apply to state courts (*Wolf v. Colorado* 1949). In *Mapp*, the Court extended the exclusionary rule and declared "that all evidence obtained by searches and seizures in violation of the Constitution is, by that same authority, inadmissible in a state court" (*Mapp* 1961, 655). Although some states had already required the exclusion of illegally seized evidence from trial, this decision applied the rule to the entire country.

The Court offered two purposes for the rule: first, "the purpose of the exclusionary rule is to deter – to compel respect for the constitutional guaranty in the only effectively available way – by removing the incentive to disregard it" (*Mapp* 1961, 656); second, even though some might complain that

> [t]he criminal is to go free because the constable has blundered ... there is another consideration – the imperative of judicial integrity. The criminal goes free, if he must, but it is the law that sets him free. Nothing can destroy a government more quickly than its failure to observe its own laws, or worse, its disregard of the charter of its own existence. (*Mapp* 1961, 659)

Eight years later, the Court further strengthened the rule in *Chimel v. California* (1969) when it ruled that, even if the police have a warrant for arrest, they may only search the area within the immediate control of the suspect.

No national public opinion surveys specifically asking respondents about their reaction to *Mapp* were conducted during the 1960s, but the ruling was probably very unpopular. In the 1964 American National Election Study, respondents were asked to name anything the Supreme Court had done in the last few years that they particularly liked or disliked. Responses in the category "protection of rights of criminals, communists" ranked third among all dislikes, behind the school prayer and civil rights rulings. Only six respondents listed decisions in this category as things they liked. This finding suggests the ruling was not popular with the public.[12]

The ruling in *Mapp* expressed the Court's preference for a complicated set of behavior outcomes. The specific policy change ordered by the Court was rather straightforward: Anytime a defendant can show that evidence was obtained illegally, trial judges should suppress the evidence from the trial. However, in the *Mapp* case, the preferences of the justices clearly extended well beyond the immediate policy change to the behavior of other actors affected by the

---

[12] Even if my assumption about popular opinion regarding the *Mapp* ruling is incorrect, it would have no impact on my study because my theory of Court power predicts the successful implementation of all rulings in vertical issues.

decision, most importantly the police. Setting aside the judicial integrity argument, the suppression of illegally obtained incriminating evidence against defendants would be almost nonsensical unless it had some effect on police search procedures.

In addition, this ruling could have numerous undesirable outcomes that were obviously not intended by the Court; however, judicial weakness and poor policy making are two very different concepts. The Court may sometimes produce normatively bad behavior outcomes, but the same could be said of Congress or the president. Producing normatively questionable outcomes only indicates a lack of power if these outcomes were contrary to the Court's preferences, but this was not necessarily the case in *Mapp*. The Court's ruling may have allowed many criminals to go free, but the Court acknowledged that this was possible and explicitly embraced the rule despite these costs. Strong evidence that the *Mapp* rule allowed criminals to go free might buttress the arguments of *Mapp*'s critics, but it would not support a claim that the Court failed to exercise power through the ruling.

I suggest that the Court intended to produce the following sequence of behavior outcomes as a result of the *Mapp* ruling:

(1) Defense attorneys file more motions to suppress evidence and judges grant a significant number of these motions.
(2) Because defendants now enjoy a relative advantage at trial, the number of guilty pleas and convictions decreases, and the number of dismissals by prosecutors increases.
(3) In an attempt to counteract defendants' new advantage at trial, police departments change their official procedures and educate their officers about the exclusionary rule.
(4) Because more police officers consider the rule, they request more search warrants and judges issue more search warrants.
(5) Because more police officers consider the rule, they also are deterred from conducting illegal searches they would have otherwise conducted.
(6) Because police officers conduct fewer illegal searches, they make fewer arrests.
(7) Because police officers make fewer arrests, crime rates increase.
(8) Eventually, police and prosecutors adapt to the new rule and discover new ways to obtain evidence without conducting illegal searches; as a result, in the long run, the number of motions to suppress filed, the number of motions to suppress granted, and the number of cases lost due to suppression of evidence all decrease.

Numerous studies over the last half century have attempted to measure the effect of *Mapp* on these different behavior outcomes. The studies vary in time period, methodology, and empirical rigor. In 1965, Stuart Nagel conducted a survey of judges, police chiefs, defense attorneys, prosecuting attorneys, and officials at the American Civil Liberties Union (ACLU) in order to measure changes in behavior and attitudes about search procedures after the *Mapp*

TABLE 5.1. *Motions to Suppress Annually, 1960–66*

	# Motions to Suppress		
	Pre-1961	1965	% granted in 1965
Boston	0	~100	~25
Cincinnati	0	~35	~40

Note: Data based on statistics gathered by Ban (1973a; 1973b) as quoted in Canon (1974, 688, footnote 36).

ruling. In 1968, law students at Columbia University conducted a study of arrest and search statistics in police reports related to misdemeanor narcotics offenses in New York City both before and after *Mapp* (Note 1968). Search and seizure scholarship proliferated during the 1970s as various scholars examined evidence related to motions to suppress evidence, evidence seizures, arrests, and convictions (Ban 1973a; 1973b; Canon 1974; 1977; Comptroller General of the United States 1979; hereafter Comptroller; Oaks 1970; Spiotto 1973). Later studies have conducted more in-depth analyses of police experiences and opinions, deterrence effects, and case flow (Orfield 1987; Perrin et al. 1997; Uchida and Bynum 1991). When considered together, the evidence collected by these scholars offers strong support for the claim that the *Mapp* decision had a causal effect on the behavior of judges, prosecutors, and police officers, and more specifically on the eight behavior outcomes described previously. I consider the evidence of *Mapp*'s effect on each of these eight outcomes.

(1) The most direct behavior outcome one could expect from the *Mapp* ruling is for judges to grant motions to suppress illegally seized evidence. Table 5.1 presents rounded numbers of motions to suppress in Boston and Cincinnati before and after *Mapp*. In both cities, the number of motions to suppress filed annually drastically increased between 1961 and 1965, and a significant number of these motions were granted (about 25 percent in Boston and about 40 percent in Cincinnati) (Ban 1973a and Ban 1973b as quoted in Canon 1974, 688, footnote 36).

The Columbia University law students found similar results in New York City (Note 1968). In the years following *Mapp*, the percent of cases in which the defendant filed a motion to suppress evidence increased, and a substantial percentage of these motions were granted. These findings are presented in Table 5.2. For example, less than 1 percent of defendants arrested by uniformed officers between January 1960 and June 1961 filed motions to suppress evidence. In the eighteen months after *Mapp*, 4.6 percent filed motions to suppress, and 58.7 percent of these motions were granted; in 1964 and 1966, about 30 percent of these defendants filed motions to suppress, and about 15 percent of these motions were granted (Note 1968, 97, table III).[13] Furthermore, later

---

[13] Statistics for 1964 and 1966 in the Columbia University study (Note 1968) are based on random samples of 100 defendants.

TABLE 5.2. *Motions to Suppress in New York City, 1960–66*

Assignment	1960–Jun. 1961	July 1961–1962	1964*	1966*
Motion to suppress evidence filed as a percent of total cases				
Narcotics Bureau	0.47	4.7	29.1	14.6
Uniform officers	0.7	4.6	31.8	30.7
Plainclothes officers	0.7	8.1	20.8	16.7
Motion to suppress evidence granted as a percent of total motions to suppress				
Narcotics Bureau	85.1	53.2	28.5	50.0
Uniform officers	100	58.7	14.2	16.6
Plainclothes officers	100	74.1	60.1	100

Note: Data based on Note (1968, 97, table III).
* Based on sample of 100 cases.

studies have demonstrated that some judges spend a considerable amount of time trying to implement the exclusionary rule (Oaks 1970, 745, tables 10 and 11).

These statistical studies confirm the findings of David R. Manwaring (1972), who conducted a qualitative analysis of the reaction to *Mapp* in state court decisions. Manwaring evaluates the degree to which courts in Pennsylvania, California, Texas, Illinois, New York, New Jersey, and Maryland complied with the intention of the Supreme Court in the *Mapp* ruling. He concludes that "[i]n its most rudimentary purpose – to impose the exclusionary rule on those states not yet applying it – *Mapp v. Ohio* was wholly successful. This command was obvious, unambiguous and unavoidable" (Manwaring 1972, 25). Accordingly, the generous estimate of conformity to the *Mapp* ruling is 100 percent.

(2) The *Mapp* ruling offered a comparative advantage to defendants in criminal cases. Accordingly, after the implementation of the rule, we might expect to see fewer convictions. Guilty pleas might also decrease as defendants and defense attorneys more willingly go to trial, and prosecutors might dismiss more cases without explanation, anticipating the suppression of critical evidence. The Columbia University study offers some evidence of these trends in New York City, presented in Table 5.3. Guilty pleas by defendants arrested by narcotics bureau officers, uniformed officers, and plainclothes officers all dropped by substantial margins after *Mapp*. Dismissals without explanation also increased for narcotics cases, but the pattern of dismissals is not as strong for arrests by uniformed and plainclothes officers (Note 1968, 97, table iii). Another study of the effect of *Mapp* in New York City found that

> [i]n calendar year 1961, convictions in New York City for illegal weapons dropped 19%, while convictions for obscene literature dropped some 46% ... In the twelve months following *Mapp*, convictions and pleas of guilty in narcotics cases in Manhattan fell off 38% from the previous twelve months. This drop

TABLE 5.3. *Guilty Pleas and Dismissals without Explanation in New York City, 1960–66*

Assignment	Percent of Cases			
	1960–61	1961–62	1964	1966
Guilty pleas				
Narcotics Bureau	89.0	70.4	39.6	29.5
Uniform officers	60.4	54.6	39.4	30.8
Plainclothes officers	50.4	35.9	20.8	33.3
Dismissals without explanation				
Narcotics Bureau	5.9	14.9	25.0	51.2
Uniform officers	31.6	29.4	22.7	17.9
Plainclothes officers	40.8	41.9	54.2	50.0

Note: Data based on study by Note (1968, 97, table III).

was accounted for by an approximate 21% drop in arrests and a 32% drop in defendants held for trial after preliminary hearing – a total decline of some 41% in the number of suspects actually reaching trial. (Manwaring 1972, 18)

(3) In an attempt to counteract defendants' new advantage at trial, we might expect police departments to change their official procedures and educate their officers about the exclusionary rule. Although statistics on changes in official police policy following *Mapp* are not readily available on a wide scale, there are credible accounts of policy change from former New York City police official Michael Murphy (1966, 941) and former Philadelphia District Attorney Arlen Specter (1962, 4). Each of these officials reported substantial policy changes within their jurisdiction in response to *Mapp*. In addition, police officers, attorneys, judges, and ACLU officials in Nagel's study overwhelmingly reported an increase in police education regarding legality in search procedures (Nagel 1965, 286, table 1). More recent studies indicate that the exclusionary rule is a major concern for most law enforcement officers (Perrin et al. 1997, 721, table 1).

More comprehensive data is available regarding the manner in which police departments responded to the *Chimel* decision. Bradley Canon's survey indicates that the majority of police departments report altering their search and seizure policy after the *Chimel* ruling to conform to the Court's preferences (1974, 715, figure 8). Of course, these reports, summarized in Table 5.4, may not accurately reflect actual field procedure, but police officers willing to lie about reports of post-*Chimel* searches might also be expected to lie about reports of pre-*Chimel* searches. At the very least, the survey reflects that police departments understood how and when they were supposed to change their policy, because lying in the survey indicates that they knew what to say in order to appear to be complying with the decision.

(4) If police officers consider the exclusionary rule when conducting searches, they should request more search warrants in order to comply with

TABLE 5.4. *Police Department Policies Regarding Searches of Premises Contemporaneous with Arrest, 1967–73*

Policy	1967–68	1973
Areas under suspect control	15 (28%)	49 (85%)
Entire premises upon suspicion	26 (48%)	7 (12%)
Routinely search entire premises	7 (13%)	0
Other	1 (2%)	1 (2%)
No clear policy	5 (9%)	1 (2%)
Total	54 (100%)	58 (101%)

Note: Data based on surveys conducted by Canon (1974, 715, figure 8).

TABLE 5.5. *Search Warrants Obtained by Police, 1958–65*

Year	Cincinnati	Boston
1958	3	176
1959	0	186
1960	7	267
1961 (Jan-May)	3	150
1961 (Jun-Dec)	25	538
1962	38	834
1963	100	940
1964	113	574
1965	89	560

Note: Data based on research by Ban (1973a; 1973b) as reproduced in Canon (1974, 709, figure 5).

the requirements of the rule. Table 5.5 reports the number of search warrants obtained by the police in Cincinnati and Boston between 1958 and 1965 (Ban 1973a and Ban 1973b as reproduced in Canon 1974, 709, figure 5). Although the use of search warrants was much more frequent in Boston than in Cincinnati before *Mapp*, both cities saw a drastic increase in the number of warrants obtained immediately following the *Mapp* ruling and continuing for years afterwards. Michael Murphy also reports a dramatic increase in the use of search warrants in New York City. Although "search warrants had been rarely used prior to *Mapp*, from the period of the summer of 1961 to [1966] some 17,889 search warrants have been obtained" (Murphy 1966, 941–2).

Bradley Canon's survey of police and prosecutors suggests that the Court's decision in *Chimel* also had a significant impact on the number of search warrants issued to police. Of the seventy-four respondents who compared 1973 figures to those five years earlier, 80 percent said that the number of search warrants issued was more than 50 percent greater; 19 percent said that the 1973

TABLE 5.6. *Changes in Search Warrants Issued in Specific Cities, 1967–73*

City	# of Search Warrants Issued		Percent Increase
	1967 or 1968*	1972	
Detroit	45	1657	3582%
Los Angeles	207	999	383%
Mobile	1208	1308	8%
St. Paul	55	118	115%

Note: Data based on records conveyed in letters from law enforcement officials as reported by Canon (1974, 712–3).
* Figures for Mobile and St. Paul are from 1967; Figures from Detroit and Los Angeles are from 1968.

figure was more than 200 percent greater than five years earlier (Canon 1974, 712, figure 6). In order to verify that the estimates by law enforcement officials were "not the products of respondents' failing memories," Canon investigated the exact number of search warrants issued in four cities (Canon 1974, 712). These figures are reported in Table 5.6. In one of the cities, Mobile, Alabama, the increase in search warrants was relatively small; in the other three cities, the increase was much more dramatic. Detroit, for example, saw the number of search warrants issued increase by more than 3,500 percent.

(5) Perhaps most importantly, if police officers comply with the exclusionary rule, they should be deterred from conducting illegal searches they would have otherwise conducted. The proliferation of search warrants after *Mapp* was matched by reports in surveys from police chiefs, judges, attorneys, and ACLU officials that more officers were adhering to constitutional standards when conducting searches (Nagel 1965, 286, table 1). In states that had the exclusionary rule before *Mapp*, 57 percent of respondents report an increase in police adherence to legality when conducting searches. In states that did not have the exclusionary rule before *Mapp*, 75 percent of respondents report such an increase. Because this is perhaps the most critical step in complying with the Court's mandate, I use this figure as the conservative estimate of behavior conformity to the exclusionary rule decision.

(6) The deterrence of illegal searches may cause police officers to make fewer arrests because they cannot find as much incriminating evidence. In fact, in addition to reporting greater adherence to constitutional standards, the members of the criminal justice community in Nagel's surveys also reported less police effectiveness, less police enthusiasm, and more conflict between police and prosecutors (1965, 286, table 1). A decrease in total arrests by police officers is probably not an intended consequence of the Court's ruling; ideally, the justices would prefer that officers find incriminating evidence through legal means rather than fail to arrest criminals. However, a drop in arrests is not necessarily contrary to the justices' preferences either. As discussed previously,

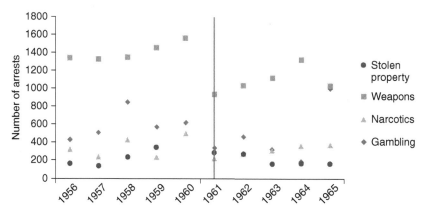

FIGURE 5.6. Arrests in Baltimore, 1956–65.

the *Mapp* decision openly acknowledges that the exclusionary rule may allow the guilty to go free. Presumably, the Court is willing to allow some criminals to escape arrest rather than sacrifice judicial integrity.

Canon attempted to collect data on arrests in four categories (stolen property, weapons, narcotics, and gambling) in fourteen cities[14] (Canon 1974, 706, figure 4) for a total of fifty-six city-category combinations. He was only able to find data for fifty-three of these fifty-six city-category combinations. Canon found that average arrest rates following *Mapp* decreased by at least 10 percent in seventeen city-category combinations. Arrests rates leveled off after increasing for years preceding 1961 in three city-category combinations. Eight cities experienced impermanent decreases, in which arrest rates declined by 20 percent or more in 1962 or 1963 and lasted at least two years, but then increased substantially above the pre-*Mapp* rates thereafter. As examples of cities that showed unusually large decreases, Canon reported specific arrest statistics for Baltimore and Buffalo (1974, 705, figures 2 and 3). These statistics are reported in Figures 5.6 and 5.7.

Although it is certainly not an intended consequence of the Court's ruling, we might expect officers to lie about searches in order to avoid a decrease in arrests. The data collected in the Columbia Law School study suggests that some officers may have lied about how they obtained evidence. As reported in Table 5.7, arrests in Narcotics Bureau cases dropped substantially after *Mapp*, but arrests by uniformed and plainclothes officers remained steady. After *Mapp*, fewer uniformed and plainclothes officers reported finding contraband hidden on arrestees; however, suspiciously, the percentage of reports that arrestees dropped contraband or held it in plain sight increased (Note 1968, 94, table II). Because the number of arrests remained steady, the increase in percentage

[14] Akron, Atlanta, Baltimore, Boston, Buffalo, Cincinnati, Cleveland, Columbus, Dayton, Denver, Newark, New Orleans, New York, and Philadelphia.

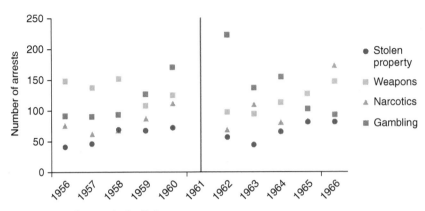

FIGURE 5.7. Arrests in Buffalo, 1956–66.

means an increase in the number of such reports. The authors conclude that the Narcotics Bureau is trying to comply with the rule change, but uniformed and plainclothes officers are probably lying about how they find evidence.[15] More recent surveys of police officers show that 75 percent of interviewees report that lying to establish probable cause is infrequent or exceedingly rare; only 19 percent described the practice as "reasonably common" (Orfield 1987, 1050, note 131).[16]

(7) Of course, if police officers make fewer arrests, crime rates might increase. An increase in crime rates is obviously not the intended result of any Court ruling, but, like decreased arrest rates, this may be an acceptable cost in the Court's mind. Regardless, an increase in crime rates may be an indication that the exclusionary rule is being enforced and having an adverse effect on law enforcement. The evidence of increased crime rates after *Mapp* is questionable at best. Stuart Nagel finds that more states affected by the *Mapp* ruling experienced above average crime rates after the decision than did states that were not affected by the ruling; in other words, those states most affected by *Mapp* saw slightly higher increases in crime rates after the decision (1965, 292, table 4). These statistics are reported in Table 5.8. If *Mapp* really did cause an increase in the crime rate, it would suggest that the Court's rulings could have far-reaching effects, even if those effects are not necessarily intended or normatively preferable.

(8) The evidence presented to this point suggests that the sudden alteration of policy announced in the *Mapp* decision caused numerous short-term consequences for the criminal justice system. Some of these changes were

[15] These findings are somewhat confusing because none of the percentages add to 100. The authors do not explain this discrepancy.

[16] The question asked: "In your experience, do police officers ever shade the facts a little (or a lot) to establish probable cause when there may not have been probable cause in fact?" (Orfield 1987, 1050, note 131).

TABLE 5.7. *Officers' Allegations Regarding Discovery of Evidence in New York City, 1960–66*

Assignment	1960–61	1961–62	1964 sample*	1966 sample*
Number of arrests				
Narcotics Bureau	1468	726	48	41
Uniform officers	316	330	22	39
Plainclothes officers	507	625	24	6
% Reporting contraband hidden on person				
Narcotics Bureau	34.7	3.0	4% of all	5% of all
Uniform officers	31.4	9.0	cases in	cases in
Plainclothes officers	23.6	3.7	the sample	the sample
% Reporting contraband dropped or thrown to ground				
Narcotics Bureau	16.8	43.2	31.3	24.4
Uniform officers	14.0	21.0	50.0	41.0
Plainclothes officers	10.6	17.0	8.3	33
% Reporting contraband in hand or in arm: in general, visible, including money passing or selling				
Narcotics Bureau	22.0	17.2	29.2	43.9
Uniform officers	13.5	18.6	22.7	25.6
Plainclothes officers	9.0	9.6	8.3	16.7
% Reporting contraband hidden in premises				
Narcotics Bureau	10.4	3.3	2% of all	0
Uniform officers	6.5	4.6	cases in	0
Plainclothes officers	16.0	9.0	the sample	0
% Reporting contraband openly exposed in the premises				
Narcotics Bureau	Less	Less	Less	Less
Uniform officers	than 5%	than 5%	than 5%	than 5%
Plainclothes officers				

Note: Data based on research conducted by Columbia University (Note 1968, 94, table II).
* All figures for 1964 and 1965 are based on a sample of 100 cases from each year.

TABLE 5.8. *Effect of Exclusionary Rule on Crime Rates, 1960–62*

Measure of Change	States with Rule before *Mapp* (N = 24)	States without Rule before *Mapp* (N = 23)
Above average crime rates in 1960	13 (57%)	8 (33%)
Above average increase in crime rates from 1960–62	9 (39%)	11 (46%)
Increase in average crime rate per 100,000 population from 1960–62	42	49

Note: Data based on research conducted by Nagel (1965, 292, table 4).

TABLE 5.9. *Arrests "Lost" Due to the Exclusionary Rule*

Study	Percentage of Arrests "Lost"			
	Police Rejections	Prosecutor Rejections	Court Dismissals	Cumulative Loss
NIJ study	0.6	0.8	0.95	2.35
GAO study	N.A.	0.2	0.6	0.8[1]
Nardulli study	N.A.	0[2]	0.6	0.6[1]
INSLAW studies	N.A.	<1	N.A.	N.A.
Feeney et al.	N.A.	N.A.	N.A.	0.5 to 1[3]

Note: Table reproduced from Davies (1983, 667, table 6).
[1] Omitting possible releases by police agencies.
[2] Interview data only.
[3] Robbery, burglary, and assault only; no breakdown by stages.

undoubtedly intended outcomes; others were accepted costs or unintended consequences. However, over time, we might expect the police and prosecutors to adapt to the rule and compensate by adopting new procedures to effectively pursue criminals without conducting illegal searches. Such adaptation was obviously the preferred outcome of the justices in *Mapp*.

Evidence collected in the decades following *Mapp* confirms that police were able to adapt and minimize the most problematic effects of the decision. For example, Manwaring found that in New York City, "the rate of successful prosecutions [came] up substantially toward the norm after the first year, as police became accustomed to their new procedures and aware of their precise powers" (1972, 20). Thomas Davies' survey (1983) of several studies on cases "lost" due to the exclusionary rule demonstrates this pattern. Each of these studies examines the extent to which suspects arrested by the police are not ultimately convicted due to the exclusionary rule, whether by police officials rejecting arrests, prosecutors rejecting arrests, or courts dismissing cases (Brosi 1979; Comptroller 1979; Feeney et al. 1983; Forst et al. 1977; 1982; Nardulli 1983; 1987). His summary of their findings is reproduced in Table 5.9.

As shown in this table, the most comprehensive study of "lost" cases (the National Institute of Justice Study) suggests that the exclusionary rule frees less than 3 percent of suspects each year. The evidence collected by Uchida and Bynum (1991) confirms this finding. In seven sites studied between 1984 and 1985, only 2 percent of defendants filed successful motions to suppress, and only about half of these cases were "lost" due to the suppression of evidence (Uchida and Bynum 1991, 1059, table 6, 1064, table 9). Of course, this long-term effect is still meaningful when considering the number of suspects arrested in the United States each year, but the effect is significantly smaller than it was immediately after the decision.

The available evidence on the effects of *Mapp v. Ohio* suggests that the Supreme Court was very successful at implementing the exclusionary rule despite strong opposition from both the public and law enforcement officials. The Court's preferences expressed in *Mapp* appear to have had a causal effect on a wide range of behavior outcomes related to the search and seizure of evidence by American law enforcement. The Court's successful exercise of power over lower courts translated into power over police department policies and police behavior, and may have had indirect effects on arrest and crime rates. Although scholars, law enforcement officials, and the public may question the Court's wisdom in *Mapp*, few can seriously question its power.

MIRANDA WARNINGS

Several years later, in *Miranda v. Arizona* (1966; hereafter *Miranda*), the Supreme Court expanded the exclusionary rule to prohibit, not only the admission of illegally obtained evidence, but also the admission of improperly obtained confessions.

> On March 13, 1963, petitioner, Ernesto Miranda, was arrested at his home and taken in custody to a Phoenix police station. He was there identified by the complaining witness. The police then took him to "Interrogation Room No. 2" of the detective bureau. There he was questioned by two police officers. The officers admitted at trial that Miranda was not advised that he had a right to have an attorney present. Two hours later, the officers emerged from the interrogation room with a written confession signed by Miranda. At the top of the statement was a typed paragraph stating that the confession was made voluntarily, without threats or promises of immunity and "with full knowledge of my legal rights, understanding any statement I make may be used against me." At his trial before a jury, the written confession was admitted into evidence over the objection of defense counsel, and the officers testified to the prior oral confession made by Miranda during the interrogation. Miranda was found guilty of kidnapping and rape. He was sentenced to 20 to 30 years' imprisonment on each count, the sentences to run concurrently. (Miranda 1966, 491–2)

When Miranda's case reached the U.S. Supreme Court, it was combined with three others, in each of which defendants were questioned "while in custody or otherwise deprived of [their] freedom in any significant way" (*Miranda* 1966, 478). Just two years earlier in *Escobedo v. Illinois* (1964), the Court had ruled that a confession obtained from a defendant who had been questioned while standing for four hours and denied access to counsel despite requests was constitutionally inadmissible. In *Miranda*, the Court extended this rule, deciding that any defendant in such custody

> must be warned prior to any questioning that he has the right to remain silent, that anything he says can be used against him in a court of law, that he has the right to the presence of an attorney, and that, if he cannot afford an attorney one will be appointed for him prior to any questioning if he so desires ... unless and until such warnings and waiver are demonstrated by the prosecution at trial, no evidence obtained as a result of interrogation can be used against him. (*Miranda* 1966, 479)

In the years since the decision, the Court has established a few minor limitations on the requirements of the *Miranda* ruling; however, in 2000, despite an increase in conservative justices on the Court, the fundamental requirements of the *Miranda* decision were upheld in *Dickerson v. United States* (2000).

The *Miranda* ruling was somewhat unpopular. A Harris Survey conducted in September 1966 found that 56.6 percent of respondents said the decision was "wrong"; only 30 percent thought it was "right." Although public opinion would change dramatically in the thirty-four years between *Miranda* and *Dickerson*, when the Court initially issued the *Miranda* ruling, it was not well received. However, the Court could rely on lower courts to directly implement the order by refusing to admit confessions from defendants who did not receive the warnings. Accordingly, I expect the Court's order to have a strong causal effect on the behavior of actors in the criminal justice system despite this public opposition.

The *Miranda* decision clearly expressed the Supreme Court's preference for lower-court judges to suppress confessions and statements obtained from defendants who had not been read these four warnings, the so-called Miranda warnings. Of course, just as they did in *Mapp*, the justices also expressed preferences about police procedure. The Court's influence on police behavior is probably of more interest and importance for the study of judicial power than the simple suppression of evidence. Presumably, the justices intended for police officers to read these rights to arrestees and for a substantial number of arrestees to understand and invoke these rights. In addition, just as in *Mapp*, the new rule may have had a negative effect on the ability of law enforcement officers to combat crime. Although these latter potential outcomes were certainly not intended by the Court, any negative effects on law enforcement should be interpreted as a calculated cost or questionable policymaking rather than a weak judiciary.

What effect did the *Miranda* ruling have on the behavior of actors in the criminal justice system? In order to answer this question, I consider the effect of the Court's ruling as a chain of events following the implementation of the rule by lower-court judges. If the preferences of the justices had a causal effect on the behavior of other actors, I suggest that it would occur in this sequence:

(1) Judges suppress confessions and statements from defendants who did not receive Miranda warnings.
(2) Police departments alter official procedures to require their officers to read the warnings and educate their officers about the rule.
(3) Police officers read Miranda warnings to arrestees.
(4) Arrestees understand Miranda warnings.
(5) Arrestees request legal representation more frequently.
(6) Arrestees invoke right to silence more frequently.
(7) Because arrestees remain silent more frequently, confession rates decrease.
(8) With fewer confessions, police solve fewer crimes.
(9) Police adapt to the new practices.

Once again, numerous scholars have attempted to address these questions in their research, and, once again, their findings are complicated and contentious. The empirical debate over the *Miranda* decision carries an unusually ideological flavor. Most authors concentrate on the "social costs" or lack thereof as part of an implicit (or in most cases completely explicit) argument for the shortcomings or merits of the ruling. In examining the data, I do not attempt to resolve many of the theoretical and methodological disputes in the literature because I am not arguing for or against the merits of the *Miranda* decision. My task is much simpler. Rather than argue that the ruling has produced more costs than benefits or more benefits than costs, I merely argue that the decision has produced costs and benefits. I claim that the ruling had a causal effect on the behavior of actors in the criminal justice system; that is, the Court successfully exercised power in implementing the decision. Whether or not this power was wisely exercised is a secondary question that I do not seek to resolve.

Despite the ideological tenor of the *Miranda* debate, its thoughtful and passionate participants have uncovered a wealth of information about the case, and the adversarial nature of the discussion has ensured that every empirical claim is thoroughly evaluated. The most prolific contributors to this debate have focused their attention on the various social costs and benefits of the *Miranda* rule (Cassell 1996a; 1996b; 1997; Davies 1982; Nardulli 1983; Schulhofer 1996a, 1996b). These scholars hope to offer empirical evidence to support normative claims about the relative merits of the rule from a policymaking perspective. Other scholars have focused specifically on the question of judicial power as exercised through the *Miranda* ruling (Leo 1996; Songer 1987; Songer and Sheehan 1990; Stephens 1965). The evidence collected by these scholars and others provides strong support for my claim that the *Miranda* ruling had a causal effect on the nine behavior outcomes listed previously.

(1) The most direct outcome intended by the *Miranda* decision was for judges to suppress confessions obtained from defendants who were not warned of their constitutional rights. Unfortunately, there are no good before-and-after studies on the number of confessions suppressed by trial-court judges; however, there is evidence that after *Miranda*, a considerable number of defendants filed motions to suppress confessions and some of these motions were granted. Peter Nardulli conducted a study of 7,767 criminal prosecutions in nine counties in Illinois, Michigan, and Pennsylvania in 1979 and found that motions to suppress were filed in about 3.6 percent of all cases (1983, 594).[17] Of these motions to suppress, 4.3 percent were granted (Nardulli 1983, 597, table 7). Nardulli conducted a similar study of 2,759 criminal prosecutions in Chicago between 1983 and 1984 (1987, 227). In this study, he found that 1.1 percent

---

[17] This figure excludes those motions filed in St. Clair County, Illinois, because "the St. Clair County public defender's office has a policy of automatically filing motions to suppress an identification and a confession along with the standard discovery motion – even in cases with no identification or confession" (Nardulli 1983, 594).

of defendants filed motions to suppress confessions, and about 3.6 percent of these motions were granted (Nardulli 1987, 228, table 1, 231).[18] Although these percentages may not seem large, they reflect a considerable number of total cases, especially if these statistics are representative of criminal prosecutions across the entire country.

The *Miranda* ruling also had a strong effect on appellate judges. Songer and Sheehan (1990) conducted a study of 250 U.S. court of appeals cases in which the court considered the admissibility of an incriminating statement in the five years following the *Miranda* decision.[19] The authors found that in these 250 cases, there was only one possible case of noncompliance and only twelve cases of limited compliance for a full compliance rate of 94.8 percent (Songer and Sheehan 1990, 307).[20] A similar study by Songer (1987) found that in 190 cases involving the admissibility of statements in five state courts of last resort, there was no evidence of defiance and very little noncompliance. These studies suggest that the *Miranda* ruling had a strong effect on the behavior of court of appeals judges and judges in state courts of last resort.[21]

---

[18] Nardulli reports the percentage of total defendants who filed successful motions to suppress (0.04%). I calculate the percentage of successful motions by dividing 0.04% by 1.1% (the percentage of defendants who file motions).

[19] Songer and Sheehan (1990) also examine decisions in libel cases after the Supreme Court's ruling in *New York Times v. Sullivan* (1964). Although I do not examine libel cases in this study, the authors make an interesting comparison between these two types of cases that reinforces my broader thesis. After finding high levels of compliance in libel cases, the authors state that "[a]lthough the *Miranda* decision evoked substantially more controversy than the libel decision of the Supreme Court, analysis of responses by the courts of appeals reveals high levels of compliance with this decision as well" (Songer and Sheehan 1990, 307). Because both of these cases were vertical issues, public opinion had little effect on the Supreme Court's power to alter behavior in these cases.

[20] Songer and Sheehan define a case as in compliance "if it required all four Miranda warnings to be given in cases involving custodial interrogation which were decided after the date of the Supreme Court's *Miranda* decision and if an intelligent waiver was executed for all admissions which were admitted into evidence. A decision was classified as being in narrow compliance if the concept of custodial interrogation was defined narrowly or if the burden of proof for showing that a waiver was made voluntarily and intelligently was not placed squarely on the prosecution. A decision was classified as noncompliant if each of the following factors was present: an incriminating statement by the defendant was admitted into evidence at a felony trial over the objection of the defense, the admission of the statement was not harmless to the defendant, the statement was the result of interrogation by law enforcement officials while the defendant was in custody, and the defendant was not informed of or did not voluntarily and knowingly waive the four rights required by the *Miranda* ruling" (Songer and Sheehan 1990, 301).

[21] Both of these studies also examine the effect of *Miranda* on "outcomes," meaning the proportion of cases in which the defense or prosecution wins. Songer (1987) finds significant changes in "outcomes" in some states, but not in others. Songer and Sheehan (1990) find no evidence of change in "outcomes." The fundamental problem with this type of analysis is that it presumes that the types of cases these courts hear did not change after *Miranda*. This assumption is highly suspect. Presumably, lower-court judges, prosecutors, and defense attorneys adapted to the new legal rules under *Miranda* and, as a result, the rulings of lower-court judges, behavior of prosecutors, and decisions by defense attorneys to appeal cases all changed. After *Miranda*,

(2) Following *Miranda*, many police departments made great efforts to explain the new rules to their officers. For example, Medalie et al. report that "[a]pproximately a month after *Miranda* was decided, the District of Columbia Police Department issued its General Order No. 9-C, an elaborate five-page, single-spaced document explaining in detail the *Miranda* requirements and reasoning" (1968, 1360). In his study of interrogations in New Haven, Connecticut, Michael Wald et al. found that a few months after the *Miranda* ruling, the New Haven Police Department held training seminars to teach the detectives about the decision and distributed cards with the Miranda warnings to the officers (1967, 1551). In a survey of four city police departments in Wisconsin in 1966–77, Neal Milner found that in less professionalized police departments, 61–69 percent of police officers learned about *Miranda* rules in conference training sessions; in the more professionalized Madison police department, 92 percent of officers learned about the rules in training sessions (1970, 123, table 2). About half of the officers reported more police education and training as a result of the ruling: 41 percent in Green Bay, 72 percent in Kenosha, 53 percent in Racine, and 50 percent in Madison (Milner 1970, 128, table 4). Lawrence Leiken's study of interrogations in Denver, Colorado, reports that by 1969 Denver police were given forms with the Miranda warnings written on them, which defendants had to sign in order to waive their rights (1970, 9).

Although these studies do not provide comprehensive statistics on the reaction of police departments across the country, at the very least they provide strong anecdotal evidence that police stations in several areas responded to the *Miranda* ruling by changing their official policies to require officers to read Miranda warnings.

(3) The education of police officers appears to have had a significant effect on their behavior. Wald et al.'s (1967) New Haven study offers an interesting picture of the immediate response to the ruling. For the Wald study, law students directly observed police interrogations of 108 suspects by the New Haven police and coded which of the four Miranda warnings defendants were given. Their study is especially interesting because it was conducted in the three months immediately following the ruling. As shown in Table 5.10, the percentage of suspects given all four warnings increased from zero to forty between June and August. Therefore, the conservative estimate of behavior conformity to the *Miranda* ruling is 40 percent. Although this study suggests that conformity was far from perfect, the *Miranda* decision appears to have had a significant, if limited, effect on police behavior.

Similar results were found in Washington, D.C. Medalie et al. conducted interviews with 260 defendants arrested before and after the *Miranda* ruling and asked them about the warnings they received (1968, 1351). Results from

judges may have ruled in favor of defendants when they otherwise would not have, and defense attorneys may have appealed cases they would never have bothered to appeal before the ruling. In fact, any evidence that outcomes did change after *Miranda* would suggest that lower-court judges were not complying with the new rules.

TABLE 5.10. *Warnings Given in New Haven, Connecticut, by Month, 1966*

# of Warnings Given	June	July	August	Total
0–2	14	31	14	59
3–4	9	22	28	49
Total	23	53	42	108
All 4 warnings	0 (0%)	8 (15%)	17 (40%)	

Note: Data based on observations of interrogations as reported by Wald (1967, 1550 Table 3).

TABLE 5.11. *Specific Warnings of Rights Given to Pre- and Post-Miranda Defendants, 1965–66*

Warnings of Rights	Pre-*Miranda* Defendants	Post-*Miranda* Defendants
No warnings	84 (48%)	21 (25%)
Silence*	25 (14%)	13 (16%)
Non-stationhouse counsel**	26 (15%)	8 (10%)
Stationhouse counsel***	4 (2%)	8 (10%)
Phone and/or bond	15 (9%)	3 (4%)
Silence & non-stationhouse counsel	12 (7%)	4 (5%)
Silence and stationhouse counsel	8 (5%)	25 (30%)
Total	174 (100%)	81 (100%)

Note: Data based on 260 defendants interviews in Washington, D.C., in 1965–66 as reported in Medalie et al. (1968, 1363, table 4).
* Combines silence warning and warning that "anything you say may be used against you."
** Combined warnings of right to counsel in court and right to telephone own counsel.
*** Combined warnings of right to presence of counsel at station house and right to appointed counsel.

their interviews are reported in Table 5.11. According to their findings, the number of defendants who received warnings of the right to silence and the right to stationhouse counsel increased by 25 percentage points after *Miranda*; the number of defendants who received no warnings at all decreased by a similar margin (Medalie et al. 1968, 1363, table 4).

It is possible that these studies severely underestimate the Court's effect on interrogation practices by focusing on the effects of *Miranda* rather than the combined effect of *Miranda* and *Escobedo*. Cyril Robinson's survey of police officers and prosecutors shortly before *Escobedo* in 1964 found that only 51 percent of large-city police reported giving silence warnings and 46 percent claimed to give counsel warnings; 71 percent of small-city police claimed to give both warnings (Robinson 1968, 434–47). After *Escobedo*, but shortly before *Miranda*, more than 90 percent of large-city police officers, small-city police officers, and prosecutors claimed to inform suspects under interrogation of the right to remain silent and the right to counsel (Robinson 1968, 507). These findings suggest that in many jurisdictions the *Escobedo* ruling had a significant impact on police procedure, and in other jurisdictions warnings were given even before *Escobedo*. For example, Seeburger and Wettick found that the Detective Branch of the Pittsburgh Police Bureau had a policy of warning defendants of the right to remain silent and the right to counsel for ten to twenty-five years prior to the *Miranda* and *Escobedo* rulings (1967, 8).

Later studies provide evidence that behavior conformity to *Miranda* was almost complete. Lawrence Leiken (1970) conducted an analysis of fifty interviews in July and August of 1969 in the Denver County Jail. Leiken found that the reading of Miranda warnings "is almost never omitted during interrogations by members of the Denver Police Department" (1970, 10); in fact, all fifty suspects in his study read or were read the warnings (1970, 14). More recently, Richard Leo's study of 182 cases in three police stations in the 1990s found that detectives provided Miranda warnings in every case in which they were legally required to do so (1996, 652–3). Based on these more optimistic reports of compliance, the generous estimate of behavior conformity to the *Miranda* ruling is 100 percent.

(4) For Miranda warnings to have any effect on the behavior of arrestees, arrestees must first understand the warnings. Leiken found that, when questioned later, 40 percent of suspects could remember both the silence warning and the right-to-counsel warning; 29 percent could remember one of the two (1970, 15). However, Leiken suspected that the ability to recall the specific warnings may not properly reflect understanding of the warnings. When prompted by a later question, 73 percent of interviewees recognized that they had the right to counsel (Leiken 1970, 15). Medalie et al. tested defendants' understanding of the Miranda warnings and found that 85 percent of "post-*Miranda* defendants" understood the right-to-silence warning, 82 percent understood the right-to-counsel warning, and 76 percent understood the right-to-appointed counsel warning (1968, 1374). Although these statistics do not reflect perfect comprehension, they suggest that the vast majority of defendants understand their rights after being warned.

(5) There is some evidence that those who receive the right-to-counsel warning request representation more frequently. Medalie et al. (1968) find that 64 percent of defendants who were warned of their right to stationhouse counsel (meaning a lawyer provided without cost) requested attorneys. Those defendants who were warned of only the right to silence, of a right to non-stationhouse counsel, or of no rights at all requested counsel at considerably lower rates (23%, 17%, and 12% respectively).

(6) One might expect those who are warned of the right to silence to remain silent more frequently; however, Medalie et al. find only weak evidence of this relationship. According to their study, those who received the silence warning made statements at only a slightly lower rate (40%) than those who did not receive the warning (46% for those warned of the right to counsel, 55% for those given no warnings). Richard Leo (1996) finds that 22 percent of arrestees

invoked their *Miranda* rights, but because all of the arrestees in his sample were read their rights, there is no way to discern the effect of the warnings.

(7) The obvious concern raised by critics of the exclusionary rule is that it will cause a decrease in the number of admissible confessions obtained by the police, which in turn will hinder law enforcement efforts. It is not clear whether a decrease in confession rates could be described as one of the Court's preferences in the *Miranda* ruling. Surely, the Court does not intend to eliminate the role of confessions in police investigation, but it does want to eliminate those confessions given because suspects did not know they had the right to remain silent. Because it is impossible to know how many confessions would still be given if suspects knew they had the right to remain silent, it is impossible to know how many confessions the Court wished to eliminate. Of course, one could also view any decline in confession rates as an unintended consequence of the Court's ruling. Regardless, it is at least plausible that the *Miranda* decision caused a decrease in confession rates.

The question of whether or not this decrease actually occurred is a highly contentious matter. Numerous scholars have conducted studies attempting to measure *Miranda's* effect on confession rates. Some of the studies discussed previously measure the confession rate by comparing those who receive Miranda warnings to those who do not in a cross-sectional analysis and conclude that the Miranda warnings have no effect on confession rates. For example, Wald et al. found that the warnings had no effect on the probability of investigators conducting "successful interrogations" (1967, 1566, table 12). Similarly, Leiken found no evidence that receiving warnings changed the probability of giving an incriminating statement or making a confession (1970, 17, table 1).

Before-and-after studies offer significantly stronger evidence that *Miranda* had a causal effect on confession rates. Several scholars test the effect of *Miranda* by examining confession rates before and after the decision. These studies are conveniently summarized in work by Paul Cassell and Stephen Schulhofer. Cassell (1996a) evaluates the findings from eleven different studies in different cities in the United States. After excluding findings from some studies due to methodological errors, he calculates the "average change" in confession rates, defined as the average percentage point change in confession rates after *Miranda*. His findings are reported in the second column of Table 5.12. For example, Cassell interprets the study in Pittsburgh, conducted by Seeburger and Wettick (1967), as finding an 18.6 percentage point decrease in the confession rate as a result of *Miranda*. Cassell concludes that, on average, the *Miranda* ruling caused a 16.1 percentage point drop in confessions (Cassell 1996a, 418, table 1).

Stephen Schulhofer challenges Cassell's interpretation of these studies based on methodological problems and repeats his analysis correcting for these problems (Schulhofer 1996a, 539, table 1). These findings are reported in the third column in Table 5.12. Schulhofer excludes the case study from New Orleans because confession rates before *Miranda* are simply estimated in this study; he excludes the study in Kings County because the study measures the decrease in statements given to police rather than confessions given to police; he excludes

TABLE 5.12. *Confession Rate Changes in Before-and-After Studies*

Study	Cassell Change Rate	Schulhofer Comparison to Regime without Warnings	Schulhofer Comparison to Regime with Some Warnings	Corrected Comparison to Regime without Warnings
Pittsburgh	−18.6	−16.2	−16.2	−16.2
New York	−34.5	excluded	excluded	excluded
Philadelphia	−24.6	−13.8	−13.8	−13.8
Seaside City	−2.0	0.0	0.0	excluded
New Haven	−16.0	−12.3	−12.3	−12.3
Washington	excluded	excluded	excluded	excluded
New Orleans	−11.8	excluded	excluded	excluded
Kansas City	−6.0	−6.0	−6.0	−6.0
Kings County	−15.5	excluded	excluded	excluded
Chicago	excluded	excluded	excluded	excluded
Los Angeles	excluded	excluded	+9.8	excluded
Average change	−16.1	−9.7	−6.4	−12.0

Note: Data based on literature review by Cassell (1996a, 418, table 1), Schulhofer (1996a, 539, table 1). All figures represent change in percentage points of confessions obtained by police before and after *Miranda*.

the New York City study because the effect in New York was exaggerated in the short term.

Schulhofer accepts each of Cassell's decisions to exclude a study. Interestingly, he agrees that the Los Angeles study should be excluded because police were required to warn suspects of their rights since the 1965 California Supreme Court case *People v. Dorado*; consequently, the study from Los Angeles does not compare a regime without warnings to a regime with warnings. Schulhofer creates a second list of confession rate changes that includes the Los Angeles study. He claims that this analysis shows the effect of *Miranda* relative to a regime with some warnings, rather than all of the *Miranda* requirements. These changes are listed in the fourth column of Table 5.12. Unfortunately, this measure is not particularly meaningful because it blurs the effect of *Miranda*. Schulhofer makes the same mistake that Rosenberg did in the area of abortion; the effect of a Supreme Court decision should be measured in those jurisdictions where the ruling was supposed to change the law. Because warnings of rights were required in California before the *Miranda* ruling, we should not expect to see any changes in this state. Averaging the effect in California with the effect in other states simply obscures the true effect of the decision.

Surprisingly, both Cassell and Schulhofer fail to apply the logic used to exclude the Los Angeles study to the Seaside City study. This study was also conducted in California after the California Supreme Court issued *People v. Dorado* (1965). Consequently, it is not surprising that this is the only study in which no effect was found on the confession rate. A proper comparison between a regime without Miranda warnings and a regime with Miranda warnings should exclude this study as well. In the fifth column of Table 5.12, I list the studies that survive all of these methodological objections and calculate a new average effect of the *Miranda* decision on confession rates. Based on my analysis, on average, *Miranda* caused a 12 percentage point decrease in the number of confessions obtained by police.

(8) The natural implication of a decrease in confession rates is a decrease in crimes solved by the police. Following this dispute over changes in confession rates, several authors published a series of articles debating *Miranda*'s effect on clearance rates – the Federal Bureau of Investigation's measure of crimes solved by investigators (Cassell 1996b; 1997; Cassell and Fowles 1998a; 1998b; Schulhofer 1996b; 1997). Cassell and Fowles employ an interrupted time series regression design to test the relationship between the *Miranda* decision and the clearance rate, controlling for a long list of other variables (1998a).[22] Based on this analysis, they conclude that the *Miranda* decision was associated with a 6.7 percent decrease in the clearance rate for violent crimes and a 2.3 percent decrease in the clearance rate for property crimes (Cassell and Fowles 1998a, 1982–3).[23] They also find statistically significant effects for the specific crimes of robbery, burglary, larceny, and vehicle theft (Cassell and Fowles 1998a, 1087–8). These findings are all robust to various specifications of the model (Cassell and Fowles 1998a, 1096).

In response to Cassell and Fowles, John J. Donohue (1998) conducted an exhaustive examination of the statistical analysis the authors employed and identified numerous causes for concern with the Cassell and Fowles study. Although Donohue points out several weaknesses in the interrupted time series analysis, the reliability of the FBI clearance data, and some of Cassell and Fowles's more ambitious claims, he does agree with the core finding that "the measured violent crime clearance rate is 10–12% lower in the post-mid-1966 period than would have been expected based on the various time-series regression models" (Donohue 1998, 1170).[24] Cassell and Fowles (1998b) respond

---

[22] Cassell and Fowles control for the crime rate per capita, the number of police employees per capita, dollars spent on police protection per capita by state and local governments, adjusted for inflation, a measure of police capacity, the number of people between the ages fifteen and twenty-four, participation in the labor force, unemployment, disposable per capita real income, births to unmarried women, urbanization, the percentage of violent crimes committed in small cities, and a standard time trend variable (1998a, 1071–81). In order to capture the effect of the *Miranda* decision, Cassell and Fowles used a "dummy" variable, a dichotomous indicator variable taking on the value one after the *Miranda* decision and the value zero before the *Miranda* decision (1998a, 1081).

[23] Both of these findings were statistically significant at the 0.01 level.

[24] See Donohue (1998) for a more complete description of the issues involved in interpreting the FBI clearance data and the statistical analysis employed by Cassell and Fowles (1998a). Although Donohue takes a rather skeptical tone in his interpretation of the findings reported by Cassell and Fowles, he subjects their work to unusually rigorous examination, and many of their findings survive this critical examination. See Cassell and Fowles (1998b) for a response to these criticisms.

to Donohue's concerns in another article defending their findings and demonstrate the robustness of their findings under various specifications.

(9) Although the *Miranda* ruling had significant effects on law enforcement behavior in the short term, these effects were probably mitigated over time as police adapted to the new rule. Nardulli's studies (1983; 1987) of *Miranda*'s effects during the 1980s demonstrate that a very small percentage of cases involve successful motions to suppress. This pattern suggests that the police adapted to the rule, and the threat of suppression motions is primarily used to deter potential violations of the rule.

The Supreme Court's ruling in *Miranda v. Arizona* had a series of direct and indirect effects on law enforcement behavior in the United States. Faced with the threat that confessions would be suppressed at trial unless the Court's new procedures were followed, police departments changed policies and educated their officers, and police officers began reading these warnings to arrestees. There is evidence that a large percentage of arrestees understood and invoked their rights. As a result, suspects may have requested attorneys more often and confessed to crimes less frequently. In the long run, the police appear to have adapted to this new set of rules, and today relatively few cases are lost as a result of *Miranda* rules.

WARRANTLESS EAVESDROPPING

Although the *Mapp* ruling prohibited the admission of evidence obtained through illegal searches, it left unanswered many questions related to search and seizure procedures. For example, were private conversations protected by the Fourth Amendment? Did surveillance of private conversations constitute a search if it did not involve physically trespassing on private property? The Court began to answer these questions in *Berger v. New York*.

In 1966, Ralph Berger was convicted of conspiracy to bribe a public official for his participation as a "go-between" in a scheme to bribe the chairman of the New York State Liquor Authority for the issuance of liquor licenses. At trial, the prosecution played several portions of recordings obtained by police through the use of recording devices placed in the office of two other conspirators. The electronic eavesdropping was authorized by a justice of the state Supreme Court under the New York Code of Criminal Procedure. The New York statute did not require law enforcement officials to believe that any particular offense had been committed, show a need for secrecy, or describe the conversations sought through the eavesdropping. Instead, the statute gave law enforcement officers a "roving commission to 'seize' any and all conversations" for a two-month extendable period, even if the conversations sought had already been seized (*Berger v. New York* 1967, 67; hereafter *Berger*).

"Eavesdropping is an ancient practice," deriving its name from the eaves of houses under which the eavesdropper would listen in order to overhear private conversations (*Berger* 1967, 45). Beginning in the 1800s, technological advances allowed more creative and effective methods of eavesdropping, including the use of concealed electronic listening devices (known as "bugging") and the surveillance of telephone conversations (known as "wiretapping"). "Since the early part of [the twentieth] century the FBI has utilized wiretapping and 'bugging' techniques in both criminal and intelligence investigations," and the "CIA and NSA have similarly used electronic surveillance techniques for intelligence purposes" (Select Committee to Study Governmental Operations 1976; hereafter Select Committee).

When the Supreme Court first considered the use of evidence obtained through electronic surveillance in the 1928 case *Olmstead v. United States*, the Court ruled that because "the interception of the suspect's telephone line was accomplished without entry upon his premises," the search was not prohibited by the Fourth Amendment (*Berger* 1967, 51). In 1942, the Court similarly found that placing a listening device against an office wall to hear conversations next door was also not prohibited because "there was no physical trespass" (*Berger* 1967, 51). However, in subsequent cases the Court took a more skeptical view of electronic eavesdropping, reversing its view on wiretapping (*Nardone v. United States* 1937) and insisting that law enforcement officials refrain from physically entering constitutionally protected areas (*Silverman v. United States* 1961). On June 30, 1965, President Johnson issued a directive to all federal agencies prohibiting the use of wiretapping "except in connection with investigations related to the national security," and then only after obtaining written approval from the Attorney General (Select Committee 1976). However, despite this order to federal agencies, state law enforcement officials continued to use wiretapping in criminal investigations.

The Court in *Berger* ruled that the language of the New York statute was too broad and essentially authorized a general search, much like the "general warrants" used by the British during colonial times (*Berger* 1967, 58). These "general warrants" had authorized almost limitless investigations without requiring just cause, and contempt for these warrants was a motivating factor behind the Declaration of Independence. The majority found that private conversations were protected by the Fourth Amendment, and the lawful seizure of such conversations required a more rigorous warrant process than that created by the New York law. In his concurring opinion, Justice Douglas praised the Court's decision for implicitly overruling *Olmstead*; six months later, in *Katz v. United States*, the Court explicitly stated that *Olmstead* was no longer good law. However, the majority in *Katz* declined to apply Fourth Amendment protection to electronic cases "involving the national security" because the question was not presented by the case before the Court (*Katz v. United States* 1967, 358, footnote 23).

Shortly after the *Berger* and *Katz* rulings, Congress passed the Omnibus Crime Control Act of 1968, which created a warrant procedure for electronic surveillance in criminal cases. The Act contained a provision explicitly denying any attempt by Congress to "limit the constitutional power of the President" to protect the nation against "hostile acts of a foreign power" or any "clear and present danger to the structure or existence of the government" (*United States v. U.S. District Court* 1972, 302; hereafter *U.S. District Court*).

The next year, three defendants were charged by the government with conspiracy to destroy government property. The defendants moved to compel the government to disclose electronic surveillance information that had led to their indictments. In response, the government submitted an affidavit by the Attorney General stating that he had approved the wiretaps to "protect the nation from attempts of domestic organizations to attack and subvert the existing structure of the Government" (*U.S. District Court* 1972, 300). Based on this affidavit, the government insisted that, despite lack of prior judicial approval, the surveillance was lawful as "a reasonable exercise of the President's power ... to protect the national security" (*U.S. District Court* 1972, 300). The district court disagreed and ordered the government to disclose the conversations. The government filed a petition for a writ of mandamus with the Court of Appeals for the Sixth Circuit, which also ruled that the surveillance violated the Fourth Amendment, and the government appealed the case to the Supreme Court.

The Supreme Court unanimously sided with the defendants. Speaking for the Court in *United States v. U.S. District Court*, Justice Powell ruled that due to "the inherent vagueness of the domestic security concept, the necessarily broad and continuing nature of intelligence gathering, and the temptation to utilize such surveillances to oversee political dissent," domestic security surveillance requires prior judicial scrutiny (*U.S. District Court* 1972, 320). In so doing, the Court invalidated the practice of warrantless eavesdropping in all domestic security cases; however, the Court expressly declined to address the issue of electronic surveillance in cases involving the "activities of foreign powers or their agents" (*U.S. District Court* 1972, 322).

The first national public opinion poll addressing the issue of wiretapping after the *Berger* ruling was conducted in 1974.[25] In this poll, 68 percent of respondents opposed giving the government the authority to use electronic surveillance against citizens suspected of criminal activity without a court order; however, 63 percent of respondents supported allowing electronic surveillance if in each case the government received permission from a court.[26] These polls may not represent public attitudes in 1967, especially considering that public opinion may have been more supportive of wiretapping before the Watergate scandal in the early 1970s. The Court's ruling in *Berger* may have been unpopular; however, because the ruling was in a vertical issue, I expect to find high behavior conformity regardless of public opinion.

---

[25] Several polls conducted in 1949 and 1950 show divided public opinion about the use of evidence obtained through electronic surveillance in court. A 1971 poll asked "has the F.B.I. (Federal Bureau of Investigation) not done enough or has it gone too far with respect to ... tapping telephones and using electronic bugs?" Respondents were fairly evenly split between the choices "not enough," "too far," "about right," and "don't know." See Appendix II for survey information and citations.

[26] See Appendix II for survey information and citations.

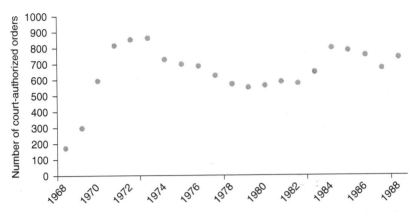

FIGURE 5.8. Court-authorized orders for the interception of wire, oral, or electronic communications, 1968–88.

There is no comprehensive source of data on the number of warrantless wiretaps conducted in the United States, but available information suggests that the practice was common prior to 1967. For example, between 1942 and 1967 the number of warrantless wiretaps conducted by the FBI ranged from 133 to 519 annually (Select Committee 1976). Beginning in 1968, the Omnibus Crime Control Act required the Director of the Administrative Office of the United States Courts to transmit to Congress a report regarding the interception of wire, oral, or electronic communications. Figure 5.8 reports the number of court-authorized orders for the interception of wire, oral, or electronic communications by state and federal judges under the Act between 1968 and 1988. The number of these orders increased rapidly following passage of the Act, reaching a high of 864 orders in 1973, before starting to decline. These eavesdropping orders produced numerous arrests and convictions. The number of arrests and convictions that eventually resulted from eavesdropping orders in each year is reported in Figure 5.9. For example, the 816 intercepts authorized in 1971 eventually resulted in 4,273 arrests and 2,273 convictions. Eavesdropping under the Omnibus Crime Control Act declined significantly following 1973, possibly due to increased public and congressional concern about wiretaps following the Watergate scandal.

There is some evidence that the number of warrantless wiretaps decreased around the time the Court issued the *Berger* ruling. Figure 5.10 reports the number of warrantless wiretaps conducted by the FBI in each year between 1940 and 1975 as reported in the testimony of Attorney General Edward H. Levi before Congress on November 6, 1975 (Select Committee 1976). According to Attorney General Levi's testimony, the pre-1968 figures include electronic surveillance for both intelligence and law enforcement purposes; those after 1968 include surveillance for intelligence purposes only, because all surveillance for law enforcement purposes were subject to the warrant procedures in the Omnibus Crime Control Act. If this testimony is accurate, it means that, at least

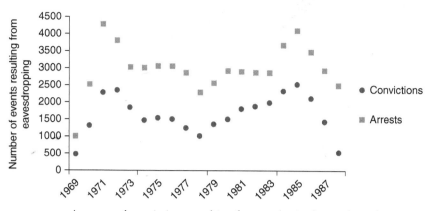

FIGURE 5.9. Arrests and convictions resulting from authorized eavesdropping, 1969–88.

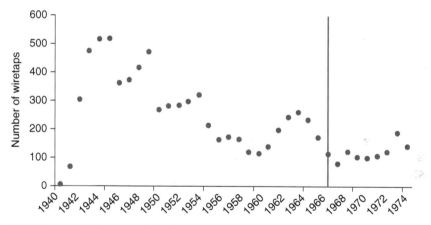

FIGURE 5.10. FBI warrantless wiretaps, 1940–75.

in the field of federal law enforcement, the Court's rulings in the *Berger* and *Katz* decisions resulted in 100 percent behavior conformity, primarily by prompting Congress to create a statutory framework to comply with the rulings.

"Between 1960 and 1972 numerous American citizens were targeted for electronic surveillance" in order to "protect the country against 'subversive' and/or violent activities" (Select Committee 1976). Most of these citizens were affiliated or supposedly affiliated with communist, anti-war, or civil rights organizations. This warrantless surveillance was conducted under the "national security" rational mentioned in the *Berger* ruling and President Johnson's 1965 executive order. The Court's ruling in *U.S. District Court* expressed the justices' preference that this practice end, except for cases involving foreign threats.

Fifteen months after the [*U.S. District Court*] case Attorney General Richardson, in a letter to Senator Fulbright which was publicly released by the

[Justice] Department, stated: "In general, before I approve any new application for surveillance without a warrant, I must be convinced that it is necessary (1) to protect the nation against actual or potential attack or other hostile acts of a foreign power; (2) to obtain foreign intelligence information deemed essential to the security of the United States; or (3) to protect national security information against foreign intelligence activities." (Levi 1975)

This letter suggests that the Court's ruling in *U.S. District Court* also produced perfect behavior conformity by the FBI.

This conclusion is cast into doubt by warrantless wiretap statistics provided by Attorney General Levi. As shown in Figure 5.10, the number of warrantless wiretaps conducted by the FBI actually increased after the Court's ruling in *U.S. District Court*; however, this increase is likely due to an unrelated event. Beginning in the early 1960s, J. Edgar Hoover, the Director of the FBI, placed a limit on the number of warrantless wiretaps and bugs that could be in operation at any one time. This policy ended when Hoover died in 1972, the same year of the Court's decision in *U.S. District Court* (Select Committee 1976). Accordingly, any decline in the number of warrantless wiretaps after 1972 due to the Court's ruling is probably masked by the simultaneous increase in wiretaps for foreign intelligence purposes.

There is no way to measure the frequency of warrantless eavesdropping among all state and local law enforcement officials before or after the Court's rulings in *Berger* and *U.S. District Court*; however, Congress's strong, prompt response to the *Berger* ruling, available statistics on authorized intercepts and warrantless FBI wiretaps, and the testimony of two U.S. Attorneys General all suggest that the Court's ruling had a strong causal effect on the behavior of law enforcement officials in seeking to obtain information through electronic surveillance. By limiting the government's ability to use evidence from warrantless electronic surveillance in criminal prosecutions, the Court created powerful incentives for lawmakers and law enforcement officials to conform to the Court's preferences.

THE RIGHT TO COUNSEL

In addition to protecting criminal defendants from improper police behavior outside the courtroom, the Court also created new rules of criminal procedure to protect them once in the courtroom. The most significant of these protections is the right to counsel, created by the Court's ruling in *Gideon v. Wainwright*. In 1961, Clarence Earl Gideon was arrested and charged with breaking and entering a poolroom in Panama City, Florida, with the intent to commit a misdemeanor. Under Florida law, this offense constituted a felony. At his trial Gideon indicated that he was unable to afford an attorney and asked that the court appoint one for him, after which the following conversation took place:

> The COURT: Mr. Gideon, I am sorry, but I cannot appoint Counsel to represent you in this case. Under the laws of the State of Florida, the only time the Court can appoint Counsel to represent a Defendant is when that person is

charged with a capital offense. I am sorry, but I will have to deny your request to appoint Counsel to defend you in this case.

The DEFENDANT: The United States Supreme Court says I am entitled to be represented by Counsel. (*Gideon v. Wainwright* 1963, 337; hereafter *Gideon*)

The trial judge disagreed and denied Gideon's request. Consequently, Gideon was forced to defend himself without the aid of legal counsel. "Gideon conducted his defense about as well as could be expected from a layman. He made an opening statement to the jury, cross-examined the State's witnesses, presented witnesses in his own defense, declined to testify himself, and made a short argument 'emphasizing his innocence to the charge contained in the Information filed in this case'" (*Gideon* 1963, 337). Nonetheless, the jury returned a verdict of guilty and sentenced Gideon to five years in prison. Writing in pencil on prison stationary, Gideon appealed his case to the U.S. Supreme Court, which granted certiorari. Gideon claimed that the denial of counsel violated his rights under the Sixth Amendment.

Unfortunately, Gideon's claim that "[t]he United States Supreme Court says I am entitled to be represented by Counsel," was not entirely accurate. In 1942, the Court said the exact opposite to a man in a remarkably similar situation to that of Clarence Gideon. In *Betts v. Brady*, the Court instead applied the "fundamental fairness" doctrine:

> the Fourteenth Amendment prohibits the conviction and incarceration of one whose trial is offensive to the common and fundamental ideas of fairness and right, and, while want of counsel in a particular case may result in a conviction lacking in such fundamental fairness, we cannot say that the Amendment embodies an inexorable command that no trial for any offense, or in any court, can be fairly conducted and justice accorded a defendant who is not represented by counsel. (*Betts v. Brady* 1942, 473)

In *Gideon*, the Court reversed this position. Writing for the Court, Justice Black said that the justices

> accept *Betts v. Brady*'s assumption, based as it was on our prior cases, that a provision of the Bill of Rights which is "fundamental and essential to a fair trial" is made obligatory upon the States by the Fourteenth Amendment. We think the Court in *Betts* was wrong, however, in concluding that the Sixth Amendment's guarantee of counsel is not one of these fundamental rights. (*Gideon* 1963, 342)

Five months later, Gideon was once again tried for his crime, this time with the assistance of counsel. After his attorney discredited the testimony of the main witness for the prosecution, the jury returned a verdict of not guilty.

Later rulings by the Supreme Court extended the right to counsel to custodial interrogation (*Miranda v. Arizona* 1966), pre-trial lineups (*United States v. Wade* 1967), some preliminary hearings (*Coleman v. Alabama* 1970), misdemeanor cases that could result in incarceration (*Argersinger v. Hamlin* 1972), the first level of appellate review (*Douglas v. California* 1963), certain parole and probation hearings (*Gagnon v. Scarpelli* 1973; *Morrissey v. Brewer* 1972), and the trial stage in a delinquency hearing (*In re Gault* 1967).

Once again, national public opinion surveys regarding the *Gideon* ruling are unavailable, but the findings of the American National Election Studies (ANES) suggest the ruling was unpopular. In addition to the general dislike for rulings protecting criminal defendants found in the 1964 study, respondents to the 1966 ANES expressed even stronger distaste for the right to counsel. In this study, responses in the category "protection of rights of accused criminals: right to counsel, fair trial, no forced confessions (*Gideon, Esposito, Miranda* cases)" ranked second after the school prayer decisions among all dislikes.[27] Strong opposition to the *Miranda* ruling in national public opinion surveys confirms this sentiment; the right-to-counsel decision was probably very unpopular. However, regardless of public opinion, I expect the *Gideon* decision to have had a strong effect on behavior because the ruling could be directly implemented by lower courts.

The Court in *Gideon* expressed a preference for the state to provide an attorney to every indigent defendant in the United States who could not afford one. An ideal measure of conformity to this ruling would compare the number of indigent defendants who were provided with free counsel before and after the ruling. Unfortunately, this data is not available. Instead, I measure the effect of the *Gideon* ruling on the criminal justice system by examining changes in organized defender systems.

Defense attorneys for indigent defendants in the United States are usually provided through one of three mechanisms: assigned counsel systems, contract attorney programs, or public defender systems. In assigned counsel systems, private attorneys are appointed by the court, either on an ad hoc basis or through a coordinated system on a rotational basis, and compensated with a flat fee or an hourly rate. In contract attorney programs, the state, county, or other jurisdictional unit contracts with private attorneys, law firms, or nonprofit organizations to provide representation for indigent defendants. Public defender programs are public or private nonprofit organizations with full- or part-time attorneys that represent indigent defendants.[28] Although there are advantages and disadvantages to each of these systems, the public defender system is the preferred method of indigent defense.[29] The existence of an organized, full- or part-time staff charged with the responsibility of providing defense counsel to those who cannot afford it greatly enhances the probability that indigent defendants are assigned counsel;[30] therefore, I will use the availability of public

---

[27] See Appendix II for survey information and citations.

[28] See Spangenberg and Beeman (1995, 32–7) for a more detailed description of these three defender systems.

[29] See, for example, Benner (1975), citing the National Advisory Commission and a survey of participants in the criminal justice system, including judges in jurisdictions utilizing assigned counsel systems.

[30] There is some evidence that the introduction of public defender systems may cause changes in the criminal justice system such as increasing dismissals, acquittals, and trial rates (Benjamin and Pedeliski 1969).

TABLE 5.13. *Counties with Public Defender Systems, 1961–94*

Year	1961	1973	1982	1986	1990	1992	1994
% of counties with public defender systems	3	28	32	37	57[1]	64[1]	. 68[1]
% of population served by public defender systems	25	64	68				
% of counties with contract defender systems		~0	6	11	11[2]	8[2]	7[2]

Note: Data compiled from Benner (1975, 669), Smith and DeFrances (1996, 2), DeFrances (2001, 1), Mounts (1986, 478), Mounts and Wilson (1986, 199), and Spangenberg and Beeman (1995, 47).

[1] These figures are based on surveys of state prosecutors' offices and include those reporting that indigents are exclusively represented by public defender systems, as well as those reporting that mixed systems are used that include public defender offices.

[2] These figures are based on surveys of state prosecutors' offices and include only those reporting that indigents are exclusively represented by contract systems.

defender systems as a proxy for the criminal justice system's conformity to the *Gideon* ruling.

Statistics on the prevalence of public defender systems in the United States are presented in Table 5.13. In 1961, two years before *Gideon*, public defender systems existed in only 3 percent of counties in the United States, serving about 25 percent of the U.S. population. The percentage of the population served far exceeds the percentage of counties because public defender systems tend to be located in densely populated areas. Twelve years later, after the *Gideon* ruling and the series of right-to-counsel cases that followed it, public defender systems were in place in 28 percent of counties serving 64 percent of the nation's population. Stated another way, although 75 percent of the population was not served by public defender systems in 1961, 52 percent of that group had access to these systems in 1973 [(64–25)/75 = 52%]; therefore, the conservative estimate of behavior conformity to *Gideon* is 52 percent. The rate of increase in public defender systems declined significantly after the decade following *Gideon*. Never since has there been such a significant jump in the number of counties using such systems, and the next large increase did not occur until the late 1980s.

The number of statewide programs that compensated assigned counsel in noncapital criminal defense cases also increased after *Gideon*, but this change may have been part of a preexisting pattern. As shown in Table 5.14, between 1951 and 1961, the number of states compensating counsel increased from twenty-three to thirty-two. By 1973, this number increased to forty and did not increase significantly again before the turn of the century.

Although it is difficult to obtain a reliable measurement of the Court's impact on the number of indigent defendants in the United States who were actually provided legal counsel, the *Gideon* ruling probably had a strong causal effect on indigent defense systems in the United States. In the decade after *Gideon*, the number of people in jurisdictions without organized defender systems was

TABLE 5.14. *States that Fund Defender Programs, 1951–99*

Year	1951	1961	1973	1995	1999
# of states that compensate assigned counsel in noncapital cases	23	32	40	41	41

Note: Data compiled from Benner (1975, 669), Smith and DeFrances (1996, 2), DeFrances (2001, 1), Mounts (1986, 478), Mounts and Wilson (1986, 199), and Spangenberg and Beeman (1995, 47).

cut in half. Furthermore, this figure represents an extremely conservative estimate of *Gideon*'s effect because the absence of organized defender systems does not mean that indigent defendants were not provided with counsel.

Numerous scholars criticize the quality and funding of indigent defense systems in the United States post-*Gideon* (Bazelon 1976; Drecksel 1991; Klien 1986; Moran 1982; Mounts 1982; Mounts and Wilson 1986; Note 2000). In fact, claims of ineffective counsel increased after the *Gideon* ruling (Strazzella 1977, 445). This outcome should not be surprising given the increased demand for attorneys and the stronger legal arguments for the right to counsel after the ruling. Interestingly though, despite the plethora of scholars lamenting the inadequacy of indigent defense in the United States, none of these scholars claim that defendants are actually denied counsel as Clarence Gideon was, suggesting a more generous estimate of 100 percent behavior conformity. The *Gideon* ruling may amount to nothing more than the right to a warm body with a law degree,[31] but even that is a significant change compared to the pre-*Gideon* status quo.

CAPITAL PUNISHMENT

On August 11, 1967, William Micke returned to his home in Savannah, Georgia, to find it being burglarized by William Henry Furman. According to Furman's later testimony, he attempted to flee the scene and, while doing so, tripped and fell. The gun Furman was carrying went off and killed Micke. Furman was charged with murder and convicted in a one-day trial. His appeal eventually reached the U.S. Supreme Court and was combined with those of two others sentenced to death, one for rape and one for both rape and murder. The Court overturned the death sentences in all three cases based on the prohibition of cruel and unusual punishment in the Eighth Amendment, made applicable to the states by the Fourteenth Amendment. The split decision, which included five different rationales from the five justices in the majority, returned the cases to the lower courts and returned the issue of capital punishment to the state legislatures, which were charged with writing new capital punishment statutes.

---

[31] Even this may be an overstatement; in some jurisdictions, law students serve as indigent defenders (*Argersinger v. Hamlin* 1972, 40–1).

The Court's decision in *Furman v. Georgia* (1972) was a clear order to lower trial courts not to sentence defendants to death under the current death penalty laws. In addition, the decision made clear that no one should be put to death in the United States until the constitutional difficulties with the current laws were resolved. The decision was unpopular with the public. A national public opinion poll conducted in July of 1972 showed that only 32 percent of Americans agreed with the Court's decision; 56 percent disagreed.[32] Opposition was even stronger in southern states, most of which permitted capital punishment (Davis et al. 2007). Four years after the *Furman* decision, the Court upheld the death penalty under a new Georgia statute in *Gregg v. Georgia* (1976).[33] Not surprisingly, this decision was very popular.[34]

Despite strong public opposition to the *Furman* ruling, the sentencing of criminal defendants is controlled by lower-court judges; therefore, I expect the ruling to have had a causal effect on the administration of the death penalty in the United States. Figure 5.11 shows the number of executions in the United States for each year between 1930 and 2006 (Bureau of Justice Statistics 2006). Beginning around 1940, the number of executions declined steadily until finally reaching zero in 1968, four years before the *Furman* ruling. In the most straight-forward sense, the Court's prohibition on the death penalty was implemented perfectly; not one execution was performed in the United States between 1972 and 1976. Therefore, I code the generous estimate of behavior conformity to the *Furman* ruling as 100 percent.

However, the data presented in Figure 5.11 do not offer strong evidence that the Court played a causal role in the capital punishment issue area. Because there were no executions in the years leading up to the *Furman* ruling, there was no possibility for the Court's decision to affect the number of executions. The Court does not fail the test of judicial power in this analysis, but it does not have the opportunity to successfully alter behavior. The most interesting finding from these data is the fact that executions did resume after the Court's ruling in *Gregg*, beginning in 1977 with the execution of Gary Gilmore by firing squad in Utah.

Because it was not possible for the Court to affect the number of executions in the United States following its decision in *Furman*, a more appropriate test of the Court's power is a measurement of its impact on those sentenced to death. Figure 5.12 shows the number of prisoners in the United States under the death sentence for each year between 1953 and 1985. In the early 1960s, around the time executions in the United States sharply declined, the number of prisoners held on death row began to steadily rise. By 1971, there were 642 prisoners in the United States waiting to be executed. In 1972, however, just a month after *Furman* had been argued before the U.S. Supreme Court,

---

[32] See Appendix II for survey information and citations.
[33] See Epstein and Kobylka (1992) for an analysis of why the Court reversed its position on capital punishment so quickly.
[34] See Appendix II for survey information and citations.

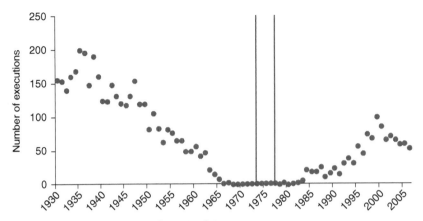

FIGURE 5.11. Executions in the United States, 1930–2006.

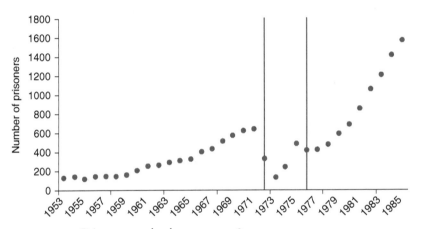

FIGURE 5.12. Prisoners on death row, 1953–85.

the California Supreme Court ruled that the death penalty violated the Cruel and Unusual Punishment Clause in the California Constitution. That ruling reversed the death sentences of 105 men and 5 women in California. Then, in June of that year, the Court issued the *Furman* ruling, and "some 631 men and 2 women then on death rows in 32 states had their sentences commuted to prison terms" (Radelet n.d., 5). Some of these prisoners, who had been in prison since the 1950s, had their sentences commuted to twenty years in prison and were actually released following *Furman*. In 1973, only 134 people were sitting on death row after being sentenced under newly enacted death penalty statutes, most of which required separate guilt and sentencing phases. In just two years, the number of people sitting on death row decreased by 79 percent; I use this figure as the conservative estimate of behavior conformity. By 1976, new death penalty laws had been enacted in thirty-five states and more than 400 people were held under the death sentence in the United States. Following the *Gregg* decision in 1976, the number of prisoners on death row increased steadily, topping 3,600 in 2002.

One might argue that the *Furman* ruling could have indirectly caused an increase in the murder rate by removing the deterrent effect of the death penalty. I decline to pursue this avenue of investigation for several reasons. First, because the justices obviously did not intend to increase the murder rate through their ruling, any increase in the murder rate would not reflect behavior conforming to the Court's preferences. Surely the Court intended for this possible outcome to be mitigated by other factors; therefore, searching for such an effect would be a perverse test of Supreme Court power. Second, because there were no executions in the United States for several years before Furman, the ruling probably had little impact on the deterrent effect. The only way the decision would have made a difference is if simply having the death penalty on the books but never enforcing it was a deterrent that the Court eliminated. Third, a brief look at the literature on the death penalty indicates that there is very little definitive evidence that it acts as a strong deterrent (Bedau 1998).

The Court's ruling in *Furman v. Georgia* presents a complicated test of judicial power. The lack of any executions in the United States in the years leading up to the *Furman* decision made it impossible for the Court to reduce the number of executions. The Court's order was not violated, but it is unclear whether it had a causal effect on the number of executions. The evidence on the number of prisoners held under the death penalty offers much stronger evidence of Court power. Following the *Furman* ruling, hundreds of prisoners on death row had their sentences commuted, and the number of prisoners on death row remained low for several years. Executions resumed in the United States only after the states rewrote their death penalty laws and these new laws were approved in *Gregg*.

FREE PRESS IN THE COURTROOM

Criminal defendants were not the only ones to win special rights in criminal trials; the Court has also expanded the rights of reporters covering these trials. In July of 1976, John Paul Stevenson was convicted of murdering a hotel manager who had been found stabbed to death the previous December. A few months later, the Virginia Supreme Court reversed Stevenson's conviction on the grounds that a bloodstained shirt allegedly belonging to Stevenson had been improperly admitted into evidence. Stevenson was retried in the same court, but this trial ended in a mistrial on May 30, 1978, when a juror asked to be excused after the trial had begun and there was no alternate juror available. Stevenson's third trial also ended in a mistrial after a juror supposedly informed other jurors of information read in a newspaper regarding Stevenson's previous trials. At the beginning of his fourth trial, Stevenson's attorney made a motion to close the trial to the public. The prosecution did not object to the motion, and the judge agreed.

Later that day, two reporters for Richmond Newspapers, Inc., sought a hearing asking the judge to vacate his closure order. The trial judge held a hearing and declined to vacate his previous order. On September 12, 1978, the prosecution presented its evidence against Stevenson for the fourth time. At the conclusion of the state's case, the defendant moved to strike the state's evidence "on grounds stated to the record"; the trial court sustained the motion, dismissed the jury, and found Stevenson not guilty (*Richmond Newspapers, Inc. v. Virginia* 1980, 562; hereafter *Richmond Newspapers*). The reporters for Richmond Newspapers, Inc., appealed the closure of the trial to the Virginia Supreme Court. After the Virginia Supreme Court dismissed their petition, they appealed to the U.S. Supreme Court.

The Supreme Court found that even though the trial that the reporters wished to cover had ended, the case was not moot because "the underlying dispute is capable of repetition, yet evading review" (*Richmond Newspapers* 1980, 563). Just four years prior, in *Nebraska Press Association v. Stuart* (1976), the Supreme Court had ruled that a defendant's Sixth Amendment right to a fair trial did not justify an order restraining members of the press from publishing or broadcasting information about a trial; however, until the ruling in *Richmond Newspapers, Inc. v. Virginia*, the Court had never addressed the First Amendment rights of members of the press or the public to attend criminal trials. Although the Court could not agree on a single majority opinion, seven justices agreed that the closure of the trial violated the First Amendment rights of the press and the public.

It is unclear whether or not the Court's decision in *Richmond Newspapers* was a popular one. In a 1977 public opinion survey, 69 percent of respondents agreed that "[r]eporters should be prohibited from publishing/broadcasting information which might affect fair trial"; and in a 1979 poll, 80 percent of respondents agreed that "[a] judge has a right to prevent newspapers from covering a trial if he thinks such coverage would make a fair trial impossible." However, when asked about the Court's 1976 ruling in *Nebraska Press Association v. Stuart*, 71 percent of respondents agreed with the Court's ruling that "judges generally cannot bar newspapers and the media from reporting on a trial as it happens."[35] These conflicting findings may reflect ambivalence in the public about this policy question, or it may reflect the drastic effects of subtle differences in question wording. Alternatively, this finding may suggest that on this particular question, the Supreme Court has a strong influence over public attitudes; consequently, support for the Court's position increased when the interviewer informed the respondent about the Court's ruling. Regardless, because free press in the courtroom is a vertical issue, I expect the Court's ruling to have had a strong effect on the behavior of lower courts.

---

[35] See Appendix II for survey information and citations.

In the *Richmond Newspapers* decision, the Court ruled that Stevenson's trial should not have been closed to the public; however, none of the four opinions offered by the seven justices in the majority suggested that trials could never be closed to the public in any circumstance. Instead, the Court's criticism focused on the failure of the trial-court judge to make specific findings to support the decision to close the trial. The closure of Stevenson's trial was unconstitutional because

> no inquiry was made as to whether alternative solutions would have met the need to ensure fairness; there was no recognition of any right under the Constitution for the public or press to attend the trial ... There was no suggestion that any problems with witnesses could not have been dealt with by their exclusion from the courtroom or their sequestration during the trial. Nor is there anything to indicate that sequestration of the jurors would not have guarded against their being subjected to any improper information. (*Richmond Newspapers* 1980, 580–1)

In other words, the Court did not express a preference for all trials to be open to the public; instead, the Court ruled that a trial-court judge could not close a trial to the public without first making findings of fact to support the need for closure in that particular case. Accordingly, even if the Court's ruling had a strong causal effect on the behavior of lower-court judges, we should not expect to see these lower courts completely stop closing trials to the public. We should simply expect a decrease in closures due to the increased burden on trial-court judges who wish to exclude the public from their courtrooms.

Unfortunately, no comprehensive data is available on the total number of criminal trials closed to the public in the United States each year. The best source of data on the closure of criminal trials around the time of the *Richmond Newspapers* decision appears in a series of articles entitled "Court Watch Summary" in a publication called *The News Media and the Law* (Reporters Committee for Freedom of the Press 1979; 1980; 1981). These articles compile reports of courtroom closures over various time periods between July 2, 1979, and May 30, 1981.[36] The data from these articles is reorganized and reported in Table 5.15.

As shown in the table, the average number of courtroom closures reported in this publication dropped from more than eleven closures per month before the *Richmond Newspapers* ruling to less than nine closures per month after the decision. If we assume that the justices intended to completely end courtroom closures, then this decrease represents a behavior conformity rate of 23.5 percent $[(11.5-8.8)/11.5]$. Of course, this is an extremely conservative estimate of the Court's effect on the behavior of lower-court judges because the justices did not intend to completely end courtroom closures. A much more

---

[36] Unfortunately, *The News Media and the Law* stopped publishing "Courtroom Watch Summary" articles after 1981. It is possible that the magazine stopped publishing reports because courtroom closures declined more drastically after May 30, 1981, but there is no way to verify this possibility.

TABLE 5.15. *Courtroom Closures, 1979–81*

	6/2/79–12/15/79	12/16/79–10/15/80	10/16/80–5/30/81
# of closures	63	112	66
Closures per month	11.5	11.2	8.8

Note: Data based on reports compiled by the Reporters Committee for Freedom of the Press as reported in *The News Media and the Law* (1979; 1980; 1981).

generous interpretation of the Court's effect would assume that this type of minor decrease in closures is exactly the type of change we should expect given the Court's heightened burden on trial-court judges; therefore, the generous estimate of behavior conformity in this issue area is 100 percent.

The limited data on courtroom closures in the United States makes it difficult to reach firm conclusions about the Court's success at altering behavior through its rulings in this area. Nonetheless, the available data suggests that courtroom closures did decline significantly following *Richmond Newspapers*. Although the conservative estimate of behavior conformity is lower in this issue area than in other vertical issues, the estimate is almost certainly lower than it should be because the Court did not intend to end all courtroom closures. Instead, the Court merely required trial judges to make findings of fact to support the need for closure. In addition to causing a decrease in closures, the ruling probably had a strong effect on the procedures judges follow when closing trials to the public that could only be detected in a more detailed, qualitative study.

SOVEREIGN IMMUNITY

Although most vertical issues involve matters of criminal law, the Court has also initiated social change by issuing rulings in matters of civil law that could be directly implemented by lower courts. The Court's rulings in sovereign immunity cases, beginning with *Seminole Tribe v. Florida*, are prominent examples of such decisions. In 1979, the Seminole Tribe of Florida opened a bingo hall, which was the first modern Native American gaming establishment in the United States. At the time, Florida law prohibited the operation of noncharitable bingo, and a county sheriff decided to enforce the law against the tribe. The Seminole Tribe filed suit in federal court seeking an injunction against the enforcement of the Florida law, and the Fifth Circuit Court of Appeals granted the request.

The Fifth Circuit ruled that states could completely prohibit gambling within their borders, including on Indian reservations; however, if they chose to merely "regulate gambling" by prohibiting the practice only in certain places or in certain situations, they could not violate the sovereignty of the Indian tribe by regulating Indian gaming (*Seminole Tribe of Florida v. Butterworth* 1981).

Because Florida allowed charitable bingo, its law was not an absolute prohibition and, therefore, could not be applied against the Seminole Tribe. Other federal courts followed the Fifth Circuit's lead, and by 1986 Indian tribes were operating more than 100 gaming facilities in the United States (Twetten 2000, 1338–40). In 1987, in *California v. Cabazon Band of Indians*, the Supreme Court endorsed the distinction between the prohibition and regulation of gaming, and ruled that states could not regulate Indian gaming unless Congress used its authority under the Indian Commerce Clause to expressly allow such regulation (207).

The next year, Congress responded by passing the Indian Gaming Regulatory Act (IGRA). The Act created three classes of Indian gaming. Under the Act, Class I games, traditional tribal games of chance, are exclusively controlled by the tribes; Class II games, including bingo and certain card games, can be operated by tribes only if they are not completely prohibited by state or federal law; Class III games, including all other games such as blackjack, slot machines, roulette, and other casino style games, can only be operated if a tribe negotiates a compact with the state in which the gaming operation resides. Once requested by Indian tribes, the Act requires states to negotiate these compacts "in good faith"; if the state refuses to negotiate or does not do so "in good faith," the tribe can file suit against the state in federal district court. The federal court then appoints a mediator to attempt to resolve the disagreement; if the mediator cannot resolve the dispute, the Secretary of the Interior can then create an enforceable tribal-state compact to provide for Indian gaming (*Seminole Tribe v. Florida* 1996, 47–50; hereafter *Seminole Tribe*).

"The tribal-state compact requirement for Class III gaming was Congress's attempt to balance competing interests of tribal and state governments" (Light and Rand 2007, 57). Through the compacting process, states could regulate Class III gaming without completely prohibiting the practice, and tribes could demand "good faith negotiation" from states that preferred to delay negotiation, prohibit only Indian gaming, or demand outrageous concessions from the tribes. The "crux" of the "balanced and careful relationship between Indian tribes ... and the various states ... was a congressional waiver of state sovereign immunity that allowed Indian tribes to sue the states and force their governors to negotiate with tribes over gaming compacts" (Fletcher 2007, 41–2).

In September of 1991, the Seminole Tribe of Florida filed suit against the State of Florida, claiming that the state had "refused to enter into any negotiation for inclusion of [certain gaming activities] in a tribal-state compact," thereby violating the "requirement of good faith negotiation" (*Seminole Tribe* 1996, 52). The State moved to dismiss the complaint, "arguing that the suit violated the State's sovereign immunity from suit in federal court" (*Seminole Tribe* 1996, 52). The district court denied the motion, and the State appealed to the Eleventh Circuit Court of Appeals. The Eleventh Circuit remanded the case back to the district court with orders to dismiss the suit. The Seminole Tribe appealed the case to the Supreme Court, which agreed to hear the case.

The concept of sovereign immunity, though tracing its origin to early English common law, finds its textual basis in the Eleventh Amendment to the Constitution, which reads:

> The Judicial power of the United States shall not be construed to extend to any suit in law or equity, commenced or prosecuted against one of the United States by Citizens of another State, or by Citizens or Subjects of any Foreign State. (U.S. Constitution, amend. XI)

Although the text of the Eleventh Amendment is clearly limited to suits commenced against a state by citizens of other states and nations, the Court has "understood the Eleventh Amendment to stand not so much for what it says, but for the presupposition ... which it confirms ... that each State is a sovereign entity in our federal system; and ... that it is inherent in the nature of sovereignty not to be amenable to the suit of an individual without its consent" (*Seminole Tribe* 1996, 54). Based on this presupposition, the Court in *Seminole Tribe* ruled that Congress did not have the power to abrogate a state's sovereign immunity; accordingly, no state could be sued under the IGRA unless it consented to be sued. Because the State of Florida had not consented by waiving its immunity, the federal court had no jurisdiction over the suit.

The *Seminole Tribe* ruling fundamentally altered the "balanced and careful relationship" that the IGRA had created between the tribes and states. By invalidating the tribe's ability to compel the state to negotiate compacts in "good faith," the ruling placed the tribes at a severe disadvantage relative to the states. Without the power to bring suit in federal court, tribes were left at the mercy of the states, which could delay negotiations indefinitely, demand huge regulatory and financial concessions from the tribes, or refuse to negotiate compacts at all. Accordingly, if the *Seminole Tribe* ruling had a causal effect on the behavior of tribes and states, then those compacts negotiated after the Court's ruling should contain provisions substantially more favorable to the states than those negotiated before the ruling.

The most beneficial provision a state can obtain in a tribal-state compact is a revenue-sharing agreement. "In a revenue-sharing agreement, a tribe commits to paying a portion of gaming revenues to the state in exchange for the right to conduct casino-style gaming in the state, sometimes including a guarantee of exclusivity; that is the state promises to limit, or at least not to expand, commercial gaming within the state" (Light and Rand 2007, 70). It is certainly not obvious that the Court in *Seminole Tribe* specifically intended to help states obtain revenue-sharing agreements in tribal-state compacts; however, it is clear that the majority sought to preserve the Court's "established federalism jurisprudence" by protecting state sovereign immunity and limiting the power of federal courts over the states (*Seminole Tribe* 1996, 64). Such an ardently pro-states' rights interpretation of the constitution was probably intended to advance the interests of the states, which in the case of the IGRA meant helping the states obtain more advantageous tribal-state compacts, such as those with revenue-sharing provisions.

No national public opinion polls have specifically asked respondents about the sovereign immunity issue or the Court's decision in *Seminole Tribe*. A poll conducted a few months after the *Seminole Tribe* ruling indicated that 57 percent of respondents would approve of their state legalizing casino gambling on Indian reservations as a way to help the state raise revenue; however, this poll sheds little light on the popularity of the *Seminole Tribe* ruling because it is unclear whether those indicating approval would do so if it did not raise revenue for the state.[37] Regardless, because the Court's ruling could be directly implemented by lower-court judges simply dismissing suits under the IGRA, sovereign immunity is a vertical issue, and I expect the Court's ruling in *Seminole Tribe* to have a strong effect on the behavior of states and tribes when negotiating compacts.

Between 1989 and 2006, 242 tribal-state compacts were signed establishing Indian gaming facilities on Native American reservations. Of these, 98 included revenue-sharing provisions. Seventy-seven of the 242 compacts were signed before the Eleventh Circuit Court's ruling upholding Florida's sovereign immunity in 1994; 40 compacts were signed between the Eleventh Circuit's ruling and the Supreme Court's 1996 ruling in *Seminole Tribe*; 124 compacts were signed between the *Seminole Tribe* ruling and 2006. Table 5.16 reports the number of compacts with and without revenue-sharing agreements in each of these three time periods. Figure 5.16 reports the number of tribal-state compacts signed each year between 1989 and 2006, broken down by whether or not the compact included a revenue-sharing agreement.

Only 3 of the 77 compacts signed before the Eleventh Circuit Court's ruling in 1994 (3.9%) included revenue-sharing provisions. One of these compacts simply required the tribe to contribute $250,000 a year, matched by the state, into a tourism promotion fund, rather than provide the state with a percentage of its revenue. Between the Eleventh Circuit Court's ruling and the Supreme Court's ruling in 1996, 14 of the 40 compacts signed (35%) included revenue-sharing provisions. Of these, 12 were compacts between various tribes and the State of New Mexico signed during 1995. Eighty-one of the 124 compacts signed after the Court's ruling in *Seminole Tribe* (65.3%) have included revenue-sharing agreements; 48 of these compacts were signed between various tribes and the State of California in 1999 and 2000.

Because there is no way to evaluate exactly how much of an advantage the Court intended to give the states in negotiating these compacts, there is no way to determine the extent to which the behavior of states and tribes conformed to the Court's preferences after the *Seminole Tribe* ruling. The most generous interpretation of the Court's power would suggest that the drastic change in behavior over this period indicates that the Court achieved 100 percent behavior conformity. The most conservative estimate of the Court's power would assume that the justices preferred that every tribal-state compact include a revenue-sharing agreement. Before the Eleventh Circuit's ruling, 96.1 percent of

---

[37] See Appendix II for survey information and citations.

TABLE 5.16. *Tribal-State Compacts, 1987–2006*

	# of Compacts with no Revenue Sharing	# of Compacts with Revenue Sharing	% of Compacts with Revenue Sharing
Pre-Eleventh Circuit ruling	74	3	3.9%
Between Eleventh Circuit ruling and *Seminole*	26	14	35.0
After *Seminole*	43	81	65.3
Total	143	98	

Note: Data based on original examination of Tribal-State Compacts as reported on the National Indian Gaming Commission Web site (http://www.nigc.gov/ReadingRoom/Compacts/tabid/760/Default.aspx).

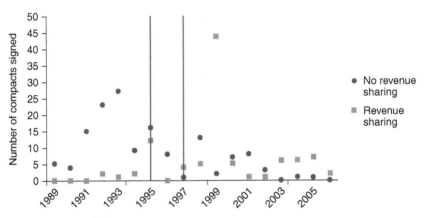

FIGURE 5.13. Tribal-state compacts, 1987–2006.

compacts had no revenue-sharing agreement; after the Supreme Court's ruling in *Seminole Tribe*, only 34.7 percent of compacts had no revenue-sharing agreement, a 63.9 percent reduction [(96.1–34.7)/96.1 = 63.9]. I use this figure as the conservative estimate of behavior conformity.

In *Seminole Tribe*, the Court waded deeply into an issue with a complicated history of litigation, federal and state legislation, and political conflict. Its ruling fundamentally altered a careful, detailed political compromise that had been negotiated between states, Indian tribes, and the federal government, and which had been operating successfully for several years. The decision gave a strong advantage to states in negotiating tribal-state compacts, and the states have used this advantage to obtain coveted revenue-sharing agreements from the tribes. As Indian gaming operations continue to proliferate around the country, the effects of the *Seminole Tribe* ruling can be felt by states and tribes that must negotiate new compacts or renegotiate old ones, tribes that must continually share their revenue with the states, and states that now enjoy a new, robust source of income.

THE GUN-FREE SCHOOL ZONES ACT

On March 10, 1992, Alfonso Lopez, Jr., a senior at Edison High School in San Antonio, Texas, carried a concealed .38 caliber handgun and five bullets into his school. Acting on an anonymous tip, school officials confronted Lopez, and he quickly confessed that he was carrying the weapon. Lopez was arrested and initially charged with violation of a Texas law making it a crime to possess a firearm on school premises. The next day, the state charges were dropped after federal agents charged Lopez with violating a federal statute, the Gun-Free School Zones Act of 1990 (GFSZ Act).

Enacted by Congress as part of the Crime Control Act of 1990, the GFSZ Act made it a federal offense for "any individual knowingly to possess a firearm at a place that [he or she] knows ... is a school zone" (*United States v. Lopez* 1995, 549; hereafter *Lopez*). For the purposes of the Act, a school zone was defined as the grounds or within 1,000 feet from the grounds of any public, parochial, or private school. Violators of the Act were subject to up to $5,000 in fines and as much as five years in prison, or both.

After being indicted by a federal grand jury, Lopez filed a motion to dismiss the indictment on the ground that the GFSZ Act was "unconstitutional as it is beyond the power of Congress to legislate control over our public schools" (*Lopez* 1995, 551). The Federal District Court denied the motion, concluding that the GFSZ Act "is a constitutional exercise of Congress's well defined power to regulate activities in and affecting commerce, and the 'business' of elementary, middle and high schools ... affects interstate commerce" (*Lopez* 1995, 551–2). Lopez was found guilty of violating the Act and sentenced to six months in prison and two years of supervised release; however, the Court of Appeals for the Fifth Circuit reversed his conviction, finding that the GFSZ Act did exceed Congress's power under the Commerce Clause (*United States v. Lopez* 1993). The government appealed the case to the U.S. Supreme Court, which granted certiorari.

On appeal to the Supreme Court, the government argued that the possession of a firearm in an educational environment would likely lead to the commission of a violent crime, which would in turn affect the national economy in several ways: first, the substantial costs of violent crimes are spread throughout the population through the mechanism of insurance; second, violent crime discourages travel to areas of the country perceived to be unsafe. In addition, the presence of guns in schools might pose a substantial threat to the educational process, which could result in a less economically productive citizenry (*Lopez* 1995, 563–4).

The Supreme Court disagreed. In an opinion by Chief Justice Rehnquist representing the views of five justices, the Court ruled that "the Act exceeds the authority of Congress 'to regulate Commerce ... among the several States ...'"

(*Lopez* 1995, 551). Rehnquist identified three categories of activity that Congress could regulate under the Commerce Clause: "the channels of interstate commerce," "the instrumentalities of interstate commerce, or persons or things in interstate commerce, even though the threat may come only from intrastate activities," and "those activities that substantially affect interstate commerce" (*Lopez* 1995, 558–9). Although the government argued that the GFSZ Act fell within this third category, the Court held that "the possession of a gun in a local school zone is in no sense an economic activity that might, through repetition elsewhere, substantially affect any sort of interstate commerce" (*Lopez* 1995, 567). In addition, the Act "contains no jurisdictional element which would ensure, through case-by case inquiry, that the firearm possession in question affects interstate commerce" (*Lopez* 1995, 561). Because the Act exceeded Congress's authority under the Interstate Commerce Clause, the Court invalidated the statute and affirmed the reversal of Lopez's conviction.

The *Lopez* decision was handed down on April 26, 1995. Two weeks later, President Clinton sent a message to Congress transmitting the proposed "Gun-Free School Zones Amendments Act of 1995" (U.S. Congress 1995). The proposed amendment was designed to rebut the criticism that the GFSZ Act did not contain a jurisdictional element by outlawing only the possession of a firearm "that has moved in or that otherwise affects interstate or foreign commerce" (Safra 2000, 638). The amendment was passed as part of the Omnibus Consolidated Appropriations Act of 1997 and signed into law on September 30, 1996 (Safra 2000, 638, footnote 9). The amended statute was never invalidated by the Court.[38]

No national opinion polls were conducted specifically asking respondents about their views on the GFSZ Act or the Supreme Court decision invalidating the Act; however, the *Lopez* ruling was probably very unpopular with the public. Public opinion surveys conducted in 1993 indicated that respondents worried more about "students bringing guns into schools" than they did about any other serious crime including having their home burglarized, being injured in a crime, or being a victim of sexual assault or gang violence. In a 1994 Gallup poll, 86 percent of respondents said that creating stronger penalties for possession of weapons by students would be a "very effective" measure to reduce school violence. More than 90 percent of respondents to a 1998 survey said that removing weapons, drugs, and gangs from schools was "absolutely essential." In a 1998 survey of registered female voters, 84 percent said they thought the federal government should play a "strong" or "somewhat strong" role in helping to guarantee that schools are safe from violence, guns, and drugs. Strong public support for restrictions on guns in schools is further evidenced by Congress's prompt and uncontroversial passage of the amendment to the GFSZ Act discussed previously.

---

[38] See Safra (2000) for a discussion of doubts as to the constitutionality of the amended GFSZ Act.

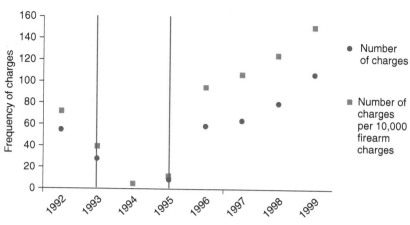

FIGURE 5.14. Defendants charged with possession of a firearm in a school zone, 1992–99.

The GFSZ Act of 1990 was initially invalidated by the Fifth Circuit Court of Appeals on September 15, 1993. The Gun-Free School Zones Amendments Act was signed into law on September 30, 1996. Consequently, if the decisions of the Fifth Circuit and the Supreme Court had any effect on the behavior of government actors, then the number of federal charges for possession of a firearm on school property should have decreased in 1993 and then returned to previous levels in 1996 after Congress corrected the law's constitutional defect. The best information available on the number of charges for this offense is reported by the Bureau of Justice Statistics (Scalia 2000, 13). Figure 5.14 reports the number of defendants charged with possession of a firearm in a school zone between 1992 and 1998 with preliminary data for 1999.

The number of charges dropped from 55 in 1992 to only 4 in 1994, and then increased to 59 in 1996. In other words, the number of federal charges filed for possession of a firearm in a school zone decreased by 93 percent after the Fifth Circuit invalidated the GFSZ Act but then returned to previous levels after the passage of the Gun-Free School Zones Amendment Act brought the law into compliance with the Court's requirements. Therefore, the conservative estimate of behavior conformity to the *Lopez* ruling is 93 percent. The number of charges steadily increased following the passage of the Gun-Free School Zones Amendments Act, reaching 108 according to the preliminary data for 1999. A similar pattern appears when considering the number of charges for possession of a firearm in a school zone as a proportion of all firearm-related federal charges. Because these figures indicate only those defendants charged with possession of a firearm on school property, it is possible that none of those charged between 1993 and 1996 were actually convicted; assuming this is correct, the generous estimate of behavior conformity is 100 percent.

A more demanding test of the Court's effect on behavior might examine the effect of the *Lopez* ruling on incidents of gun violence in schools. I decline to pursue this analysis for four reasons.[39] First, just as in the case of the capital punishment ruling, I assume that the Court did not intend to encourage violent crime through the *Lopez* decision. Because the Court surely does not prefer an increase in violence, testing whether the Court was able to increase gun violence in schools as a result of its ruling would be a perverse test of judicial power. Second, because carrying a gun in a school would normally constitute a violation of state law, there is reason to believe that the marginal deterrent effect of the GFSZ Act would be minimal. Third, because the GFSZ Act was only invalidated for approximately three years and the Supreme Court's ruling was only in effect for about sixteen months, it is unlikely that the full consequences of the decision had time to take effect. Finally, and perhaps more importantly, for the *Lopez* rulings to have any effect on deterrence, potential violators would have to be aware of the ruling; however, it is highly unlikely that most elementary and secondary school students were aware of the Fifth Circuit or Supreme Court rulings invalidating this law.

Nonetheless, a realistic depiction of the *Lopez* ruling must conclude that it had little impact on gun control policy. Congress quickly replaced the invalidated statute with a new and nearly identical law, and, in the meantime, state laws continued to criminalize the activity that the Gun-Free School Zones Act had targeted. The Court's ruling achieved almost total behavior conformity, but it was inconsequential because the Court did not ask for a significant policy change. This finding does not contradict my theory of Supreme Court power, but it does suggest that some Court rulings – even "important" Court rulings – have little impact on social policy because they do not attempt to alter social policy. I will consider circumstances in which the Court asks for little or no policy change again in the sections on Congressional Exclusion and the Brady Bill.

If anything, this analysis raises doubts as to whether the *Lopez* decision should be considered an "important" ruling that belongs in this study. It is possible that the decision received media attention because it signaled a significant legal change rather than policy change, and that legal change could have led to future Court rulings, which would subsequently cause significant policy change. Indeed, this expectation was borne out when the Court invalidated the Violence Against Women Act in *United States v. Morrison* (2000) five years later.

Regardless of the broader policy impact, when considered on its own terms, the Supreme Court's ruling in *United States v. Lopez* had a strong causal effect on the behavior of federal prosecutors in charging defendants under the GFSZ Act. After the initial invalidation of the law by the Fifth Circuit, prosecutions drastically declined and did not return to previous levels until Congress amended the statute to comply with the Court's requirements. There is little

---

[39] For an analysis of indicators of school crime and safety, see DeVoe et al. (2004). There is some evidence that serious violent crimes in schools peaked briefly in 1994, but this trend started to decline in 1995, before the GFSZ Act was amended. It is unlikely this trend was caused by the *Lopez* decision. However, it is possible that the subsequent decline in violent crime was due to the Court's decision in *Roe v. Wade* (see *infra* Chapter 5, Abortion section).

reason to suspect that the Court's ruling had indirect effects on the behavior of potential violators of the Act, or that the Court intended to have such an effect. Nonetheless, the *Lopez* ruling is another example of the Court's strong influence over issue areas controlled by lower courts.

SUMMARY: UNPOPULAR VERTICAL ISSUES

In the eleven unpopular vertical issues under examination, I consistently find evidence of the Court altering the behavior of state and private actors through its rulings. In direct contrast to Gerald Rosenberg's examination of the Court's abortion cases, I find that the Court's decision in *Roe v. Wade* had dramatic and immediate effects on the behavior of women seeking abortion. Once accounting for differing state laws at the time of *Roe*, the evidence clearly shows the profound impact of the Court's decision. Perhaps the most drastic effect of the ruling was the decrease in the proportion of women crossing state lines to receive an abortion. Other studies suggest that the ruling may have had indirect effects on adoption rates and, though this claim is very contentious, may partially account for the drop in the crime rate in the early 1990s.

In contrast to Rosenberg's conclusion that the Court's criminal rights "revolution failed" (2008, 335), I find that the Court caused numerous, significant changes in the behavior of state and private actors in the criminal justice system. Although methodological difficulties and limited data hampered much of my analysis in those issues related to criminal procedure, the best evidence available suggests that the Court was highly successful at exercising power through these rulings. Conformity to the controversial capital punishment ruling appears to be perfect. The Court achieved high behavior conformity in those cases involving improperly obtained evidence, whether as the result of illegal searches, confessions obtained without informing suspects of their *Miranda* rights, or warrantless eavesdropping. In each of these cases, not only does the available evidence indicate that lower-court judges complied with the Court's instructions and stopped admitting such evidence, but it also suggests that non-court government actors adapted to these new rules by obtaining warrants for searches and eavesdropping, and by warning suspects of their *Miranda* rights. In addition, the Court's right-to-counsel rulings prompted the creation of numerous public defender systems to ensure basic legal defense for indigent defendants.

The Court was also highly successful at altering behavior through its First Amendment rulings. The Court's rulings in the flag desecration and obscenity cases caused the discontinuation of criminal convictions under state and federal laws and prompted the public to engage in or continue engaging in this constitutionally protected behavior. By far the weakest evidence of Supreme Court power in a vertical issue is that found in my examination of the Court's free press rulings; although the Court may have caused significant changes in the behavior of trial judges when closing their courtrooms to the press, the data supporting this claim is very limited.

Finally, the Court successfully exercised power through several rulings enhancing states' rights that could be implemented through lower courts. In the Gun-Free School Zones Act and sovereign immunity cases, the Court dramatically limited the power of the federal government to exert authority over gun control and Indian gaming.

Considered together, these studies demonstrate the expansive power of the Supreme Court to alter behavior in a wide range of issues when its rulings can be directly implemented by lower courts. Furthermore, the Court's decisions in these cases were extremely unpopular with the public, suggesting that in these situations the Court is not dependent on popular opinion or support from elected officials. When the implementation of a Supreme Court ruling depends only on the cooperation of lower-court judges, the Court's influence can extend well outside the courtroom, into abortion clinics, police stations, federal agencies, public protests, and the Internet.

6

Popular Lateral Issues

> Those in power need checks and restraints lest they come to identify the common good for their own tastes and desires, and their continuation in office as essential to the preservation of the nation.
>
> Justice William O. Douglas[1]

In this chapter, I examine popular Supreme Court rulings in lateral issues – those issues in which the Court must rely on non-court actors to implement its rulings. I find that when Court rulings faced little popular opposition, the justices' preferences had a strong causal effect on the behavior of state and private actors. These findings call into question the common assumption that popular Court decisions are insignificant because popular policies could always be enacted through the democratic process. On the contrary, my findings suggest that the manifestation of some popular policies may require prompting from the judiciary. Regardless, the case studies in this chapter demonstrate that the Court can wield significant power even when its decisions cannot be implemented by lower courts.

REAPPORTIONMENT

Although rarely receiving as much attention as rulings on abortion, free speech, or criminal rights, the reapportionment decisions inaugurated a revolutionary transformation of American government. Before the Court intervened in the process of drawing legislative districts, the representation of American citizens through democratic institutions at every level of government was extremely unbalanced. Legislative apportionment, which usually reflected historical trends more than the current population, drastically underrepresented those living in major metropolitan areas where population growth had not been met by a commensurate increase in representation. Legislators from rural districts often represented a mere fraction of the population represented by legislators

---

[1] Douglas (1956).

from urban areas. Consequently, voters in rural areas held a disproportionate influence over Congress and most state legislatures.

In 1959, Charles W. Baker and other Tennessee citizens filed suit in the U.S. District Court for the Middle District of Tennessee, claiming that the Reapportionment Act of 1901 arbitrarily appointed representatives in the Tennessee General Assembly in violation of the Equal Protection and Due Process Clauses of the Fourteenth Amendment. The trial court dismissed the case, finding that it lacked jurisdiction over legislative apportionment and that the complaint failed to state a claim on which it was possible for the court to grant relief. Baker and his associates appealed the dismissal, and the Supreme Court agreed to hear the case. The Court, in a six-to-two ruling, declared that legislative apportionment is not a "political question," but rather a "justiciable issue," and that if the Tennessee citizens could prove their case, they would be entitled to appropriate relief (*Baker v. Carr* 1962). Chief Justice Warren would later describe the *Baker* decision as "the most important case of [his] tenure on the Court" (Bravin 2005). Two years afterward, the Court ruled that the Equal Protection Clause required "equal representation for equal numbers of people" in the House of Representatives (*Wesberry v. Sanders* 1964). A few months later, the Court applied the same rule to both chambers of state legislatures in *Lucas v. Forty-Fourth General Assembly of Colorado* (1964).

Numerous lawmakers around the country, in both the federal House of Representatives and in nearly all of the state legislatures, had a lot to lose from the reapportionment rulings. The redistricting of all these legislative bodies would force many lawmakers out of office and result in considerably reduced political influence for their constituents. Perhaps more importantly, control of legislative apportionment rested in the hands of the very lawmakers who would be disadvantaged by this decision.

Those legislators and congressmen representing highly populated areas also had little to gain; the reapportionment of the Congress and the state legislatures would mean more political strength for their urban constituents, but it would not directly benefit their own political fortunes. If anything, it might reduce their political stature as they would be reduced from the only legislator in a large city to just one of several. The jostling of the legislative body might also hurt their political party, which could significantly decrease their influence. At the most, it would mean a seniority bump for the urban lawmakers as turnover increased due to redistricting changes. In addition, even if all the urban representatives did want the change to take place, the existing districting rules denied them sufficient numbers to enact reform. If they wanted to initiate reapportionment on their own and had the political power to do so, then the Court's intervention would have been unnecessary.

In spite of these obstacles stacked against reapportionment, it did have one thing going for it: the strong support of the public. A public opinion poll conducted in 1966 revealed that 57 percent of respondents supported the Court's ruling; only 18 percent disagreed.[2] Another poll that did not allow respondents

---

[2] See Appendix II for survey information and citations.

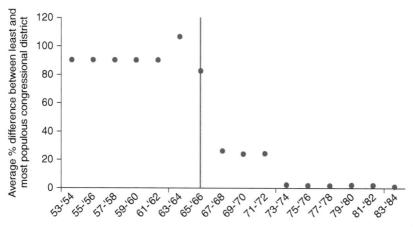

FIGURE 6.1. Reapportionment in Congress, 1955–84.

to answer "not sure" indicated that 76 percent of respondents thought the decision was "right" and 24 percent thought it was "wrong." Strong public support for the Court's ruling created a disincentive for lawmakers to openly resist the mandate. In order to defy the Court's ruling, elected officials would have to simultaneously defy the will of the people.

Figure 6.1 shows the effect of the reapportionment rulings on Congress. The graph reports the average percent difference between the least and most populous congressional district in each state for each congressional term between 1953 and 1984 (Adler 2003). For example, in the 1953–54 term, the congressional district with the fewest people in Alabama had a population of 250,726 people. The most populous district in Alabama contained 558,928 people, 123 percent more than the least populous district. This percent difference was calculated for each state for the 1953–54 term, and the average of these figures was about 90 percent. Therefore, on average the most populous congressional district was about 90 percent more populous than the least populous district in each state during this term.

Normally, Congress is only reapportioned every ten years, following the decennial census. After Congress was reapportioned following the 1960 census, the average percent difference increased to 107 percent for the 1963–64 term; however, for the 1965–66 term, the first term after the *Wesberry* ruling, that figure fell to 86 percent due to five states redrawing their congressional districts in compliance with the ruling. The following term, after an additional twenty-four states redrew their districts (Cox and Katz 1999, 812), that figure plummeted to 26 percent where it remained until the next regular reapportionment following the 1970 census. After the 1970 reapportionment, the average difference between the least and most populous congressional districts in each state fell to just 2.3 percent. This change indicates 97.9 percent behavior conformity $[(107-2.30)/107 = 97.9\%]$. Little more than a decade after the Supreme Court had first asserted the power to review legislative

TABLE 6.1. *Average Minimum Percentage of State's Population that Could be Represented by the Majority in a State Legislative Chamber, 1955–64*

Year	1955 (%)	1964 (%)	1966 (%)
House of Representatives	34.4	36.4	46.7
Senate	32.3	33.2	47.8

Note: Data based on reports in the Congressional Quarterly Almanac ("Senate Lets Reapportionment Stand" 1966). No data was available for North Dakota in 1955 or Alabama in 1965.

districting, it had achieved a complete reorganization of the congressional electoral system.

The Court's reapportionment rulings also had a strong causal effect on the apportionment of state legislative districts. When state legislative districts are badly malapportioned, it is theoretically possible for the majority of a legislative chamber to be controlled by lawmakers who represent only a small minority of the state's population. For example, in 1955 it was possible for a major-ity of the members in the Alabama House of Representatives to come from districts containing only 27 percent of the population. This figure was only slightly below the average for states in 1955; on average, districts with only 34.4 percent of a state's population could control the House of Representatives in the state legislature. Table 6.1 reports the average minimum percentage of a state's population that could control a majority in the House and Senate of the state legislature in 1955, 1964, and 1966. As reported in the table, little change occurred in the apportionment of state legislatures between 1955 and 1964; however, this situation changed drastically in the two years following the *Lucas* ruling. In this period, forty-six of the fifty state legislatures were reapportioned to conform to the Court's preferences.[3] By 1966, the average minimum percentage of a state's population that could control a majority in a state legislative chamber was nearly 50 percent.

In *The Hollow Hope*, Gerald Rosenberg, though arguing against the Court's ability to initiate political change, concedes that the Court did reapportion the House of Representatives and state legislatures. However, Rosenberg contends that this measure of political transformation is inadequate for an appropriate evaluation of the Court's power. According to Rosenberg, the advocates of reapportionment were interested in much more than mere population equity in legislative districts; they hoped to alter the balance of political power in Congress and the state legislatures by shifting legislative power away from traditionally conservative rural districts toward more liberal urban districts in order to enact new liberal policies. Finding no evidence that these new poli-cies were enacted, Rosenberg dismisses the "Reapportionment Revolution" as

[3] See "Legislative Reapportionment Completed in 46 States," *Washington Post*, June 23, 1966. E15.

creating only "small" effects because the "procedural victory ... didn't automatically lead to substantive effects" (2008, 296–302).

Rosenberg's test sets an extremely high bar for evaluating Supreme Court power. After all, the Court did not order a shift away from rural political interests toward urban interests, nor did it order the passage of new, liberal policies. The Court ordered the equalization of legislative districts by population, and that is what occurred. One might nonetheless find it surprising that social scientists found no evidence of more indirect consequences following the reapportionment rulings. However, since Rosenberg wrote the first edition of the *The Hollow Hope*, several impressive studies have established that reapportionment did indeed have numerous indirect consequences.

For example, in their study of the reapportionment cases, Gary Cox and Jonathan Katz (1999) find that congressional redistricting during the 1960s primarily benefited nonsouthern Democrats. The authors conclude that the reapportionment revolution "substantially affected two important macro-features of postwar congressional elections": the disappearance of the "long-time pro-Republican bias of about 6 percent in nonsouthern congressional elections" and "abruptly increasing margins" of congressional victories (Cox and Katz 1999, 834; see also Cox and Katz 2002).[4]

The effects of reapportionment at the state level have been studied by Stephen Ansolabehere, Alan Gerber, and James Snyder (2002; see also Ansolabehere and Snyder 2008). These authors find that, prior to redistricting, counties with relatively more legislative seats per person received relatively more monetary transfers from the state per person. After the reapportionment rulings, those counties that lost legislative seats received a smaller share of state transfers; in other words, the shift in political power produced a commensurate shift in policy outcomes. The authors conclude that "[t]he amount of redistribution that followed from *Baker* was substantial ... The cumulative effect was to shift approximately $7 billion annually toward counties that had been underrepresented prior to the imposition of one person, one vote" (Ansolabehere et al. 2002, 775).

In fact, as early as 1988, Mathew McCubbins and Thomas Schwartz explored the effect of reapportionment on policymaking in Congress. McCubbins and Schwartz (1988) argue that changes in the representation of rural and metropolitan constituents have a significant effect on federal spending for metropolitan distributive programs, metropolitan-oriented agricultural programs, and traditional farm programs. The effect of redistricting on federal spending varied widely across time periods and programs, from about $20 million per year to almost $1 billion per year (McCubbins and Schwartz 1988, 408). The authors conclude that the change in congressional representation ordered by the one person, one vote rule reallocated benefits from rural to metropolitan voters.

[4] This second phenomenon helps explain Mayhew's "famous puzzle: the case of the vanishing marginals" (Cox and Katz 1999, 834; see Mayhew 1974).

The story of reapportionment lends strong support to my theory of Supreme Court power. In situations in which the Court depends on non-court actors to implement policy, elected officials may be able to defy the Court; however, without public opinion on their side, politicians tend to comply with the Court's instructions. In this case, not only did the Court affect public policy, it fundamentally altered the structure of power in some of the most important policymaking institutions in the country.

MAJORITY-MINORITY CONGRESSIONAL DISTRICTS

The Supreme Court has also affected the creation of legislative districts by regulating the use of race in that process. Between 1980 and 1990, Georgia had ten congressional districts, one of which was a "majority-black" district, meaning that a majority of the district's voters were African-Americans. The 1990 decennial census revealed that Georgia's population entitled it to an eleventh congressional seat, which meant that the state legislature would have to redraw the state's congressional districts. Under the Voting Rights Act of 1965, Georgia must submit redistricting plans for preclearance by the U.S. Attorney General. In August of 1991, the Georgia State General Assembly submitted a congressional redistricting plan to the Attorney General that created two majority-black districts. The Attorney General refused preclearance, objecting that the plan did not properly recognize the minority population and therefore did not properly represent the 27 percent of Georgians who were African-American. The General Assembly submitted a second plan that increased the black population in certain districts, but this plan was also rejected for failing to create a third majority-minority district. In its third attempt, the legislature remedied this problem by creating the Eleventh District, which stretched 260 miles from Atlanta to the Atlantic Ocean, covering 6,784.2 square miles, splitting eight counties and five municipalities, combining four separate urban centers, rural counties, and narrow swamp regions. The Almanac of American Politics called the district a geographic "monstrosity" (*Miller v. Johnson* 1995, 909).

On January 13, 1994, five white voters from the new Eleventh District filed suit in the Federal District Court, challenging the plan as a racial gerrymander in violation of the Equal Protection Clause. In *Shaw v. Reno*, the Supreme Court had ruled that "redistricting legislation that is so bizarre on its face that it is 'unexplainable on grounds other than race' ... demands the same close scrutiny that we give other state laws that classify citizens by race" (1993). The district court found that the Georgia plan failed to meet this scrutiny. On appeal the Supreme Court agreed, finding that "race was ... the predominant, overriding factor explaining the General Assembly's" redistricting plan and that the plan did not meet the requirements of the strict scrutiny test (*Miller v. Johnson* 1995, 920–2). The next year, the Court struck down similar "racial gerrymandering" plans in North Carolina (*Shaw v. Hunt* 1996) and Texas (*Bush v. Vera* 1996).

The available data on the public response to *Miller* is limited and contradictory. The only poll asking respondents directly about the *Miller* ruling was an ABC/Washington Post Poll conducted in July of 1995. It found that 61 percent of respondents disapproved of the Court's decision. Unfortunately, the question wording was somewhat confusing; respondents who disapproved of using race as a factor in drawing congressional districts were expected to say that they approved of the Court's ruling and vice versa. In addition, the question wording may have biased the responses. The poll described the decision as "a recent ruling by the Supreme Court [that] has made it harder for states to create congressional districts where blacks make up the majority of residents."[5] By describing the probable effect of the ruling as making it "harder" for a state to perform a task rather than explaining the reasoning or context of the decision, the question wording may be responsible for the results of the poll.

The interpretation of the ABC News/Washington Post Poll is cast into further doubt by a Washington Post/Kaiser/Harvard Racial Attitudes Survey conducted in March of 2001. The poll asked, "In order to elect more minorities to public office, do you think race should be a factor when boundaries for U.S. Congressional voting districts are drawn, or should it not be a factor?" Eighty-six percent of respondents said that race should not be a factor.[6] Of course, the wording of this poll may also bias the results by suggesting that using race as a factor will ensure the election of more minorities to public office, but the wording is clearer than the earlier question. This second poll is also more consistent with other polls that show strong support for Court decisions that bar race-conscious policies in hiring decisions, promotion decisions, business contracting, college admissions, and public elementary and secondary school assignment. Given the questionable wording of the ABC News/Washington Post Poll, it seems unlikely that the public's opinion on race-conscious policies was radically different regarding congressional redistricting and changed drastically following the Court's ruling. Consequently, I assume that the Court's decision in the majority-minority district cases did not face strong opposition and expect to see these decisions have a causal effect on congressional districts.

It might be unfair to say that the Court in *Miller* was expressing a preference for the creation of fewer majority-minority congressional districts; however, the Court certainly did show a preference for restrictions on the redistricting process that would make it harder to create such districts. As a consequence, if the Court's preference had a causal effect on the behavior of state legislatures, then the number of majority-minority congressional districts should have decreased following the *Miller* decision. Did the decision have this effect?

Beginning in the 1960s, the number of majority-minority congressional districts in the United States steadily increased. As shown in Figure 6.2, the number of districts with a majority of African-American residents increased from about

---

[5] See Appendix II for survey information and citations.
[6] See Appendix II for survey information and citations.

FIGURE 6.2. Majority-minority congressional districts, 1962–2004.

six during the 1960s, to twelve during the 1970s, to about seventeen during the
1980s, and then jumped to thirty-two in the redistricting following the 1990
decennial census, an increase of fifteen seats. The number of majority-Hispanic
congressional districts also increased during this period. However, after the
Miller decision in 1995, the number of majority-black districts decreased from
thirty-two to twenty-six by 1998; the number of majority-Hispanic districts
dropped from twenty to eighteen in the same period. Although not overwhelming numerically, these changes were the first decrease in majority-minority
congressional districts in more than half a century, and the number of majority-
black districts has not rebounded to this day.[7]

The change in the number of majority-black districts from thirty-two to
twenty-six erased 40 percent of the fifteen-seat increase that occurred after the
1990 census; therefore, I code behavior conformity to the majority-minority
district rulings as 40 percent. This is an extremely conservative estimate of
behavior conformity because the Court did not specifically order a return to the
number of majority-black districts during the 1980s. A more generous interpretation of the Court's power in this issue area would conclude that because
every district the Court ordered redrawn was redrawn, the Court achieved 100
percent behavior conformity.

Obviously, altering the structure and composition of the U.S. House of
Representatives has numerous important consequences. Several studies have
demonstrated some of these consequences. Not surprisingly, the creation of
majority-minority districts has been shown to increase the proportion of minorities elected to the House of Representatives in a state (Gay 2001; Grigg and
Katz 2005; Lublin 1999). In addition, an increase in these districts is associated

[7] The number of majority-Hispanic congressional districts did increase again following the
2000 census, which is not surprising given the steady increase in the Hispanic population in the
United States.

with increases in voter turnout among minority populations (Barreto, Segura, and Woods 2004; Gay 2001).

The effect of majority-minority districts on partisan electoral advantages, the ideology of House members, and "substantive" representation of minority interests is a highly contentious subject. Some authors argue that the creation of these districts moves congressional ideology to the left (Grose 2005; Sharpe and Garand 2001; Shotts 2001; 2002; 2003a; 2003b). Others claim that race-conscious redistricting has the "perverse" effect of giving Republicans an electoral advantage and moving congressional ideology to the right (Hill 1995; Lublin 1997; 1999; Lublin and Voss 2000; 2003). Along a similar vein, some argue that black representation in Congress is maximized by distributing African-American voters into districts without a majority-black population (Cameron, Epstein, and O'Halloran 1996). Others deny that the creation of majority-minority districts has any effect on partisan advantages (Grigg and Katz 2005; Petrocik and Desposato 1998).

Just as in the reapportionment rulings, the Court in *Miller v. Johnson*, *Shaw v. Hunt*, and *Bush v. Vera* faced little public opposition in issuing an order that changed the way we elect members to the U.S. House of Representatives. Although the scope of the Court's order was more limited in the majority-minority district rulings, the effect of these rulings on the electoral system was immediate and meaningful. The number of majority-minority districts in the House of Representatives decreased for the first time in fifty years following the Court's actions. This change has probably had meaningful effects on electoral and lawmaking behavior, as well as on the role of minorities in American political life.

THE LEGISLATIVE VETO

Not only has the Supreme Court altered the manner in which members of Congress are elected, it has also altered the manner in which Congress operates. For example, the Court invalidated the frequently used legislative veto in *Immigration and Naturalization Service v. Chadha*. Jagdish Rai Chadha was born in Kenya to Indian parents, but neither Kenya nor India recognized him as a legal citizen. He was lawfully admitted to the United States in 1966 on a nonimmigrant student visa so that he could attend college in Ohio as a foreign exchange student. His visa expired on June 30, 1972, and on October 11, 1973, the District Director of the Immigration and Nationalization Service (INS) initiated deportation proceedings against him. Chadha conceded that he had overstayed his visa but requested suspension of deportation, as provided under the Immigration and Nationality Act for aliens who have resided in the United States for more than seven years, have proven during that period to be of "good moral character," and whose deportation would result in extreme hardship. After a hearing and a character investigation conducted by the INS, an Immigration Judge found that Chadha met the requirements and ordered that Chadha's deportation be suspended.

The Immigration and Nationality Act included a provision commonly known as a "legislative veto." The legislative veto is an oversight mechanism through which Congress delegates power to the executive branch on the condition that Congress may nullify or suspend the actions of the administrative agency by some type of legislative action other than a statute (Fisher 1993, 273; Levinson 1987, 116). The Immigration and Nationality Act required the Attorney General to convey to Congress his recommendation for the suspension of an alien's deportation and to deport such an alien if "either the Senate or the House of Representatives passes a resolution stating in substance that it does not favor the suspension of such deportation" (*Immigration and Naturalization Service v. Chadha* 1983, 925; hereafter *Chadha*). On December 12, 1975, Representative Eilberg, the Chairman of the Judiciary Subcommittee on Immigration, Citizenship, and International Law, introduced a resolution opposing "the granting of permanent residence in the United States to [six] aliens," including Chadha (*Chadha* 1983, 926). Four days later, the House of Representatives passed the resolution without debate or a recorded vote based primarily on Representative Eilberg's opinion that Chadha and the other five aliens in question did not meet the hardship requirement of the statute.

After the House's veto of the Attorney General's decision, the Immigration Judge reopened the deportation hearings and ordered that Chadha be deported. Chadha filed a petition for review in the Ninth Circuit Court of Appeals, arguing that the legislative veto provision of the Immigration and Nationality Act was unconstitutional. The Ninth Circuit agreed, and the U.S. Supreme Court affirmed the Ninth Circuit's ruling. The Supreme Court ruled that the legislative veto provision was unconstitutional because it violated Article I, Section 7 of the Constitution, which requires passage of legislative proposals by a majority of both Houses of Congress and presentation to the president. In doing so, it violated "integral parts of the constitutional design for the separation of powers" (*Chadha* 1983, 946). The Court's decision attracted so little public interest that no national opinion polls were ever conducted on the use of the legislative veto or the Supreme Court decision invalidating its use. Due to a lack of public interest and therefore a lack of public opposition, I expect the Court achieved a high degree of behavior conformity to the *Chadha* ruling.

The Court's decision in *Chadha* invalidated nearly 200 statutory provisions in which Congress had reserved the right to exercise a legislative veto (Fisher 1993, 275). The ruling invalidated a common legislative tool that had been in use for more than five decades; legislative veto provisions appeared in legislation covering "the war power, national emergencies, impoundment, presidential papers, federal salaries, and agency regulations" (Fisher 1993, 284). Following the *Chadha* ruling, Congress amended several statutes by deleting legislative veto provisions and replacing them with provisions for joint resolutions, which require passage by both houses and the signature of the president. Affected issues included the executive reorganization statute, the District of Columbia Home Rule Act, national emergencies law, export administration, federal pay increases, and the War Powers Act (Fisher 1993, 286). For other statutes, such as the Nuclear Non-Proliferation Act of 1978, Congress left the legislative veto provision in the law, but no longer attempted to utilize that provision (Fisher 1993, 287).

Nonetheless, Congress continued to add legislative veto provisions to bills after the *Chadha* decision, and presidents continued to sign them into law; however, presidents usually indicate through signing statements that they will treat the legislative veto provisions as having no legal force or effect due to the *Chadha* ruling. Between 1983, when the Court issued the *Chadha* ruling, and 2005, more than 400 legislative veto provisions were signed into law, most of which required administrative agencies to seek approval from specific congressional committees (Fisher 2005, 5).[8]

It is possible that Congress includes these provisions in the hope that the Court will one day overrule the *Chadha* decision, in which case these legislative vetoes will once again have legal force. However, it is more likely that these legislative veto provisions support a system of "informal and nonstatutory understandings" between administrative agencies and the congressional committees that control their funding (Fisher 2005, 3). Although presidents are often willing to engage in high-profile confrontations with Congress, administrative agencies must "work closely with their review committees, year after year, and have a much greater need to devise practical accommodations and honor them" (Fisher 2005, 5). These accommodations often take the form of informal clearance procedures, informal agreements, and nonstatutory documents. By engaging in this type of informal cooperation, administrative agencies are able to obtain more latitude and flexibility from oversight committees. These informal practices do not conflict with the *Chadha* ruling; in fact, the U.S. Court of Appeals for the Federal Circuit has explicitly endorsed such practices, noting that "our separation of powers makes such informal cooperation much more necessary than it would be in a pure system of parliamentary government" (*City of Alexandria v. United States* 1984, 1026).

Despite the undisputed continuation of these informal practices, the *Chadha* ruling did forbid the use of legislative provisions that allowed one or both houses of Congress to exercise formal control over executive actions. If this ruling had a causal effect on Congress's behavior, then we should expect Congress to conform its behavior to the Court's preferences by ceasing to exercise the legislative veto after the *Chadha* ruling. An investigation of the use of legislative veto provisions suggests that Congress did just that.

In order to assess the Court's effect on the use of legislative vetoes in Congress, I utilized the THOMAS search engine on the Library of Congress Web site to search for instances in which Congress passed simple (one-house) or concurrent (two-house) resolutions disapproving of specific executive branch actions. This search revealed 111 instances in which Congress exercised the legislative

---

[8] See Korn (1996) for a more detailed description of the legislative veto and its invalidation, especially regarding the constitutionality of legislative action before *Chadha*, the usefulness of the legislative veto to legislators, and the proper structure of the separation of powers system.

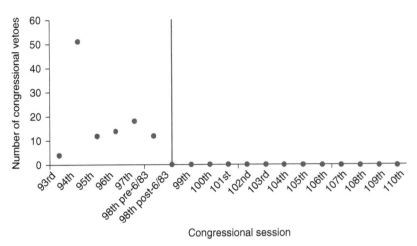

Congressional session

FIGURE 6.3. Congressional vetoes, 1973–2008.

veto between 1973 and 2008, all of which fell before the Supreme Court's ruling in *Chadha*. The findings of this search are reported in Figure 6.3. Before the *Chadha* decision, Congress exercised the legislative veto between four and fifty-one times during each congressional session; since *Chadha*, Congress has not used a formal one- or two-house legislative veto once. Accordingly, I code both the generous and conservative estimates of behavior conformity to the legislative veto ruling as 100 percent.

The Court's ruling in the *Chadha* case invalidated more federal legislative provisions than any Supreme Court ruling in history. In a single stroke, the Court altered the legislative landscape of numerous domestic and foreign policy issues and put an end to a common lawmaking device that had been in use for decades. However, it is important to note that informal cooperation between congressional committees and administrative agencies continued unabated after *Chadha*. These "voluntary accommodation procedures" allow Congress to "delegate substantial discretion to executive agencies if they accept a system of review and control by the committees of jurisdiction" (Fisher 2005, 6). The Court successfully restructured the formal dynamic between the legislative and executive branches, but it did not disturb the common practice of cooperation between these branches, nor did it intend to.

PUBLIC AID TO RELIGIOUS SCHOOLS

In addition to regulating the behavior of the national legislature, the Supreme Court has also intervened in the operations of local political institutions. One example is the Court's effort to restrict the use of public resources to promote private religious schools. These restrictions are certainly not absolute. For example, the Supreme Court has upheld state laws that reimbursed the parents of parochial school children for bus transportation (*Everson v. Board* of *Education* 1947), supplied secular textbooks to parochial schools (*Board of Education v. Allen* 1968), and provided tax exemptions for real property owned by religious organizations and used for religious worship (*Walz v. Tax Commission of the City of New York* 1970). However, in subsequent cases, the Court has made clear that the government's authority to promote religious institutions is limited by the First Amendment. The most prominent of these cases was *Lemon v. Kurtzman* (1971; hereafter *Lemon*).

Lemon involved statutes in Pennsylvania and Rhode Island that provided public financial support to nonpublic schools for teacher salaries, textbooks, and instructional materials for secular subjects. Both laws made financial aid available to "church-related educational institutions" (*Lemon* 1971, 607). Taxpayers from each state separately challenged the statutes. A three-judge federal district court ruled that the Rhode Island statute violated the Establishment Clause, but a three-judge panel in Pennsylvania upheld that state's law. The Supreme Court granted certiorari and heard both cases together. In deciding the case, the Court created what later came to be known as the "*Lemon* test," a three-pronged test to evaluate government action under the Establishment Clause. In order to pass the test, "[f]irst, the statute must have a secular legislative purpose; second, its principal or primary effect must be one that neither advances nor inhibits religion; finally, the statute must not foster an excessive government entanglement with religion" (*Lemon* 1971, 612–3).[9] Applying this test, the Court found that both statutes were unconstitutional.

Perhaps the most important consequence of the *Lemon* decision was its application to Title I of the Elementary and Secondary Education Act of 1965.[10] This statute provided "financial assistance to local educational institutions to meet the needs of educationally deprived children from low-income families," including those enrolled in private schools (*Aguilar v. Felton* 1985, 404; hereafter *Aguilar*). Many school districts used funds from this program to support private religious schools, including a program paying employees who teach in parochial schools in New York City (*Aguilar* 1985) and a "Shared Time and Community Education" program in Grand Rapids, Michigan, that provided classes to nonpublic school students in classrooms located in and leased from the nonpublic schools (*Grand Rapids v. Ball* 1985). In *Aguilar v. Felton* and *Grand Rapids v. Ball*, the Supreme Court ruled that both programs were unconstitutional; however, both of these decisions were overruled twelve years later in *Agostini v. Felton* (1997).

The *Lemon* ruling was greeted with divided public opinion. The year before the ruling, a Gallup/Kettering Poll of Public Attitudes Toward Public Schools showed that 48 percent of the public favored giving some government tax

---

[9] Internal quotation marks and citations omitted.

[10] "Title I was superseded by Chapter I of the Education Consolidation and Improvement Act of 1981 ... The provisions concerning the participation of children in private schools under Chapter I are virtually identical to those in Title I" (*Aguilar v. Felton* 1985, 414). As such, following the Supreme Court, I will refer to the program as "Title I."

money to help parochial schools; 44 percent opposed this practice.[11] In 1974, the same polling organization found that 53 percent of respondents favored amending the U.S. Constitution to permit government financial aid to parochial schools; however, these polls did not distinguish between giving financial support to private schools in the forms permitted by the Court (bus transportation, textbooks, etc.) and using public funds to pay teachers to teach classes in private schools.

The *Aguilar* and *Grand Rapids* rulings received substantially more public support. In September of 1985, 61 percent of respondents to an Associated Press/Media General Poll said that tax funds should not be used to send public teachers into religious private schools to teach nonreligious courses; only 29 percent of respondents supported this practice.[12] Given the lack of strong opposition to the Court's rulings in *Aguilar* and *Grand Rapids*, I expect the Court to have successfully altered the behavior of government officials operating Title I programs.

The Supreme Court's rulings in *Aguilar* and *Grand Rapids* expressed the Court's preference for school districts to refrain from using Title I funds to have "publicly funded instructors teach classes composed exclusively of private school students in [religiously affiliated] private school buildings" (*Aguilar* 1985, 409). Therefore, if the ruling had a causal effect on the behavior of school administrators, then (1) the school districts should have used different locations and methods to deliver Title I services to sectarian school students following the decision. The ruling may also have had indirect and unintended consequences on two other behavior outcomes: (2) the number of private school students receiving Title I services and (3) the cost of providing these services.

(1) A few months after *Aguilar* and *Grand Rapids*, the Department of Education (DOE) issued initial guidance on how school districts should comply with the rulings. The DOE suggested that Title I services be provided by busing private sectarian school students to public schools or other neutral sites. In June of 1986, the DOE "supplemented its guidance, allowing the use of computer-assisted instruction and mobile vans or other portable units located on public or leased property on or near the grounds of private sectarian schools" (General Accounting Office 1987; hereafter GAO).

The next year, the General Accounting Office conducted the first of three studies evaluating the effects of the *Aguilar* ruling on Title I programs (GAO 1987; 1989; 1993). The first of these studies examined "15 school districts that varied in size, geographical setting, and number of students attending private sectarian schools" (GAO 1987, 1). These school districts responded to the ruling in a variety of ways. Nine districts temporarily discontinued their services for periods ranging from one month to the entire school year (GAO 1987, 2, 32). Two districts obtained court orders to temporarily continue providing

---

[11] See Appendix II for survey information and citations.
[12] See Appendix II for survey information and citations.

TABLE 6.2. *Delivery Location/Method of Title I Services in Districts Visited by the GAO, 1986–87*

Delivery Location/Method	% of Private School Students
Portable classrooms	57.6
Mobile vans	26.7
Computer technology	11.8
Neutral sites	2.3
Public schools	1.5

Note: Data based on study conducted by GAO (1987, 26–7, table 2).

TABLE 6.3. *Delivery Location/Method of Title I Services for All States, 1991–92*

Delivery Location/Method	% of Private School Students
Portable classrooms	19
Mobile vans	39
Computer technology	17
Neutral sites	9
Public schools	13
Other (such as take-home computers)	4

Note: Data based on study conducted by GAO (1993, 26–7, appendix VI).

Title I services in private schools; one continued operating its program in private schools without a court order (GAO 1987, 32). However, by the 1986–87 school year, all Title I services for private school students in these districts were provided in compliance with *Aguilar*. As shown in Table 6.2, the vast majority of students received these services in portable classrooms or mobile vans. A significant percentage also received services from computer-based instruction in private schools. The 1993 GAO study conducted an exhaustive examination of delivery locations and methods for Title I programs in every state and found total compliance with the ruling. These statistics, presented in Table 6.3, show that by the 1991–92 school year, mobile vans had become the most popular methods of delivering Title I services (GAO 1993, 26–7). Both of these studies suggest that the *Aguilar* ruling achieved 100 percent behavior conformity shortly after it was issued.

(2) The *Aguilar* ruling also had several negative and presumably unintended consequences on the administration of Title I programs in the United States. The most significant of these consequences was the dramatic effect of the ruling on private school student enrollment in Title I programs. As shown in Figure 6.4, the number of private school students receiving Title I services declined from about 185,000 in the 1984–85 school year to about 123,000 in the 1985–86 school year, after the *Aguilar* ruling. This change represents

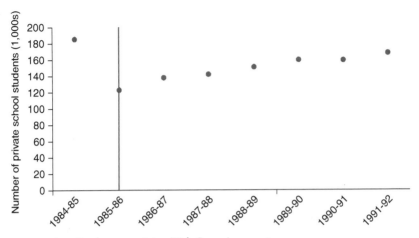

FIGURE 6.4. Students receiving Title I services, 1984–92.

a 34 percent decrease. In the years following the ruling, enrollment in Title I programs slowly rebounded; however, seven years after the ruling, enrollment had climbed to only 168,000, which is 9 percent less than the pre-*Aguilar* figure (GAO 1993, 32).

(3) The rebound in Title I enrollment in the years following *Aguilar* is primarily due to Congress investing more money in the program (GAO 1993, 3). Although conformity to the *Aguilar* ruling was nearly universal, it was not cheap. The 1987 GAO study found that ten of the districts studied spent a combined $7.3 million in initial costs and $1.9 million in recurring costs to ensure the continuation of their Title I programs. Most of these costs were for capital expenditures, such as constructing portable buildings, purchasing mobile vans, or obtaining computers and computer programs. In 1987, Congress passed the School Improvement Act, which provided an additional $30 million for Title I programs in fiscal year 1988 (GAO 1987, 2). In fiscal year 1989, Congress appropriate $19.8 million for eligible capital expenditures to help schools comply with the ruling (GAO 1989, 2). Overall, the GAO estimated that it would eventually cost approximately $105 million to comply with the *Aguilar* decision (1989, 19).

The Supreme Court's ruling in *Lemon v. Kurtzman* and its subsequent rulings applying the *Lemon* test in *Aguilar v. Felton* and *Grand Rapids v. Ball* had a profound impact on the administration of Title I programs for private school students in the United States. Very shortly after the ruling, every school district administering Title I funds ceased to use these funds to pay for teachers to instruct students within religiously affiliated school buildings. The school districts responded in a variety of ways, such as suspending programs, utilizing alternate locations, and relying on computerized instruction. These changes had significant financial costs and severely limited the number of private school students who received Title I services for years to come. As expected, given the popularity of these rulings, the Court's decisions in these cases had a strong causal effect on the behavior of school officials in administering Title I programs.

AFFIRMATIVE ACTION IN COLLEGE ADMISSIONS

The Supreme Court has also issued important rulings affecting post-secondary education in the area of affirmative action. In 1973, Allan Bakke applied to the University of California, Davis, Medical School. At the time, the school used a dual admissions process, in which regular applicants were considered separately from those who identified themselves as "economically and/or educationally disadvantaged" applicants or members of a "minority group." Regular applicants were required to have a minimum undergraduate grade point average of 2.5 or higher, but applicants in the special admission program were not. These special applicants were not ranked against candidates in the general admissions process and instead competed among themselves for sixteen of the one hundred seats in the entering class. During a four-year period, no whites were admitted through the special admissions program, although many applied.

Despite earning a higher admissions score than several minority applicants, Bakke was denied admission to the special program. In 1974, he applied again and was once again rejected. Bakke filed suit in the Superior Court of California for mandatory, injunctive, and declaratory relief to compel his admission to the medical school. Bakke lost at the trial-court level but won in the California Supreme Court. The Board of Regents of the University of California then appealed the case to the U.S. Supreme Court.

The Court was deeply divided over the issue, with four justices opposing the use of race in college admissions, four justices supporting the Davis plan, and Justice Powell splitting the difference. Powell agreed with Justices Brennan, Marshall, Blackmun, and White that the goal of achieving a diverse student body was sufficiently compelling to justify consideration of race in admission decisions under some circumstances, but he disagreed that the Davis admissions program was a necessary means to achieve that compelling goal. According to Powell, the Davis program was constitutionally problematic because it used a quota system in which "a specified percentage of the student body is in effect guaranteed to be members of selected ethnic groups" (*Regents of the University of California v. Bakke* 1978, 315; hereafter *Bakke*). Instead, Powell argued that the Harvard College admissions program that took into account all of an applicant's qualities, including race, as part of a "holistic review" would serve the state's interest in promoting diversity without using a strict quota. Accordingly, he voted with Chief Justice Burger and Justices Stevens, Stewart, and Rehnquist to compel Bakke's admission to the medical school.

The constitutionality of affirmative action in college admissions was not seriously challenged again until the 2003 Supreme Court cases *Grutter v. Bollinger* and *Gratz v. Bollinger*. Barbara Grutter was a white Michigan resident whose admission application was rejected by the University of Michigan Law School. She filed suit against the university, claiming that the law school's consideration of race as part of an individualized review of each applicant in the admissions process constituted a violation of the Equal Protection Clause. Similarly, Jennifer Gratz was denied admission to the University of Michigan undergraduate program. Under the undergraduate admission system, applicants from "underrepresented" racial groups, including African-Americans, Hispanics, and Native Americans, received an automatic 20-point bonus out of 100 points needed for admission. Gratz also filed suit against the university.

The Supreme Court upheld the law school admissions program, but struck down the undergraduate program as violating the Equal Protection Clause. In a 5–4 decision written by Justice O'Connor, the Court ruled that the law school's admissions process was narrowly tailored to further the compelling state interest in obtaining the educational benefits that flow from a diverse student body because it conducted an "individualized inquiry into the possible diversity contributions of all applicants" (*Grutter v. Bollinger* 2003, 341). In a 6–3 decision written by Chief Justice Rehnquist, the Court ruled that the undergraduate admissions program did not withstand strict scrutiny because it did not provide the individualized consideration contemplated by Justice Powell (*Gratz v. Bollinger* 2003).

Measuring public opinion toward affirmative action programs is extremely difficult; responses to questions on this topic vary widely depending on question wording. For example, a series of polls conducted by different organizations in 2003, the year *Grutter* and *Gratz* were decided, offer several conflicting depictions of the public's attitudes. According to a Pew News Interest Index Poll, 60 percent of respondents thought the existence of "affirmative action programs designed to increase the number of black and minority students on college campuses" was a "good thing"; only 30 percent thought it was a "bad thing." More respondents said the programs were fair than those who said they were unfair (Pew News Interest Index Poll: 47%–42%). In a 2001 Gallup/CNN/USA Today Poll, a majority of respondents favored "affirmative action programs for minorities and women for admission to colleges and universities" (56%–39%). Respondents also consistently supported affirmative action programs when asked about the general use of affirmative action in "hiring, promoting and college admissions" (Associated Press Poll: 53%–35%; CBS News/New York Times Poll: 54%–37%).[13]

During the same year, different polls revealed strong opposition to affirmative action programs. Respondents said they agreed with President Bush's opposition to the University of Michigan's admissions policy (New Models National Brand Poll: 58%–29%; Los Angeles Times Poll: 56%–26%) and opposed the use of race in university admissions to "increase diversity in the student body" (Quinnipiac University Poll: 67%–28%; NBC News/Wall Street Journal Poll: 65%–26%). Respondents also disapproved of "affirmative action programs at colleges and law schools that give racial preferences to minority applicants" (Time/CNN/Harris Interactive Poll: 49%–39%). A Princeton

---

[13] See Appendix II for survey information and citations.

Survey Research Associates/Newsweek Poll reported that respondents thought colleges and universities "should not give preferences in admissions for" blacks (68%–26%), Hispanics (70%–25%), or Asians (71%–23%). Respondents also opposed "college scholarship programs available only to black or minority students" (NBS News/Wall Street Journal Poll: 78%–19%).[14]

Given these conflicting survey results, determining whether a majority of the public opposed the Court's affirmative action rulings is a difficult task. For the purposes of my study, I assume the Court's ruling in *Gratz* did not face strong opposition. I base this assumption on three points. First, most polls that show support for affirmative action programs in 2003 do so by very narrow margins, but those polls that show opposition to these programs do so by larger margins. If my assumption is wrong and a majority of the public did oppose the Court's rulings, it was a very slim majority. Second, none of the affirmative action polls conducted in 2003 differentiate between the consideration of race in a holistic review and a rigid point system. It is likely that a significant number of respondents indicating support for affirmative action programs support the former but not the latter, meaning that they would agree with the Court's decision in *Gratz*. Third, the large swings in poll results might indicate that a significant number of respondents are ambivalent or apathetic about the issue. If this is true, then the Court does not face genuine opposition from the public, and I would expect the Court's ruling to have a causal effect on the behavior of university admissions officers and policymakers.

Measuring the effects of the Court's rulings on university admissions is also an exceptionally complicated task for several reasons. First, in order to avoid criticisms and give themselves increased flexibility, university admissions offices are not eager to reveal their admissions process. Second, there is no national organization that compiles available information about university admissions processes. Finally, because the Court's ruling proscribed only a particular type of affirmative action, measuring compliance with the ruling requires a detailed understanding of a school's admissions process rather than a general understanding of whether the school gives some preference to minority applicants.

The only specific preference expressed by the majority in *Gratz* was for universities that use public funds, which is almost all universities, to stop using point systems in admissions that automatically give a certain number of points based on race.[15] According to a report by the National Association for College

---

[14] See Appendix II for survey information and citations.

[15] Throughout this study, I have focused my examination of each issue area on one Supreme Court ruling. For example, my study of abortion rulings focused entirely on the Court's decision in *Roe v. Wade*. Although it's possible that the Court's decisions in *Hodgson v. Minnesota*, *Planned Parenthood v. Casey* and *Sternberg v. Carhart* had significant effects on behavior, I have attempted to limit these studies to a manageable scope. For some issue areas, such as abortion, the selection of a particular case on which to focus is relatively uncontroversial; however, in other issue areas this choice is more subjective. For example, it is unclear whether my examination of the Court's affirmative action rulings should focus on *Bakke* or on *Gratz*. I have chosen to focus on *Gratz* due to the recency and the availability of data related to this decision; nonetheless, I do not want to appear as if I am cherry-picking cases to support my arguments.

Admission Counseling, this type of point system was only "used by a relative handful of institutions – generally large public universities" (2003, 31; hereafter NACAC). The only universities that used such systems mentioned in the report were the University of Michigan, Ohio State University, and the University of Massachusetts at Amherst. Following the *Gratz* decision, all three of these universities changed their admissions policies. The University of Michigan modeled its new admissions system after its law school program (NACAC 2003, 31; Perry 2007, 160). Both Michigan and Ohio State University replaced the point system by asking applicants to "write essays intended to show what they may be able to contribute to diversity on campus" (Schmidt 2004). The University of Massachusetts at Amherst also stopped awarding extra points to applicants based on race (Perry 2007; Schmidt 2004). The specific mandate in the *Gratz* ruling only affected a few schools; however, measured by this standard, behavior conformity to the ruling was 100 percent.[16]

The ruling may also have had indirect effects on the enrollment of minority students in these universities. The year after the *Gratz* ruling, minority applications decreased at slightly larger rates than total applications at the University of Michigan and Ohio State and increased at a smaller rate than total applications at the University of Massachusetts at Amherst (Schmidt 2004). These patterns indicate that some minority applicants may have declined to apply to these schools anticipating a rejection because of changes in policy. More importantly, the African-American enrollment in the freshmen class dropped at all three of these schools between 2002 and 2004 (Selingo 2005). As shown in Table 6.4, the greatest decrease was at Ohio State where the number of African-American freshmen dropped by 31 percent. Hispanic enrollment dropped slightly at the University of Michigan and Ohio State during this period but increased dramatically at the University of Massachusetts.

The holding in *Gratz* technically applied only to university admissions, but the decision also had obvious implications for other race-conscious university policies. Before it was issued, 73 percent of chief admissions officers expected the Court's decision to affect recruitment practices (NACAC 2003, 30). After the ruling, Travis Reindl, director of state policy analysis at the American Association of State Colleges and Universities estimated that as many as half of the four-year colleges in the United States had reviewed or modified scholarship and fellowship programs that use race as a criterion (Glater 2006). According to Roger Clegg, general counsel for the Center for Equal Opportunity, "the overwhelming majority of colleges that we have contacted – Carnegie Mellon University, Harvard University, Indiana University, the Massachusetts Institute

---

Accordingly, I encourage the skeptical reader to examine alternative sources that explore the effects of the *Bakke* decision (Ball 2000; Dreyfuss and Lawrence 1979). For example, in a study of student enrollment in law and medical schools, Gruhl and Welch find that *Bakke* had a negative effect on African-American and Hispanic applications and a positive effect on acceptance rates and ratios for both groups (1990, 469).

[16] Because the measurement of behavior conformity is very straightforward for this issue area, I use this figure as both the conservative and generous measure of behavior conformity.

TABLE 6.4. *Changes in Minority Enrollment in Freshman Class in Universities that Discontinued Point Systems after* Gratz, 2002–04

University	# of Students in 2002 (Proportion of Class)	# of Students in 2004 (Proportion of Class)	Change in # of Students (% Change in # of Students)
University of Michigan			
African-American students	442 (7.3%)	350 (5.8%)	−92 (−20.8%)
Hispanic students	305 (5.0%)	264 (4.4%)	−41 (−13.4%)
Ohio State University			
African-American students	572 (9.7%)	393 (6.6%)	−179 (−31.3%)
Hispanic students	180 (3.1%)	165 (2.8%)	−15 (−8.3%)
University of Massachusetts at Amherst			
African-American students	172 (5.2%)	153 (3.6%)	−19 (−11.0%)
Hispanic students	101 (3.0%)	153 (3.6%)	+52 (+51.5%)

Note: Data based on statistics gathered by the Chronicle of Higher Education as reported in Selingo (2005).

of Technology, Northwestern University, Princeton University, the University of Illinois at Urbana-Champaign, Williams College, Yale University, and dozens of others – have opened up racially exclusive programs to all students, regardless of race" (Clegg 2005). Some of these schools, such as Princeton and the Massachusetts Institute of Technology, changed their policy before *Gratz* in response to investigations by the Department of Education (Schmidt and Young 2003). Others, including Harvard, Yale, and Carnegie Mellon, in response to the Court's ruling, opened to students of all races programs and scholarships that were once limited to minorities (Selingo 2005).

The Supreme Court's decision in *Gratz v. Bollinger* required only a few universities to change their admission policies, and each of these institutions complied with the ruling. As a result of *Gratz*, universities no longer use point systems to give preference to certain racial minorities, and as an indirect and possibly unintended consequence, minority enrollment has dropped in most of the schools that changed their policies. The Court's opinion also appears to have had a causal effect on the behavior of university administrators in the operation of scholarships and summer programs; after *Gratz*, numerous universities opened these programs to all of their students.

STUDENT RELIGIOUS PUBLICATIONS AT PUBLIC UNIVERSITIES

The Court has also prohibited public schools and universities from discriminating against various forms of student expression based on its religious content. For example, in *Widmar v. Vincent* (1981) the Court ruled that the University of Missouri at Kansas City could not prohibit religious student groups from using forums generally open for use by other student groups. In *Board of Education of Westside Community Schools v. Mergens* (1990) and *Lamb's Chapel v. Center Moriches School District* (1993), the Court issued similar rulings in the context of a public secondary school. The Court extended the logic of these rulings to require the University of Virginia to provide funding for religious student publications on the same basis as other student publications in *Rosenberger v. University of Virginia* (1995).

In 1990, Ronald Rosenberger, an undergraduate at the University of Virginia, along with several other students, established a student publication called *Wide Awake*, "a magazine of philosophical and religious expression" designed to "facilitate discussion which fosters an atmosphere of sensitivity to and tolerance of Christian viewpoints" (*Rosenberger* 1995, 825–6). The organization applied to the student activities funding board, requesting nearly $6,000 in printing costs, but the application was denied because *Wide Awake* was deemed to be a "religious activity" that "promoted or manifested a particular belief in or about a deity or an ultimate reality" (*Rosenberger* 1995, 827). *Wide Awake* appealed the decision within the university, but the denial was ultimately approved by the dean of students on the grounds that the university did not fund religious activities.

Having exhausted his options within the university, Rosenberger contacted the Center for Individual Rights, which filed suit against the school, claiming that the denial of funding to *Wide Awake* was unconstitutional content and viewpoint discrimination. The district court granted summary judgment to the university. The Fourth Circuit Court of Appeals affirmed its decision, finding that the university had engaged in viewpoint discrimination, but the decision was justified because funding a religious publication would violate the Establishment Clause. The Supreme Court granted certiorari and reversed the Fourth Circuit. In a 5-to-4 decision, the Court ruled that the denial of funding to Rosenberger violated his freedom of speech. Furthermore, providing funds to a religious publication based on neutral criteria would not violate the Establishment Clause. Accordingly, the university was required to provide funding to student religious publications on the same basis as all other student publications.

No national public opinion surveys were conducted regarding the *Rosenberger* decision, suggesting that it attracted little public attention and, therefore, little popular opposition. Accordingly, I expect the Court to have been fairly successful in altering the behavior of public universities through this ruling. There is anecdotal evidence to suggest that the ruling had some effect; for example, several months after the Court's ruling in *Rosenberger*, the university's Board of Visitors amended its guidelines to make religious publications eligible for funding (Dudley 1995). Did the Court's ruling alter behavior on a larger scale?

The most comprehensive examination of *Rosenberger's* effects can be found in a study by Pamela Joy Van Zwaluwenburg (2004). Van Zwaluwenburg sent surveys to administrators in charge of student organizations at 523 four-year, public, accredited colleges and universities, of whom 242 ultimately responded. Sixty-nine percent of these schools were behaving consistently with *Rosenberger's* requirements before the ruling was issued; 57 percent had always funded religious student organizations and 12 percent did not fund any student organizations at all (Van Zwaluwenburg 2004, 98).[17] However, her results suggest that *Rosenberger* had a very limited effect on funding practices in the remaining universities. Of those schools that excluded religious groups from their funding pools before the decision, only 29 percent stopped these practices after the ruling. Because this is the only available measurement of the effects of the Court's ruling, I code both the conservative and generous estimates of behavior conformity to *Rosenberger* as 29 percent.

My findings in this issue area stand in stark contrast to those in other popular lateral issues. Why did the Court achieve so little conformity to this ruling? One possibility is that my assumption regarding popular opposition to the ruling is simply inaccurate; perhaps significant opposition did exist, despite the lack of any public opinion polls related to the issue. Alternatively, this issue area might simply reveal my model's inability to explain all variation in the Court's power over lateral issues. For example, the implementation of *Rosenberger* might have relied on the attitudes of university officials, the clarity of the Court's ruling, or the means by which it was communicated to universities, rather than attitudes in the general public.[18] Regardless, the findings from this case study clearly cut against the expectations of my theory and suggest that the Court might sometimes fail to cause behavior changes even when its rulings face little popular opposition.

MINIMUM WAGE FOR STATE EMPLOYEES

The Supreme Court found much greater success at altering federal-state relations through its rulings regarding the federal minimum wage. In 1938, Congress passed the Fair Labor Standards Act (FLSA), which required most employers to pay their employees an hourly minimum wage and overtime pay when working more than 40 hours in a week. The act originally excluded state and local governments from its coverage; however, in 1961 and again in 1966, Congress began amending the FLSA, extending the Act's coverage to certain public employees. In 1974, Congress extended its coverage to almost all

---

[17] For the purposes of this analysis, I consider only the Court's effects on the funding of religious student organizations. Van Zwaluwenburg extends her analysis to the Court's effects on the funding of political organizations as well. Accordingly, her summary of the data is slightly different than mine. I reconstruct her data based on table 5.1 on page 98 of her dissertation. This table is somewhat confusing because the first line of the table is mislabeled. The category labeled "Have never funded religious organizations" should be labeled "Still exclude both religious and political organizations." I clarified this issue with Dr. Van Zwaluwenburg by phone on December 17, 2009. My thanks to her for her assistance in this matter.

[18] Van Zwaluwenburg finds little evidence for any of these theories.

state and local government employees. In response, several cities and states, as well as the National League of Cities and the National Governor's Conference, brought action in the District Court for the District of Columbia challenging the constitutionality of these amendments. The District Court upheld the validity of the amendments, and the cities and states appealed their case to the Supreme Court, which granted certiorari. In *National League of Cities v. Usery*, the Court ruled that the amendments to the FLSA unconstitutionally exceeded Congress's power under the Commerce Clause by interfering with "the States' ability to structure employer employee relationships" in areas of traditional governmental functions, such as "fire prevention, police protection, sanitation, public health, and parks and recreation" (1975, 851; hereafter *National League of Cities*).

Four months after the Court's ruling in *National League of Cities*, the San Antonio Transit System informed its employees that it was no longer bound by the FLSA's overtime provisions, but it continued to follow the minimum wage requirements because basic wage levels in mass transit employment were traditionally higher than the minimum wage (*Garcia v. San Antonio Transit Authority* 1985, 534, footnote 3; hereafter *Garcia*). On September 17, 1979, the Wage and Hour Administration of the Department of Labor issued an opinion that the operation of San Antonio's public transportation system, now named the San Antonio Metropolitan Transit Authority (SAMTA), were "not constitutionally immune from the application of the Fair Labor Standards Act" (*Garcia* 1985, 534). SAMTA filed suit against the secretary of labor in federal court. The same day Joe G. Garcia and several other employees of SAMTA brought their own suit in the same court seeking to recover overtime pay they claimed they were owed. The district court stayed that action but allowed Garcia to intervene as a defendant in support of the secretary of labor.

After losing at the district court level, Garcia and the secretary of labor appealed the case directly to the Supreme Court. The Court ruled that

> the attempt to draw the boundaries of state regulatory immunity in terms of "traditional governmental function" is not only unworkable but is also inconsistent with established principles of federalism and, indeed, with those very federalism principles on which *National League of Cities* purported to rest. That case, accordingly, is overruled. (*Garcia* 1985, 531)

By overruling *National League of Cities*, the *Garcia* Court once again made the FLSA's minimum wage and maximum hour requirements applicable to state and local government employees.

Neither *National League of Cities* nor *Garcia* attracted much public attention; accordingly, no national public opinion polls were conducted regarding either one of these rulings. Public opinion polls in the late 1970s and 1980s showed strong support for raising the minimum wage;[19] however, a lack of any polling data on the application of the minimum wage to state and local

---

[19] See Appendix II for survey information and citations.

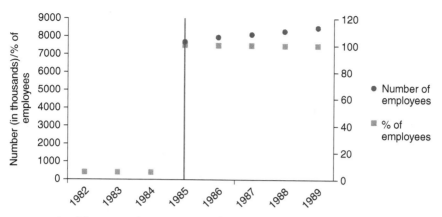

FIGURE 6.5. Non-supervisory state and local government employees subject to minimum wage provisions of the FLSA, 1982–89.

government employees suggests that there was not strong opposition to the Court's ruling in *National League of Cities*. The lack of public interest may be due to the fact that only a small percentage of the labor force is employed in the public sector, and many of these employees are employed by the federal government or states that have their own minimum wage laws. For example, at the time *Garcia* was handed down, the state minimum wage exceeded the federal minimum wage in twenty-four states; therefore, the amendments to the FLSA and their invalidation by the Court should not have had any effect on wages paid to state and local government employees in these states. Regardless of the reason, given the lack of public interest in and therefore a lack of strong opposition to the *National League of Cities* ruling, I expect the decision to have had a strong effect on the behavior of state and local governments.

The best data available on the application of the FLSA to state and local employees can be found in a series of reports submitted to Congress by the Employment Standards Administration of the Department of Labor during the 1980s (Employment Standards Administration 1983–90). These reports provide data on the estimated number of nonsupervisory state and local government employees and their status under the minimum wage provisions of the FLSA. Because data is not available for years prior to 1982, the best way to evaluate the effects of the Court's decision in *National League of Cities* is to observe the effects of the Court reversing its decision in *Garcia*. As shown in Figure 6.5, prior to the *Garcia* ruling in 1985, only 5.3 percent of state and local government employees were subject to the minimum wage provisions of the FLSA; however, after the Court's ruling in *Garcia*, 100 percent of state and local government employees were subject to these provisions. Accordingly, this data suggests that the *National League of Cities* ruling was preventing the application of the FLSA to 94.7 percent of state and local government employees. I use this figure as both the conservative and generous estimates of behavior conformity to *National League of Cities*.

The Court's rulings in the minimum wage cases were inherently limited to those state employees working in states with minimum wages below the federal minimum wage. This subset of employees comprises only a small percentage of the total labor force. Nonetheless, the Court's ruling in *National League of Cities* exempted almost all of these workers from coverage under the FLSA for a decade before the Court reversed itself in *Garcia*. Without opposition from the public, the Court was able to successfully alter the behavior of numerous state agencies for years, despite opposition from the federal government.

BUSH V. GORE

Shortly before 8 p.m. Eastern time, on November 7, 2000, each of the major news networks and CNN projected that Vice President Al Gore would carry the state of Florida and its twenty-five electoral votes. Gore's projected win in Florida, combined with his decisive victory in Michigan, left little possibility that his competitor, Texas Governor George W. Bush, would be able to defeat him in the presidential election. Some of Gore's top advisers and friends were so confident of Gore's victory that they took a break from the television news reports to eat dinner. Governor Bush changed his plans for the evening and returned home to the Governor's Mansion rather than watching the election returns with relatives and friends as he had planned (Bruni 2000).

Ninety minutes later, a group of reporters were ushered into the upstairs living room in the Governor's Mansion. Mr. Bush was still skeptical about the Florida projection. "I don't believe some of these states that they've called," he said. "I'm upbeat" (Bruni 2000). A few minutes later, his doubts were vindicated. At 9:54 p.m. CNN withdrew their projection for Florida; the other major networks quickly followed suit. Over the next several hours, Governor Bush took the lead in the Florida returns and his margin of victory continued to increase. At 2:15 a.m., the networks called Florida and the election for Bush. Shortly after, Vice President Gore called to concede the election and congratulate the Governor. Gore wrote a short, gracious concession speech and proceeded to War Memorial Plaza in Nashville where several thousand supporters awaited him. However, before he could deliver the speech, he was stopped by an aide, Michael Feldman, who had received a call from a man named Michael Whouley. According to Whouley, who was monitoring the Florida election results, Governor Bush's 50,000 vote advantage had dwindled to just 6,000 votes, with many more left to tally.

At 3:30 a.m., Vice President Gore once again called Governor Bush to tell him that circumstances had changed and there would be an automatic recount in Florida. "You mean to tell me, Mr. Vice President, you're retracting your concession?" Bush asked. "You don't have to be snippy about it," Gore responded (Sack and Bruni 2000). Snippiness between the candidates would continue for another thirty-six days.

Later that day, the Florida Division of Elections reported that out of almost six million votes cast, Governor Bush led Vice President Gore by only 1,784 votes. Because the margin was less than one-half of 1 percent, the results triggered an automatic machine recount, which yielded an even smaller margin for Bush – only 327 votes. Gore exercised his right under state law to request manual recounts in four Florida counties: Volusia, Palm Beach, Broward, and Miami Dade; however, despite this statutory right, a minor inconsistency in Florida election law set a seven-day deadline for counties to submit their election returns and allowed the state's Secretary of State, Katherine Harris, to use her discretion in accepting late returns. Each of the four counties submitted statements indicating their intention to submit late returns on November 15th, but Harris, who had been the Florida co-chair of Bush's campaign, refused to accept any late returns.

Vice President Gore and the Florida Democratic Party filed suit in state court, claiming that Harris had acted arbitrarily in denying the late submissions. The state circuit court ruled against Gore, but he appealed the decision to the Florida Supreme Court, which ordered Harris to accept manual recounts submitted until November 26th at 5 p.m. Bush appealed the decision to the U.S. Supreme Court, which ruled that it had "considerable uncertainty" as to the reasons for the Florida court's decision, and returned the case to that court for further consideration.

Meanwhile, on November 26th, the Florida Elections Canvassing Commission certified the election results and declared Bush the winner of Florida's twenty-five electoral votes. Gore filed a complaint contesting the certification. A state circuit court denied relief, but Gore once again appealed to the Florida Supreme Court. On December 8th, the Florida Supreme Court, which was dominated by Democratic appointees, partially reversed the decision of the circuit court, ruling that 9,000 ballots in Miami-Dade County on which machines had failed to register a vote for president (so-called undervotes) probably contained "legal votes ... sufficient to place the results of this election in doubt" (*Gore v. Harris* 2000, 47). The Florida Supreme Court ordered the Circuit Court of Leon County to supervise the tabulation by hand of those 9,000 ballots and any other manual recounts from other counties that were necessary.

The next morning, election judges in Miami-Dade county began sorting through thousands of ballots, placing them in labeled shoeboxes as the world waited with anticipation (Gillman 2000, 120). Around the state, numerous other counties began the complicated task of separating "undervotes" from other ballots. The Bush campaign appealed the Florida Supreme Court's ruling to the Eleventh Circuit Court of Appeals, which refused the campaign's request for an emergency injunction to stop the recount. Bush filed an emergency application to the U.S. Supreme Court for a stay of the mandate to conduct the recount. The Court, in a surprise move, granted the application, "treated the application as a petition for certiorari, and granted certiorari" by a 5–4 vote with the most conservative justices in the majority (*Bush v. Gore* 2000). Just hours after the recount had begun, election officials stopped their work.

On December 12, 2000, the U.S. Supreme Court issued its historic ruling in *Bush v. Gore*. The Court, by a 7–2 margin, ruled that the recount ordered by the Florida Supreme Court violated the Equal Protection Clause because a state may not, by "arbitrary and disparate treatment, value one person's vote over that of another" in a manner that "dilute[es] the weight of a citizen's vote ... The recount mechanisms implemented in response to the decisions of the Florida Supreme Court do not satisfy the minimum requirement for non-arbitrary treatment of voters ..." (*Bush v. Gore* 2000, 104–5). By a vote of 5 to 4, the Court ruled that no constitutional recount could be completed in the time remaining (110).

For several hours, Gore's lawyers and adviser's scrambled, trying to decipher the opinion and look for opportunities to extend their challenge. Although some lawyers in Florida saw a "glimmer of hope" for the vice president, most thought his options were limited and his chances of success were slim. Overnight, several prominent Democrats began calling on Gore to withdraw. The public was evenly divided in their agreement with the Court's ruling in *Bush v. Gore*. Polls showed that between 42 and 48 percent of respondents disapproved of the Court's ruling; however, despite this ambivalence about the Court's decision, the public would probably not have supported Gore continuing to contest the election. When asked whether they approved of Gore's decision to concede, more than 72 percent of respondents answered in the affirmative; only 26 percent wanted Gore to fight the Court's decision.[20] Because the vast majority of survey respondents wanted Gore to follow the ruling, I code the Court's decision as facing little public opposition, and I expect it to have had a significant effect on behavior.

The next morning at 10 a.m., a Gore campaign spokesman issued a short statement: "The vice president has directed the recount committee to suspend activities" (McManus and Miller 2000). That night at 9 p.m., less than twenty-four hours after the Court's ruling, Vice President Gore withdrew from the presidential election: "Just moments ago, I spoke with George W. Bush and congratulated him on becoming the forty-third president of the United States, and promised him that I wouldn't call him back this time" (Gillman 2000, 151).

Any analysis of the Court's effect in *Bush v. Gore* must be simple and obvious: George W. Bush became president of the United States. It takes no special insight or careful analysis to know that the Court was 100 percent successful at altering behavior through this ruling.[21] In this sense, my analysis is – by necessity – fairly uninteresting. However, from another perspective, the Court's decision in *Bush v. Gore* is the most dramatic example of Supreme Court power of any case I have examined. After five weeks of political posturing, election recounts, intense media scrutiny, and seemingly endless legal

---

[20] See Appendix II for survey information and citations.
[21] See Banks et al. (2005) for an analysis of the consequences of the Court's decision for jurisprudence, electoral politics, and judicial selection.

battles, a single decision by the Supreme Court – issued by a closely divided bench, based on questionable legal reasoning that shocked and befuddled scholars for years to come[22] – ended a bitter contest for the most powerful political office in the world in a single day.

The Court's ruling in *Bush v. Gore* was one of the most complete and impressive displays of judicial power ever; however, its fit with the expectations of my theory is dependent on my claim that the ruling faced little popular opposition. One might argue that the ruling should be treated as at least somewhat unpopular because 42–48 percent of the public expressed disapproval of the decision. Although I believe the public's overwhelming approval of Gore's decision to concede is the more relevant evidence on this question, I must concede that my claim is highly contestable. If the ruling did face significant opposition, my findings in this case simply cut against the predictions of my theory and suggest that the Court is even more powerful than I have argued.

On January 6, 2001, Congress met in a joint session to open and count the electoral votes. Acting in his role as President of the Senate, Vice President Gore presided over the joint session. When the ballots from Florida were presented, a group of representatives from the Congressional Black Caucus rose to object; however, because Senate rules required objections to be made by at least one representative and one senator, and not a single senator had agreed to object, each objection was dismissed. "We did all we could," said Alcee Hastings, a Democratic representative from Florida. "The chair thanks the gentleman," Gore replied, a smile on his face. Asked later why no senators had joined in objecting to the Florida electors, Senator Patrick Leahy explained: "There is a great deal of frustration that the Supreme Court decided the election by stopping the count in Florida. As much as I disagree with the court's decision, I uphold it as the law of the land and won't object" (Gillman 2000, 171).

SUMMARY: POPULAR LATERAL ISSUES

My examination of Supreme Court rulings in popular lateral issues lends strong support to my theory of Court power: The Court is generally successful at altering behavior when it issues popular rulings, even if those rulings cannot be implemented by lower courts. For example, the Court has successfully altered the behavior of Congress and numerous state legislatures through several opinions related to the membership and operations of these institutions. The Court's decisions in the reapportionment, majority-minority legislative districts, and legislative veto issues all faced little public opposition, either because the rulings were popular or because they attracted little public interest. In each of these cases, Congress and the state legislatures altered their behavior to conform to the Court's preferences. The reapportionment and majority-minority legislative districts rulings have radically altered congressional and state legislative elections in the United States, and the legislative veto ruling invalidated

[22] See Ackerman (2002) and Dworkin (2002).

hundreds of federal statutory provisions and ended the use of a common law-making tool that had been frequently utilized for decades.

My theory of Supreme Court power has also been validated by the Court's rulings in other issues. In its popular decisions regarding public aid to religious schools and affirmative action in college admissions, the Court was very successful at altering behavior. Similarly, the Court's ruling invalidating a federal minimum wage for state employees garnered little public interest and appears to have had a strong effect on the regulation of wages for state employees. Finally, and perhaps most importantly, in *Bush v. Gore* the Court single-handedly resolved a dispute over the election of the President of the United States. The only popular lateral issue in which I find little evidence of Court power is its ruling on funding for student religious publications in public universities.

My analysis of Supreme Court rulings in popular lateral issues poses a serious challenge to traditional conceptions of judicial power. Many normative and empirical studies of judicial review proceed from the premise that popular Court decisions are insignificant because these popular policies could be obtained without the Court's assistance. However, I find that in some cases judicial action may be necessary to enact popular policies in the face of unresponsive public officials. These findings also suggest that public officials tend to implement judicial decisions about which the public is indifferent, rather than waste the political capital necessary to resist the ruling. When the Court faces little popular opposition, either because its rulings are supported by the public or because they simply attract little public interest, the institution can have a profound impact on a wide range of policies.

7

Unpopular Lateral Issues

I often wonder whether we do not rest our hopes too much upon constitutions, upon law and upon courts. These are false hopes, believe me, these are false hopes. Liberty lies in the hearts of men and women; when it dies there, no constitution, no law, no court can save it; no constitution, no law, no court can even do much to help it. While it lies there it needs no constitution, no law, no courts to save it.

Judge Learned Hand[1]

In this chapter, I continue my examination of lateral issues by examining those Court rulings that faced significant public opposition. In each of these cases, I find that the successful implementation of the Court's ruling depended on popular support. When opposition to the ruling was strong, the Court's power was significantly diminished; the stronger the opposition, the less effect the ruling had on behavior. Because non-court actors are unconstrained by the numerous institutional controls placed on lower-court judges, they are often willing to openly defy the Court's rulings or at least quietly ignore them. Furthermore, the implementation of Supreme Court rulings is much more difficult when the rulings are directed at local government actors, because these officials depend on support from local constituencies. As a result, a ruling will not be successfully implemented in regions where the decision is unpopular, even if it enjoys strong support nationally.

SCHOOL DESEGREGATION

Perhaps the most important and controversial area in which the Supreme Court has intervened in American politics during the last half century has been the desegregation of public schools. The Court's continued insistence since the 1950s that public schools not discriminate between students on the basis of race has prompted more praise, controversy, and scholarly interest than any other decision since the *Dred Scott* case. In the states of the old Confederacy, the Court's

---

[1] Hand (1960, 190).

ruling in *Brown v. Board of Education* was so poorly received that it prompted many opponents to insist that the justices be impeached (Klarman 2004, 367). In 1956, more than one hundred southern politicians signed the "Southern Manifesto" to protest the Court's ruling (*Congressional Record* 1956, 4515). Numerous elected officials in the South openly refused to enforce the Court's mandate. This open resistance sometimes prompted tense confrontations. On September 24, 1957, after a protracted desegregation dispute in Little Rock, Arkansas, President Dwight Eisenhower ordered the 101st Airborne Division of the United States Army to the city and federalized the entire 10,000-member Arkansas National Guard to ensure that nine African-American students could attend Little Rock Central High School (Klarman 2004, 326).

The *Brown* decision did not go unquestioned in northern states either. As late as 1959, Herbert Wechsler, a famous liberal law professor, questioned the wisdom of the Court's ruling in *Brown* in an address to the Harvard Law School (Wechsler 1959). After the civil rights movement of the 1960s, the decision became canonized in both the public and academic culture as an irreversible, unquestionable tenet of American political life (Hall 2010). The opinion has played an important role in the confirmation hearings of numerous Supreme Court justices. For example, during the confirmation hearing for John Roberts, more than a half century after the ruling, the future Chief Justice was asked to confirm his fidelity to *Brown* (Senate Committee on the Judiciary 2005). As recently as 2007, in *Parents Involved in Community Schools v. Seattle School District No. 1*, the Court invoked the principles established in *Brown* to invalidate school assignment systems in Seattle and Louisville. This time the Court extended those principles to prohibit race-conscious plans designed to promote rather than prohibit school integration. The dissenters condemned the majority's ruling, claiming that their position was the true heir to *Brown's* legacy.

Despite support for the *Brown* decision by a slim majority of the American public in 1954,[2] the decision was fiercely opposed in southern states. Given this strong opposition, and the fact that the Court was dependent on local school officials to implement the ruling, it would not be surprising if the Court failed to successfully exercise judicial power through this order. However, opposition to the Court's order was not uniform across every state in which segregation was practiced. "According to 1956 Gallup polls, more than 70% of whites outside the South thought that *Brown* was right ... In the South ... only 16 percent of whites agreed with *Brown*" (Klarman 2004, 365–6). These polls suggest that opposition to the Court's ruling was much stronger in states in the Deep South than in Border States. Based on this difference in public opinion, I expect to see a significant difference in the effect of the Court's ruling in these two regions.

This expectation is confirmed by looking at the available data on school desegregation. Figure 7.1 presents statistics on school desegregation for Southern and Border States from 1954 to 1965. The graph shows the percentage of African-American students attending public school with any white

---

[2] See Appendix II for survey information and citations.

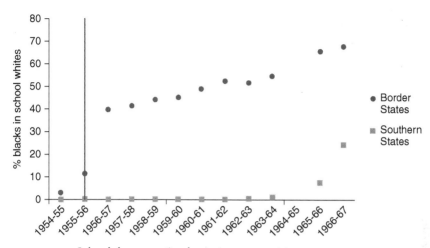

FIGURE 7.1. School desegregation by region, 1954–66.

students in these states for each year. Although *Brown* was decided in 1954, *Brown v. Board of Education II*, in which the Court identified the means by which desegregation should be implemented, was not handed down until May 31, 1955. Although little changed in the few months between the ruling and the start of the 1955–56 school year, a significant change occurred in the Border States before the following school year. Between the 1955–56 school year and the 1956–57 school year, the percent of African-American students in school with whites increased from 11.3 percent to 39.6 percent. Of the 97.1 percent of African-American students in the Border States in segregated schools before *Brown*, 37.8 percent of this group attended school with whites during the 1956–57 school year. I use this statistic as the conservative and generous estimates of behavior conformity to the desegregation ruling in the Border States. School desegregation in the Border States continued to increase during the next decade, reaching more than 50 percent before the Civil Rights Act of 1964 was passed.

In the Deep South, the Court was not nearly as successful at altering the behavior of school administrators. As late as the 1963–64 school year, less than 2 percent of African-American students in these states attended schools with white students. Improvement in these schools occurred only after passage of the Civil Rights Act of 1964, in which Congress empowered the Attorney General to file suit on behalf of African-American students denied access to public schools.

The struggle to desegregate public schools in America highlights the distinction between the Court's power when issuing popular and unpopular rulings. When the Court relies on non-court actors to implement its decisions, its success in altering behavior outcomes depends on the presence or lack of public opposition. Court rulings in lateral issues can have significant impact on behavior change if they are not strongly opposed by the public, as was the case for the desegregation ruling in the Border States. However, these rulings have little chance for success when facing strong popular resistance, such as the Deep South's reaction to *Brown v. Board of Education.*

SCHOOL PRAYER

Regional patterns are also evident in behavior outcomes following the Court's school prayer rulings. On July 8, 1958, the Board of the Union Free School District Number Nine voted to require that a prayer written by the New York Board of Regents be read daily in each of their schools. On instructions from the Board, the District Principal required each teacher in the school district to read the following prayer aloud at the beginning of each day: "Almighty God, we acknowledge our dependence upon Thee, and we beg Thy blessings upon us, our parents, our teachers and our Country" (*Engel v. Vitale* 1959; hereafter *Engel*). Shortly after the prayer readings started, the parents of ten students, including members of the Jewish faith, the Society for Ethical Culture, the Unitarian Church, and one nonbeliever, challenged the practice as violating the prohibition of the establishment of religion in the First Amendment to the U.S. Constitution. After losing at the trial-court level and in the New York Court of Appeals, the parents brought their case before the U.S. Supreme Court, which reversed the lower courts and held that the practice of reading the prayer was unconstitutional. Writing for the majority, Justice Black ruled that "[t]he New York laws officially prescribing the Regents' prayer are inconsistent both with the purposes of the Establishment Clause and with the Establishment Clause itself" (*Engel* 1962, 433).

Despite the Court's clear language, the *Engel* decision did not resolve the debate about the role of religion in public schools. In a series of decisions during the next half century, the Court repeated its rejection of religious activities in public schools. The next year, the Court struck down a Pennsylvania law requiring Bible readings in public schools and a school district policy requiring the recitation of the Lord's Prayer in *Abington School District v. Schempp* (1963). Two decades later, in *Wallace v. Jaffree*, the Court invalidated an Alabama statute authorizing a one-minute period of silence in all public schools "for meditation or voluntary prayer" (1985, 40). In *Lee v. Weisman*, the Court ruled that a school principal inviting a rabbi to deliver a prayer at a high school graduation ceremony created "a state-sponsored and state-directed religious exercise in a public school" (1992, 587). In *Santa Fe Independent School District v. Doe* (2000), the Court held that a school's policy permitting a student-led, student-initiated prayer at football games violated the Establishment Clause.

The school prayer decisions were extremely unpopular. The first public opinion poll related to *Engel*, conducted in 1964, reported that 77 percent of Americans favored a constitutional amendment to legalize prayers in public schools. A 1966 poll found that 65.5 percent of respondents thought the *Engel* ruling was "wrong"; only 26.9 percent thought it was "right."[3] Other polls showed similar patterns.[4] Public opposition remained strong for years to come. Polls conducted in the mid-1980s, after *Wallace*, and in the early 1990s, after *Lee v. Weisman*, continued to report strong opposition to the Court. When the justices handed down their decision in *Santa Fe Independent School District* in 2000, 68 percent of the public disagreed with it.

Opposition to the school prayer decisions, though persistent in every region, has been consistently concentrated in the South. According to the 1964 American National Election Study, 88 percent of respondents in the South thought schools should be allowed to start each day with a prayer. Support for school prayer was slightly lower in other regions, but still extremely high (81% in New England, 75% in the Mid-Atlantic, 68% in the Midwest, and 62% in the West). Regional data from the Social Science Survey is only available starting in the 1970s, but since that time support for school prayer in the South has frequently topped 70 percent. By contrast, support for religious practices in school is almost always weaker in the Northeast, the Midwest, and the western states.[5]

The justices in *Engel* obviously expressed their preference that teachers not read the prayer adopted by the New York Board of Regents, but they also expressed disapproval of other religious exercises in public schools: "When the power, prestige and financial support of government is placed behind a particular religious belief, the indirect coercive pressure upon religious minorities to conform to the prevailing officially approved religion is plain" (*Engel* 1962, 431). If this preference had a causal effect on the behavior of teachers and school administrators, then the frequency of all religious activities should have decreased following the decision; however, given the strong opposition to the school prayer decisions, I expect the ruling to have very limited effects, especially in the South.

This expectation is generally confirmed by the available data on religious practices in schools. Just as in the case of school desegregation, the effects of the *Engel* and *Schempp* decisions varied widely by region. The most reliable data on religious practices in schools during the 1960s comes from surveys conducted by social scientists. For example, Richard Dierenfield conducted a survey of 4,000 school superintendents (54.57% response rate) in 1960 that

---

[3] See Appendix II for survey information and citations.
[4] A national 1966 Louis Harris and Associates Survey showed that 70% of respondents thought the Court's decision was "wrong"; 30% thought the decision was "right." A national 1971 Gallup Poll showed that 67% of respondents disapproved of the Court's decision; only 27% approved. See Appendix II for survey information and citations. A survey conducted by the Survey Research Center at the University of Michigan before the 1964 elections found that 74% of respondents expressed approval of school devotionals. The Center's post-election survey found that 68% had only negative things to say about the Court, and there were more negative mentions of the prayer decision (252) than any other issue (Laubach 1969, 138).
[5] See Appendix II for survey information and citations.

TABLE 7.1. *Bible Readings in Public Schools, 1960–65*

Region	% of Schools Districts with Bible Readings in 1960	% of School Districts with Bible Readings in 1965	Behavior Conformity (%)
East	67.56	4.27	93.7
West	11.03	2.29	79.2
Midwest	18.26	5.19	71.6
South	76.84	49.48	35.6
Total	41.74	12.90	69.1

Note: Data based on surveys of 4000 superintendents (54.57% response rate) about religious practices in schools within their jurisdiction in 1960 and 1965 as reported in Dierenfield (1962, 51) and Laubach (1969, 139). Survey question: "Is Bible reading conducted in the schools of your system?"

TABLE 7.2. *Devotional Exercises in Public Schools, 1960–65*

Region	% of Schools Districts with Devotional Exercises in 1960	% of School Districts with Devotional Exercises in 1965	Behavior Conformity (%)
East	80.16	7.28	90.9
West	8.62	2.29	73.4
Midwest	25.95	11.28	56.5
South	88.69	61.74	30.4
Total	50.24	18.62	62.9

Note: Data based on surveys of 4,000 superintendents (54.57% response rate) about religious practices in schools within their jurisdiction in 1960 and 1965 as reported in Dierenfield (1962, 56) and Laubach (1969, 139). Survey question: "Are homeroom devotional services held in the schools of your system?" Percentages include superintendents reporting devotional exercises in "some" or "all" of their schools.

asked about religious practices in schools. The survey found that in 1960, about 68 percent of school districts in the Northeast conducted regular Bible readings; by 1965, only 4 percent conducted these readings (Dierenfield 1962, 51; Laubach 1969, 139). In the South, the percentage of schools reporting Bible readings fell from 77 percent to 49 percent (see Table 7.1). Despite a meaningful decrease in the South, about two-thirds of school districts in this region reporting Bible readings in 1960 continued this practice after *Schempp*. Reports of other devotional exercises in public schools showed a similar regional pattern during this same time period (see Table 7.2).

Dolbeare and Hammond (1971) confirmed this regional pattern in a follow-up to the Dierenfield surveys conducted in 1967. Dolbeare and Hammond surveyed 1,100 superintendents who had reported conducting religious activities in Dierenfield's survey. They found that of the 295 school districts in the Northeast

TABLE 7.3. *Termination of Devotional Exercises, 1960–67*

Region	Schools Districts with Devotional Exercises in 1960	% of School Districts Stopping Devotionals after 1963*
East	295	93
West	21	62
Midwest	165	54
South	171	21
Total	652	n/a

Note: Data based on surveys of 1,100 superintendents that reported religious activities in Dierenfield's (1962) 1960 survey (57% response rate) as reported in Dolbeare and Hammond (1971).
*I use these figures as the conservative estimates of behavior conformity to the school prayer decisions.

TABLE 7.4. *Relation of Compliance Rates to State-Level Policy Actions, 1960–67*

State Agency Affirming-Negating Score	Number of States	Number of Districts	Dierenfield's Compliance Rate (%)
+3	5	180	91
+2	7	141	89
+1	10	61	52
0	14	169	42
−1 or −2	6	78	22

Note: Data based on a survey of 1,100 superintendents that reported religious activities in Dierenfield's (1962) 1960 survey (57% response rate) and a survey of actions taken by relevant state-level agencies as reported in Dolbeare and Hammond (1971). The survey of actions taken by state-level agencies coded the actions of state legislatures, attorneys general, courts, and state superintendents of education as either affirming or negating the Supreme Court's school prayer decisions.

that had reported conducting devotional exercises in 1960, 93 percent of these districts discontinued the practice after 1963 (see Table 7.3). The compliance rate was 62 percent in the West and 54 percent in the Midwest; in the South, only 21 percent of school districts complied with the ruling. Because these statistics conform less closely to my expectations than other estimates, I use these figures as the conservative estimates of behavior conformity to the school prayer rulings.

Dolbeare and Hammond also found a correlation between compliance and the level of support for the school prayer decisions in different states. They collected data on actions taken by state-level agencies (state legislatures, attorneys general, courts, and state superintendents of education) relating to school prayer and coded each action as either affirming or negating the Court's decisions. They then constructed an "affirming-negating score" for each state and examined the compliance rates of districts in states with similar scores. The results of this analysis are presented in Table 7.4. States with high affirming-negating scores contained school districts with high compliance rates; states with low scores contained school districts with low compliance rates. For example, of the 180 school districts in the five states with scores of +3, 91 percent reported discontinuing their devotional exercises. Of the 78 districts in the six states with scores of -1 or -2, only 22 percent reported complying with the Court's order.

Even if we assume that these state-level actions were driven by public opinion, it is not clear whether the actions of these state-level agencies caused the differential conformity patterns. The relationship between actions by state-level agencies and school district conformity may be causal or both patterns may be caused by a third variable, such as public opinion regarding the school prayer issue. Regardless, Dolbeare and Hammond's analysis of regional patterns and state-level action lends strong support to the claim that the school prayer decisions had a greater effect on behavior outcomes in states where support for the Court's decision was stronger.

H. Frank Way (1968) conducted a similar survey studying religious practices in public schools in 1965. Way's survey might be more accurate because it was sent to teachers rather than superintendents, and teachers might provide a more accurate depiction of actual school practices. However, Way's survey suffers from the disadvantage that it was not conducted in two waves. Because the survey was sent after the *Engel* and *Schempp* decisions, Way relies on the teachers to accurately remember and report religious practices before the rulings. Despite using very different methodology, Way's findings are remarkably similar to those of Dierenfield, Dolbeare, and Hammond. Because Way's results are slightly more supportive of my theory, I use these statistics as the generous estimates of behavior conformity to the school prayer decisions.

The Court's effect on prayer in public schools as reported by teachers is shown in Table 7.5. The Court's ability to cause change in the behavior of school teachers varied widely by region. In New England, 95 percent of teachers reported conducting morning prayers before 1962; only 27 percent continued this practice in the 1964–65 school year (71.6% conformity).[6] The Mid-Atlantic States saw a similar effect; reports of morning prayers dropped from 80 percent to 7 percent (91.3% conformity). Reports in the West indicated that prayers decreased from 14 percent to 5 percent (64.3% conformity). The effect of the Court's decisions was significantly weaker in the Midwest and the South. In the Midwest, although only 38 percent of teachers reported conducting prayers before 1962, 21 percent continued to lead prayers in 1965 (44.7% conformity). In the South, reports of school prayer dropped from 87 percent to 64 percent, leaving the majority of teachers unaffected by the Court's ruling (26.4% conformity).

---

[6] I calculate the generous estimates of behavior conformity for the school prayer decisions by dividing the percentage-point decrease in school prayer reports by the percent reporting school prayer before the ruling. I average the New England and Mid-Atlantic compliance rates to provide a comparison to the Northeast figures reported by Dolbeare and Hammond (1971).

TABLE 7.5. *Morning Prayers in Public Schools, 1962–65*

Region	% of Teachers Reporting Prayers before 1962	% of Teachers Reporting Prayers in 1964–65	Behavior Conformity* (%)
New England	95	27	71.6
Mid-Atlantic	80	7	91.3
West	14	5	64.3
Midwest	38	21	44.7
South	87	64	26.4

Note: Data based on survey of 2,320 public elementary school teachers in 464 schools (74% response rate) as reported in reported in Way (1968, 199).
*I use these figures as the generous estimates of behavior conformity to the school prayer decisions.

TABLE 7.6. *Bible Reading in Public Schools, 1962–65*

Region	% of Teachers Reporting Bible Readings Before 1962	% of Teachers Reporting Bible Readings in 1964–65	Compliance Rate (%)
New England	64	20	68.8
Mid-Atlantic	62	5	91.9
West	14	6	57.1
Midwest	28	12	57.1
South	80	57	28.8

Note: Data based on survey of 2,320 public elementary school teachers in 464 schools (74% response rate) as reported in Way (1968, 199).

The Court's effect on Bible reading in public schools is reported in Table 7.6. The regional patterns are very similar to those for morning prayers. In New England, more than two-thirds of teachers who reported Bible readings before 1962 discontinued this practice in the 1964–65 school year (Bible reading dropped from 64% to 20%). In the South, little more than one-fourth of teachers heeded the Court's instructions (Bible readings dropped from 80% to 57%).

The Court's decisions on religious activities in public schools had profound effects on daily practices in some parts of the country; in other regions, the effects of the rulings were more limited. Where the rulings faced the strongest public opposition, school officials often ignored the Court's decisions. In Indiana, fewer than 6 percent of school boards changed their policies that permitted Bible reading and prayer; in Texas, a survey conducted by the Council of Churches found that "the change was negligible" (Wasby 1970, 131). In Kentucky, only 34.4 percent of school districts surveyed reported discontinuing Bible readings and school prayer (Reich 1968, 50). More interestingly, the decisions often met outright defiance. For example, twenty-seven school boards rewrote policies on Bible reading and school prayer after 1963. Of them, eleven authorized these practices, directly contradicting the Supreme Court (Reich 1968, 50). Beaney and Beiser (1964) find several examples of defiance and careful avoidance in Kentucky, Rhode Island, Delaware, and New Jersey.

The pattern of conformity to the school prayer decisions partially confirms my theory of Supreme Court power: Because school prayer is a lateral issue, the Court's rulings had little causal effect in those areas where the decision was least popular.[7] Local public opinion was especially important for these decisions because "actual implementation of the decisions[s] was essentially a local matter" (Katz 1965, 401). As Beaney and Beiser emphasize, although compliance was limited in every region, "[m]ost of the instances of outright defiance occurred in the South," where the decision faced strong public opposition (1964, 486). Compliance was slightly higher in the West and the Midwest, where the ruling was slightly more popular.

More surprisingly, the Court achieved a high degree of success in the Northeast. In contrast to the expectations of my theory, I found drastic behavior changes in this region, despite strong opposition to the ruling. This finding is difficult to explain. This regional pattern might be the result of differences in public opinion that were not captured by the National Election Study; for example, support for school prayer in the Northeast might have been widespread, but less intense than in the South. Alternatively, this finding might simply cut against the strength of my argument, suggesting that the Court is even more powerful than my theory suggests.

CENSORSHIP IN PUBLIC EDUCATION

The Supreme Court has also intervened in the administration of public elementary and secondary schools by prohibiting various forms of censorship in these institutions. The first of these rulings arose from a dispute between three public school students and their principals in Des Moines, Iowa. The students, 15-year-old John Tinker, his 13-year-old sister, Mary Beth Tinker, and 16-year-old Christopher Eckhardt, wore black armbands to school in December of 1965 to protest United States involvement in the Vietnam War. Each student was suspended and told not to return to school until they removed the armbands. The Court ruled that the school's actions violated the freedom of speech because the wearing of armbands in the case was entirely divorced from actually or potentially disruptive behavior ... [and] was closely akin to 'pure speech' ..." (*Tinker v. Des Moines Independent School District* 1969, 505). Unfortunately, no public opinion polls were ever taken regarding the *Tinker* decision, and no study has ever systematically measured the ruling's effects on school disciplinary programs. Due to a lack of information about

---

[7] See Johnson (1967) and Dolbeare and Hammond (1971) for examples of other scholars who claim that the efficacy of the Court's decisions regarding school prayer and Bible reading was strongly influenced by local public opinion.

the popularity and consequences of this ruling, I have chosen to focus my attention in this section on the Court's intervention in the context of school library censorship.

In February 1976, the Board of Education of the Island Trees Free Union School District No. 26 in New York issued an "unofficial direction" to the superintendent of schools and the principals of the district's high school and junior high to remove eleven books from the school libraries. After the removal of the books became public, the Board issued a press release defending its actions and characterizing the books as "anti-American, anti-Christian, anti-Semitic, and just plain filthy" (*Board of Education v. Pico* 1982, 857; hereafter *Pico*). The Board concluded, "It is our duty, our moral obligation, to protect the children in our schools from this moral danger as surely as from physical and medical dangers" (*Pico* 1982, 857). The Board later appointed a "Book Review Committee" to read the books and recommend whether they should be retained in the school libraries. The committee recommended that only two of the books should be removed and a third restricted to use only with parental approval, but the Board substantially rejected the committee's report. Instead, the Board removed nine of the books and restricted access to a tenth book.

Several students in the school district brought suit in federal district court, claiming that the Board's decision to remove the books violated their First Amendment rights. The district court granted summary judgment in favor of the Board, noting its broad discretion to formulate educational policy; however, the Second Circuit Court of Appeals reversed the district court and ruled against the school. The Supreme Court granted certiorari and affirmed the court of appeals. Speaking for a plurality of the Court, Justice Brennan ruled that, although "school boards do have broad discretion in the management of school affairs," this discretion "must be exercised in a manner that comports with the transcendent imperatives of the First Amendment" (*Pico* 1982, 863–4); "local school boards may not remove books from school library shelves simply because they dislike the ideas contained in those books and seek by their removal to prescribe what shall be orthodox in politics, nationalism, religion, or other matters of opinion" (*Pico* 1982, 872).

Public reaction to the *Pico* decision was mixed. In a 1982 Roper Report public opinion poll, respondents opposed banning books in schools and libraries that "some people consider objectionable" by a two-to-one margin; however, in this poll, before asking for the respondent's opinion, the questioner suggested that the proposal may violate "various Constitutional Guarantees, such as freedom of the press ..."[8] In addition, describing the potentially banned material as books that "some people consider objectionable" may have encouraged the respondents to assume that other people found the books objectionable, but the respondent would not. The General Social Survey (GSS) found that national majorities opposed banning anti-religious books, communist books, homosexual books, and racist books from public libraries, but these surveys

---

[8] See Appendix II for survey information and citations.

are also problematic because the public may have very different opinions about banning books from public libraries and banning books from school libraries.

Other surveys provide a different picture of the public's attitude toward book banning in school libraries. A 1982 Merit Report poll revealed that, when asked who should control what books are available in public school libraries, just as many respondents trusted school boards, superintendents, and school principals as those who preferred to let teachers and librarians decide. A series of surveys conducted by Times Mirror between 1987 and 1990 consistently found that roughly half of respondents agreed with this statement: "Books that contain dangerous ideas should be banned from public school libraries."[9] In addition, the GSS revealed important geographical differences in response rates. Although national majorities opposed removing objectionable books from public libraries, majorities in the South Atlantic and East South Central supported removing the objectionable books. Given these divided poll results, I expect the *Pico* ruling to have some limited effects on school boards banning books from school libraries in most parts of the country but very little effect in the southern states.

The justices in *Pico* expressed a preference that school boards and school administrators refrain from removing or restricting school library books due to objectionable content. There are two different ways to collect information on the frequency of censorship in school libraries: (1) to count reports of censorship in media outlets; (2) to survey school librarians and ask about their experiences with censorship. I consider each of these methods in the following pages.

(1) The longest running tabulation of censorship attempts in school libraries is compiled by *The Newsletter on Intellectual Freedom* (NIF), a publication of the Intellectual Freedom Committee of the American Library Association (1970–95; hereafter ALA). The *NIF* reports brief descriptions of censorship challenges in a section entitled "Censorship Dateline." Each of these descriptions was read and coded as an instance of censorship in school libraries if the challenge occurred at a public school library and resulted in the removal or restriction of the book in question. Removals or restrictions were counted as acts of censorship whether ordered by school boards or school administrators. Reports were not counted as acts of censorship if the challenge was not yet resolved at the time of the report, the material was briefly removed or restricted but later retained, or if material was destroyed or stolen by private individuals without the approval of school officials.

Instances of censorship in school libraries reported in *The Newsletter on Intellectual Freedom* between 1970 and 1995 are reported in Figure 7.2. The *Pico* ruling had only a small effect on the frequency of censorship as reported in the *NIF*. There was a slight dip in reports a few years after *Pico*, but the frequency of reports rebounded strongly in the early 1990s. A regression discontinuity analysis reveals that the change in censorship reports after the *Pico*

---

[9] See Appendix II for survey information and citations.

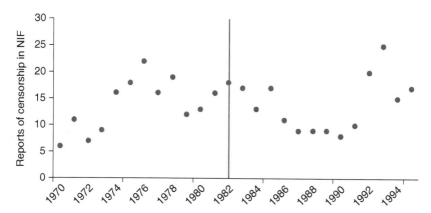

FIGURE 7.2. Censorship in school libraries, 1970–95.

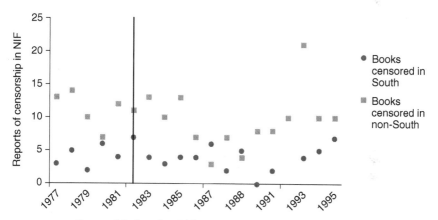

FIGURE 7.3. Censorship in school libraries by region, 1977–95.

ruling is statistically significant; the *Pico* ruling is associated with a decrease of 7.5 censorship reports each year.[10] This change reflects a 41.7 percent decrease (7.5/18). I use this figure as the generous estimate of behavior conformity to the censorship rulings. Interestingly, the decrease in censorship in the late 1980s appears to be completely concentrated in non-southern states. As shown in Figure 7.3, censorship in southern states remained constant during this period, while censorship in non-southern states dropped significantly. This pattern was short-lived though; censorship in non-southern states returned to previous levels and spiked to an all-time high in 1993.

Media reports of censorship in libraries have also been compiled by The People for the American Way in a report called *Attacks on the Freedom to*

---

[10] See Appendix IV for regression analysis.

Learn beginning in 1982 (1982–1991; hereafter PAW). This series of reports includes similar descriptions of challenges to library material and their resolutions, but it combines reports of censorship in public and school libraries. The report tracks a steady increase in challenges in the decade after *Pico*, from 57 in 1982 to 347 in 1992 (PAW 1986, 1; 1993, 9). The study also finds a steady increase in the rate of successful challenges to library material, from 23 percent in 1982 (Reichman 1993, 10) to 41 percent in 1993 (PAW 1993, 17); however, only a fraction of these successful challenges were in schools. *Attacks on the Freedom to Learn* reported around fifty cases of censorship each year during the mid-1980s, but less than half of these were in schools [7 in 1985, 17 in 1986, 24 in 1987, and 17 in 1988 (PAW 1985–88)] and around a third of these school censorship cases were in the South [2 in 1985, 7 in 1986, 24 in 1987, and 17 in 1988 (PAW 1985–88)]. Unfortunately, it is impossible to determine whether *Pico* had an effect on these figures because these reports offer little information on censorship before the ruling.

Media reports of censorship incidents suggest that *Pico* may have had very little effect on censorship in school libraries, but the reports are limited in several ways. First of all, the great majority of censorship practices in school libraries go unreported in media outlets. Only if a parent, school official, or civic group brings the issue to the attention of local media is it possible for censorship to be tabulated through these reports. Second, the frequency of reports may be affected by the media's interest in the subject. It is possible that censorship did drop dramatically after *Pico*, but media reports increased because the media became more interested in the topic after the decision. Undoubtedly, a school board banning a book is much more interesting and newsworthy after the Supreme Court has forbidden the practice.

(2) To avoid these methodological concerns, several scholars have attempted to measure the frequency of censorship in school libraries by surveying school librarians or administrators and asking about their experiences with censorship. These surveys have the advantage of obtaining information about censorship activities even when they are not reported by the media; however, they have the disadvantage of relying on school personnel to return the survey and accurately report instances of censorship. If certain types of schools are less likely to return the survey or if respondents have an incentive to consciously or unconsciously alter their recollection of censorship in their school, these surveys may provide inaccurate information. Nonetheless, this alternative methodology offers another vantage point from which to evaluate *Pico*'s effects.

In *Battle of the Books: Literary Censorship in the Public Schools, 1950–1985*, Lee Burress (1989) reports an interesting series of surveys of school personnel conducted between 1966 and 1982. "The basic question on these surveys was: 'Has someone objected to a book or other learning material used in your school in the last year?'" (Burress 1989, 50). The findings of these surveys are reported in Table 7.7. The most recent of the surveys, conducted in 1982, indicates that 34 percent of school personnel surveyed indicated that someone had objected to a book in the last year. Unfortunately, Burress does

TABLE 7.7. *Challenges to Books in School Libraries, 1966–82*

	1966	1973	1977	1982
% reporting challenges	20	28	30	34

Note: Data based on surveys of school personnel reported in Burress (1989, 50).

not report any surveys conducted after the *Pico* ruling. A 1991 survey conducted by Dianne McAfee Hopkins (1996) found that 36 percent of respondents reported receiving challenges to their materials between 1986 and 1989. These statistics are difficult to compare because they cover different lengths of time; however, if every school reporting a challenge experienced only one challenge during this period, then the rate of censorship reports per year dropped to about 12 percent in the late 1980s. Of course, this is a big assumption; if any of these schools experienced challenges in multiple years, then the rate would be higher. For this reason, 12 percent marks a lower boundary on the yearly challenge rate during this period; nonetheless, these figures suggest the *Pico* ruling may have discouraged challenges to school library material.

A possible decrease in challenges to school library material is only interesting because it suggests that *Pico* affected the challengers' attitudes or that the challengers were deterred from challenging because they anticipated less success. The more important question is whether actual censorship activity deceased after *Pico*. The frequency of censorship activity can be measured by multiplying the percentage of schools reporting challenges by the percentage of challenges that succeeded. The only national surveys to collect this information are the Hopkins (1996) study mentioned previously and a study conducted jointly by the American Association of Publishers, the American Library Association, and the Association for Supervision and Curriculum Development (1981; hereafter AAP) in April of 1980. The relevant findings from both of these surveys are reported in Table 7.8.

Both surveys report similar percentages of challenges resulting in restriction or removal (52.9% in AAP; 48% in Hopkins). The Hopkins study revealed a higher challenge rate than the AAP Study (22.4% in AAP and 36% in Hopkins), but the Hopkins study covered a longer time frame. After correcting for this time difference and making the same assumptions I did for the challenge rate comparison, I find that the percentage of schools reporting restriction or removal per year was slightly higher between 1978 and 1980 (7.1% of schools per year) than between 1986 and 1989 (5.8% of schools per year). This change is an 18.3 percent decrease [(7.1−5.8)/5.8]; I use this figure as the conservative estimate of behavior conformity. The *Pico* ruling may have had a very small effect on censorship practices, but this conclusion relies on the assumption that schools are not experiencing challenges in multiple years.

Although media reports of censorship incidents indicate that the *Pico* ruling may have had some effect on school censorship, surveys of school librarians offer only limited evidence to support this claim. The evidence that is available

TABLE 7.8. *Frequency of Censorship Activity, 1978–89*

Region	AAP Study Sept. 1978–April 1980	Hopkins Study Jan. 1986–Dec. 1989
% of schools reporting challenges	22.4	36
% of challenges resulting in restriction	30.7	22
% of challenges resulting in removal	22.2	26
% of challenges resulting in restriction or removal	52.9	48
% of schools reporting restriction or removal	11.8	17.3
# of years under consideration	1.67	3
% of schools reporting restriction or removal per year	7.1	5.8

Note: Data based on survey of 7,572 public elementary and secondary school librarians, library supervisors, principals, and district superintendents in the 50 states and the District of Columbia in April 1980 as reported in AAP (1981, 2, 7) and survey of 4,682 (72% response rate of 6,500 questionnaires) public secondary school libraries and media centers as reported in Hopkins (1996).

depends on assumptions that cannot be proven due to vague question wording in surveys of school personnel. This finding is consistent with my theory of judicial power because the public reaction to *Pico* was mixed. There is some weak evidence that during the late 1980s public reports of censorship declined in non-southern states, where the ruling was more popular, but this trend reversed itself in the early 1990s. Overall, the evidence suggests that the Supreme Court only partially altered behavior through its ruling in *Board of Education v. Pico*.

MINORITY SET-ASIDE PROGRAMS

As discussed in the last chapter, the Supreme Court faced little opposition to its rulings on affirmative action in college admissions; however, the Court faced somewhat stronger opposition to its affirmative action rulings in the context of government contracting. Many states and federal agencies give general contractors on government projects a financial incentive to hire subcontractors owned by "socially and economically disadvantaged individuals" (*Adarand Constructors v. Pena* 1995, 204; hereafter *Adarand*). These contract policies are commonly referred to as minority set-aside programs.

In 1989, the Supreme Court ruled that the City of Richmond's minority set-aside plan was unconstitutional because it failed to meet strict scrutiny under the Equal Protection Clause, meaning that the racial classification was not narrowly tailored to meet a compelling government interest (*City of Richmond v. J.A. Croson Co.* 1989). Although the city could use race-based legislation to eradicate the effects of past discrimination in the construction industry, "generalized assertions" of past racial discrimination could not justify "rigid" racial quotas for awarding public contracts. However, "[i]f the statistical disparity between eligible MBE's [Minority Business Enterprises] and MBE membership were great enough, an inference of discriminatory exclusion could arise. In such a case, the city would have a compelling interest in preventing its tax dollars from assisting these organizations in maintaining a racially segregated construction market" (*Adarand* 1995, 503).

That same year, the U.S. Department of Transportation awarded a highway construction contract to Mountain Gravel and Construction Company. Under the terms of the federal contract, the prime contractor would receive additional compensation if it hired disadvantaged small businesses, and "the contractor shall presume that socially and economically disadvantaged individuals include Black Americans, Hispanic Americans, Native Americans, Asian Pacific Americans, and other minorities" (*Adarand* 1995, 205). Mountain Gravel solicited bids for a subcontract for highway guardrails. The lowest bid was submitted by Adarand Constructors, but the subcontract was awarded to Gonzales Construction, a minority-owned business certified as disadvantaged by the Small Business Administration.

Adarand filed suit against Federico Pena, the U.S. Secretary of Transportation, alleging that the minority set-aside program violated the Equal Protection Clause of the Fourteenth Amendment. The district court granted the government's motion for summary judgment, and the Court of Appeals for the Tenth Circuit affirmed its decision. The Supreme Court granted certiorari and reversed the lower courts. In an opinion written by Justice O'Connor, the Court ruled that all racial classifications, whether imposed by local, state, or federal agencies, were subject to the strict scrutiny standard. The case was remanded back to the district court, which found that the Department of Transportation program did not meet this standard.

The *Adarand* decision received a mixed response from the public. In an ABC News/Washington Post poll, 55 percent of respondents approved of the decision, whereas 41 percent disapproved. This poll was consistent with a poll taken a few months before the ruling, in which 59 percent of respondents said they opposed minority set-aside programs. These polls suggest that the *Adarand* decision faced significant but limited public opposition.[11]

The Supreme Court's rulings in *Croson* and *Adarand* expressed the Court's clear preference for local, state, and federal agencies to carefully consider race-neutral alternatives and prove the existence of past discrimination before enacting race-conscious programs. The existence of past discrimination could only be proven by conducting disparity studies, which measure the disparity between the awarding of contracts to minority business enterprises and other businesses. If these decisions had a causal effect on the behavior of government

---

[11] See Appendix II for survey information and citations.

officials administering these programs, we should expect to see two behavior outcomes:

(1) The implementation of disparity studies or discontinuation of minority set-aside programs at the state and local level after the *Croson* decision in 1989.
(2) The evaluation of whether federal minority set-aside programs meet strict scrutiny and the elimination of programs that do not after the *Adarand* decision in 1995.

(1) Before the Supreme Court's decision in *City of Richmond v. J.A. Croson*, 236 state and local minority set-aside programs existed in the United States (Plaus 1991, 644).[12] Following the *Croson* decision, numerous jurisdictions, including state governments, particular state agencies, cities, school districts, and other governmental units, adjusted their practices to comply with the ruling. Just a year after *Croson*, more than fifty challenges had been leveled against minority set-aside programs, and at least forty-six jurisdictions had abandoned their programs either as the result of legal action or anticipating such action (Simms 1990; see Rice 1999, 1020). By 1999, Mitchell Rice was able to identify more than sixty jurisdictions in the U.S. that had conducted disparity studies at a cost of more than $13 million (1999, 1012). The individual studies ranged in cost from $60,000 to $791,000, indicating the significant financial burden placed on these jurisdictions by the Court's ruling. At least twenty-seven of these disparity studies were conducted in jurisdictions that had not yet discontinued or revised their set-aside program. Taking this information together, at least 73 of the 236 jurisdictions operating set-aside programs before *Croson* terminated their programs, revised their programs, or justified their programs through a disparity study after the ruling. Consequently, the most conservative estimate of conformity to the *Croson* ruling by state and local authorities is 31 percent (73/236).

Behavior conformity may have been much higher. In 1994, James Ward conducted a survey of 171 cities. Of the fifty-two cities that responded to the survey, only ten reported operating a set-aside program before *Croson*. Four of these cities had dismantled their set-aside programs (two by court order and two voluntarily). The other six were conducting disparity studies as required by the ruling.[13] This finding would suggest 100 percent behavior conformity,

---

[12] This estimate is taken from a letter from Tyrone D. Press, Chief, Investigation and Research, Office of Chief Counsel for the Minority Business Enterprise Legal Defense and Education Fund (MBELDEF), to Marie Carlin, Articles Editor, Loyola of Los Angeles Law Review (Jan. 10, 1991) (discussing research compiled by the MBELDEF from verbal and written correspondence with various sources). "In addition to state legislative initiatives, over 150 localities established programs which constitute the bulk of available contracting opportunities" (Plaus 1991, 664, footnote 64).

[13] Ward's (1994) main argument is that actual spending on "set-asides" and "goal programs" designed to promote minority businesses only slightly decreased between 1988 and 1990 (from

but cities that were defying the Court's ruling may have been less likely to return the survey; consequently, this generous estimate should be interpreted with caution.

The limited data available suggests that discontinuing minority set-aside programs caused minority business participation to drop substantially (Rice 1999, 1020–1). In Atlanta, participation dropped from 37 percent in 1989 to 24 percent in 1990. In Richmond, participation dropped from 32 percent in 1989 to 11 percent in 1990 and to less than 5 percent in 1991 (Ward 1994, 1101). In Philadelphia, participation dropped from 25 percent in 1990 to 3.5 percent in 1991. Tampa, Florida, saw a 99 percent decrease in participation by African-American firms and a 50 percent decrease in participation by Hispanic firms. Minority business participation dropped by 50 percent in the State of Illinois and by 99 percent in Hillsborough County, Florida (Rice 1999, 1020–1). Although data is not available for every jurisdiction that discontinued a set-aside program, there is no reason to believe that the experiences of these jurisdictions were unusual.

(2) The Clinton administration took several steps in response to the *Adarand* ruling. The Department of Justice (DOJ) conducted a review of affirmative action in federal procurement programs and issued guidance on applying the requirements of *Adarand* to these programs (General Accounting Office 2001, 6; hereafter GAO). The DOJ identified components of Disadvantaged Business Enterprise (DBE) programs that needed to be reformed and several acceptable, race-conscious contracting mechanisms (United States Commission on Civil Rights 2005, 14, 17; hereafter USCCR). The DOJ also decided that the Department of Commerce, in consultation with the General Services Administration and Small Business Administration, would develop benchmarks and determine acceptable strategies to limit race measures to certain areas of government procurement (USCRC 2005, 15).

In response to these suggestions, several agencies revised their DBE programs (USCCR 2005, 14). For example, after *Adarand*, the Federal Communications Commission "decided to reexamine, and ultimately reconstruct, its preferential auction program for licensing radio stations" (Enemark 1997, 216). Similarly in 1999, the Department of Transportation, which had been the target of the *Adarand* suit, issued new regulations that "significantly altered" its DBE program:

> The regulations designated 10 percent as a national aspirational goal for disadvantaged businesses, but mandated actual participation goals at levels based on the local market availability of DBEs, not a set percentage. Moreover, the regulations required states to use race-neutral measures, including outreach and technical assistance, to meet as much of their goals as possible. (USCCR 2005, 14)

$188,492,345 in 1988 to $181,977,082 in 1990); however, the Court did not invalidate "goal programs," and Ward offers no reason why we should expect to see any changes in cities that never had set-aside programs or whose programs were undergoing a disparity study.

These new regulations led to "numerous state and local governments conduct[ing] disparity studies to support their minority contracting programs and to help set up their federal DBE participation goals" (GAO 2001, 6). Most of these studies revealed disparities between availability and utilization of minority- and women-owned business in transportation contracts, but a few federal DBE programs were discontinued by court order (GAO 2001, 38). The limited data available suggests that DBE's participation in federal transportation contracting dramatically decreased after the discontinuation of these programs (GAO 2001, 39).

In a study conducted ten years after the *Adarand* ruling, the U.S. Commission on Civil Rights found that "agencies do not engage in the activities that constitute serious consideration [of race-neutral alternatives], such as program evaluation, outcomes measurement, empirical research and data collection, and periodic review" (USCCR 2005, iii); however, in his dissenting statement, Commissioner Michael Yaki denied this was the appropriate standard by which to measure compliance with *Adarand*. The Commission Majority claimed that *Adarand* requires agencies to "consider, and employ, race neutral strategies before resorting to race-conscious ones" (USCRC 2005, 18), but Yaki insisted that this reading is inconsistent with Justice O'Connor's opinion. Instead, Yaki highlighted Justice O'Connor's assurance that

> [t]he unhappy persistence of both the practice and the lingering effects of racial discrimination against minority groups in this country is an unfortunate reality, and government is not disqualified from acting in response to it…. When race based action is necessary to further a compelling interest, such action is within constitutional constraints if it satisfies the 'narrow tailoring' test … (USCCR 2005, 82; *Adarand* 1995, 237)

Yaki leveled a series of additional charges against the Commission Majority, pointing out methodological, logical, and factual flaws in the report (USCCR 2005, 87–9). Unfortunately, Yaki concluded that he was unable to measure the impact of the *Adarand* decision and the DOJ's response to the ruling for two reasons. First, because the Commission used flawed procedures to produce the report, the data uncovered by the study was inadequate to answer this question. Second, and perhaps more importantly,

> [t]he *Adarand* decision was only one of many developments affecting federal contracting in the 1990s. Legislative changes, which had both positive and negative influences on small business opportunities to compete for federal government contracts, include the Federal Acquisition Streamlining Act of 1994, the Federal Acquisition Reform Act of 1996, and the Small Business Reauthorization Act of 1997. (USCCR 2005, 104)

These legislative changes complicate any assertions about the causal effects of the *Adarand* ruling.

Nonetheless, Yaki's dissenting statement highlights a few interesting points about patterns in federal procurement following the *Adarand* ruling. First, the number of new Small Disadvantaged Business Contracts awarded by the federal government decreased around the time of the filing of the *Adarand* case, perhaps suggesting that the number of new contracts was suppressed due to uncertainty after the case was filed and before it was decided (USCCR 2005, 109–10). Second, procurement through small disadvantaged businesses increased steadily between 1992 and 2003, except for the years 1995 through 1997, when it remained essentially steady. Procurement through the Small Business Administration's Section 8(a) Business Development Program increased steadily from 1992 to 1998 and then started to decline in 1999 (USCCR 2005, 107–8). Finally, minority-owned firms with paid employees were much less likely to survive between 1997 and 2001 than from 1992 to 1996, suggesting that some minority-owned firms may have gone out of business as a result of the *Adarand* ruling. However, it is important to emphasize that none of these effects can be confidently attributed to the *Adarand* decision, because of the limited available data and the possibility of confounding the effects of *Adarand* with the effects of new legislation.

The Court appears to have had a limited causal effect on the behavior of state and private actors through its rulings on minority set-aside programs. Because the Supreme Court was dependant on non-court actors to implement its decision, the *Croson* ruling may have caused policy changes in only about 31 percent of jurisdictions operating such programs; however, the *Adarand* ruling prompted the Clinton administration to alter Disadvantaged Business Enterprise programs in a number of different departments. Facing significant public opposition, the Supreme Court's actions in these cases caused limited but substantial changes to a wide variety of contracting decisions at all levels of government, and available data suggests that these changes may have had negative effects on minority-owned business.

CONGRESSIONAL EXCLUSION

In addition to altering the manner in which members are elected to Congress through its reapportionment and majority-minority districts rulings, the Court has also limited Congress's authority to exclude its members. During the 89th Congress, a Special Subcommittee on Contracts of the Committee on House Administration conducted an investigation into the activities of Congressman Adam Clayton Powell, the chairman of the Committee on Education and Labor. Powell had been widely criticized for mismanagement of his committee's budget, missing committee meetings, and traveling abroad at public expense, including trips to his retreat on the Bahamian isle of Bimini. The Special Subcommittee found that Powell and several committee staffers had engaged in illegal and inappropriate behavior regarding travel expenditures and salary payments. No formal action was taken against Powell during the 89th Congress, and in 1966 he was reelected to his twelfth term in the U.S. House of Representatives. When the 90th Congress met in January 1967, the House, by a vote of 363 to 65, ordered the Speaker to appoint a Select Committee to determine Powell's eligibility to serve. The resolution prohibited Powell from taking his seat until the

House acted on the Special Committee's report but allowed Powell to continue receiving his salary during the interim period.

The Select Committee invited Powell to testify regarding his "qualifications as to age, citizenship, and residency; his involvement in a civil suit (in which he had been held in contempt), and 'matters of ... alleged official misconduct since January 3, 1961'" (*Powell v. McCormack* 1969, 490; hereafter *Powell*). Powell agreed to appear before the Committee, but he refused to testify about any subject other than his age, citizenship, and residency. Two days later, the Committee issued a second invitation for Powell to testify, in which it claimed that it had "the authority to report back to the House recommendations with respect to ... seating, expulsion or other punishment" (*Powell* 1969, 491); this time Powell refused to testify, maintaining his contention that the age, citizenship, and residency restrictions were the exclusive requirements for membership and that neither expulsion nor punishment was possible until he had been seated.

The Select Committee issued its report on February 23, 1967, in which it found that Powell met the eligibility requirements but had wrongfully diverted House funds and made false expenditure reports to the Committee on House Administration. The Committee recommended that Powell be sworn in and seated as a member of the 90th Congress but that he be censured and stripped of his seniority. The House disagreed and amended the Committee's proposed resolution to exclude Powell and declare his seat vacant. The Speaker of the House ruled that a majority vote was sufficient to pass the resolution, and the House adopted the amended proposal by a vote of 307 to 116.

Powell and thirteen voters from his congressional district subsequently filed suit in the U.S. District Court for the District of Columbia. Powell claimed that the House resolution violated the Constitution because it was inconsistent with the requirement that House members be elected by the people of each state and because the age, citizenship, and residency requirements are the exclusive requirements for membership. He asked that the District Court order the Speaker of the House, John McCormack, to administer the oath of office, the Clerk of the House to perform services due a Representative, the Sergeant at Arms to pay his salary, and the Doorkeeper to admit him to the Chamber. The District Court dismissed the complaint "for want of jurisdiction of the subject matter" (*Powell* 1969, 494), and the Supreme Court granted certiorari.

By the time the case reached the Supreme Court, Powell had been reelected in 1968 and seated in the 91st Congress. Consequently, the targets of Powell's action claimed that the issue was moot. They also argued that the Court had no jurisdiction in the matter for various reasons. Despite these claims, the Court, in an eight-to-one decision, ruled that the case was not moot, Congress's denial of membership could not be treated as an expulsion, the courts did have subject matter jurisdiction, and the case was "justiciable," meaning that it was not an inherently political question. The Court further held that in judging the qualifications of its members, Congress is limited to the age, citizenship, and residency requirements. Accordingly, the House had no power to exclude Powell from its membership.

No national public opinion polls were conducted regarding the Court's decision in *Powell v. McCormack*, but several surveys asked respondents about the exclusion of Adam Clayton Powell in 1967. Respondents to these surveys generally opposed seating Powell. According to a Gallup Poll, 61 percent of respondents felt that Powell should not be allowed to keep his seat; according to a Harris Survey, 54 percent of respondents thought that Powell should not be given his seat.[14] Opposition to seating Powell does not necessarily indicate opposition to the Court's ruling; just because a respondent did not want Powell to be seated does not mean they would want the Congress to have the power to exclude members for any reason. If the respondents were more fully informed of the issue at stake, they may prefer that Congress simply seat and then expel Powell, or they may simply prefer that his constituents not reelect him. Nonetheless, I assume that opposition to seating Powell indicates opposition to the Court's ruling; therefore, because the popularity of the ruling was mixed, I expect the Court's ruling to have only limited effects.

The intended consequences of the *Powell* decision were simple and clear: Powell should be allowed to retain his congressional seat, and Congress should refrain from excluding members-elect for any reason other than failure to meet the age, citizenship, and residency requirements. Both of these consequences were borne out in the years following the Court's ruling. Most directly, Adam Clayton Powell retained his seat in Congress, although he was stripped of his seniority. In this sense, the Court appears to have achieved 100 percent behavior conformity despite some public opposition; however, popular opposition caught up to Powell in the end. He was defeated for reelection by Charles Rangel in 1970, less than a year and a half after his Court victory. He retired to Bimini and resided there until his death in 1972.

Prior to Adam Clayton Powell, Congress rarely exercised its power to exclude members.[15] The first exclusion of a member-elect from Congress occurred in the aftermath of the Civil War; in 1868, the House refused to seat two elected representatives on the grounds that they allegedly gave aid and comfort to the Confederacy (*Powell* 1969, 544). "In 1882 and again in 1900, the House excluded a member-elect for practicing polygamy" (*Powell* 1969, footnote 83). Avowed socialist Victor L. Berger was twice excluded before he was reelected and seated following the reversal of his criminal conviction for

---

[14] See Appendix II for survey information and citations.

[15] The eligibility of several members-elect has been challenged at various points in our nation's history: William McCreery in 1807, another Maryland member-elect in 1808, John M. Niles in 1844, Samuel Marshall and Lyman Trumbull in 1856, several members-elect accused of being disloyal between 1862 and 1867, a Texas Congressman accused of criminal acts in 1870, John W. Langley in 1925, a Minnesota Representative who had been convicted of sending defamatory matter through the mail, and Senator Theodore G. Bilbo in 1947 (*Powell* 1969, 542, footnotes 79 and 83).

giving aid and comfort to the enemy. In 1929, the Senate excluded a member-elect due to improper campaign expenditures (*Powell* 1969, footnote 83). For almost four decades prior to this incident, Congress refrained from exercising the exclusion power for any reason; therefore, the Court's ruling prohibiting certain types of exclusions was not an especially difficult test of judicial power, because it was proscribing a practice that was almost never used anyway. Nonetheless, Congress has not excluded a single member since the Court's ruling in *Powell v. McCormack*; therefore, I code both the generous and conservative estimates of behavior conformity in the congressional exclusion case as 100 percent.

The possibility of congressional exclusion arose once again in December of 2008 when Illinois Governor Rod Blagojevich named Roland Burris, a former state attorney general, to fill a vacancy created by the election of President Barack Obama. Although legally empowered to fill the vacant Senate seat, Governor Blagojevich had come under intense public scrutiny and outrage after being arrested for allegedly trying to sell the appointment. Initially, Senate leaders announced that they would not seat anyone appointed by the corrupt governor, but constitutional scholars challenged their authority to do so, citing the *Powell* case (Hulse 2008). Little more than a week after their initial statements, Senate leaders reversed their position due to the legal questions involved, their eagerness to add a reliable Democratic vote to the chamber, and pressure from African-American lawmakers to seat Burris, who would be the only African-American in the Senate (Hulse 2009). Burris was sworn in on January 15, 2009; Blagojevich was removed from office exactly two weeks later.

THE BRADY BILL

On March 30, 1981, just 69 days after Ronald Reagan was sworn in as president of the United States, a man named John Hinckley Jr. shot and wounded the new president and three others outside the Washington Hilton Hotel in Washington, D.C. The first shot hit White House Press Secretary James Brady in the head, paralyzing him for life. After the incident, Brady and his wife, Sarah, became ardent champions of gun control. Their work culminated in the passage of the Brady Handgun Violence Prevention Act of 1993, more commonly known as the Brady Bill.

The Brady Bill amended the Gun Control Act of 1968 (GCA), which prohibits the transfer of firearms to, among others,

> convicted felons, fugitives from justice, unlawful users of controlled substances, persons adjudicated as mentally defective or committed to mental institutions, aliens unlawfully present in the United States, persons dishonorably discharged from the Armed Forces, persons who have renounced their citizenship, and persons who have been subjected to certain restraining orders or been convicted of a misdemeanor offense involving domestic violence (*Printz v. United States* 1997, 902; hereafter *Printz*).

The Brady Bill required the Federal Bureau of Investigation to create an instant background check system by November 30, 1998, to assist in the enforcement of the GCA. Until the instant background check system become operational, the interim provisions of the Brady Bill required gun dealers who wished to sell a handgun to notify the "chief law enforcement officer" (CLEO) of the purchaser's residence and wait five days before completing the transfer. In states that issued handgun permits after background checks or used instant background check systems ("Brady-alterative states"), the sale could be made immediately without the waiting period. In states without these systems CLEOs were required to "make a reasonable effort to ascertain within 5 business days whether receipt or possession would be in violation of the law, including research in whatever State and local recordkeeping systems are available and in a national system designated by the Attorney General" (*Printz v. United States* 1997, 903).

Between February 1994, when the Brady Bill came into effect, and October 1995, eight sheriffs and the Wyoming Sheriff's Association, which represents each of that state's twenty-three county sheriffs, initiated court cases challenging the constitutionality of the law (General Accounting Office 1996, 47; hereafter GAO). These sheriffs alleged that the law exceeded Congress's authority under the Commerce Clause and violated the Tenth Amendment to the Constitution (GAO 1996, 47, footnote 44). After several inconsistent rulings by lower federal courts, the U.S. Supreme Court agreed to resolve the issue in *Printz v. United States* in 1997.

In *Printz*, the Court sided with the sheriffs challenging the law and ruled that the interim provision of the Brady Bill requiring CLEOs to conduct background checks was unconstitutional, because "[t]he Federal Government may not compel the States to enact or administer a federal regulatory program," and such a power could not be justified under the Necessary and Proper Clause (*Printz* 1997, 924, 933). Although "States and CLEOs may voluntarily continue to participate in the federal program," (*Printz* 1997, 936) Congress may not commandeer state officials to execute federal law.

Although no public opinion poll was conducted regarding the Court's ruling in *Printz*, several national opinion surveys measured the public's support for the Brady Bill. The same month the Court handed down the *Printz* decision, a Gallup/CNN/USA Today Poll showed that 84 percent of respondents supported the law. Similar levels of support existed both before and after the ruling (87% in 1995 and 89% in 1999).[16] In addition, despite challenges to the law from a few sheriffs, "the law enforcement community has strongly supported Brady" and the International Association of Chiefs of Police was a leading proponent of the five-day waiting period to allow time for background checks (GAO 1996, 47). Therefore, among those local officials responsible for implementing the interim provisions of the Brady Bill and among the general public, the Court's ruling in *Printz* was probably extremely unpopular.

---

[16] See Appendix II for survey information and citations.

The Court's ruling in *Printz* neither prescribed nor proscribed any behavior on the part of local law enforcement officials; instead, the decision allowed CLEOs to freely choose whether to cooperate with the interim provisions of the Brady Bill. The ruling simply prohibited the federal government from compelling CLEOs to conduct background checks, and there is no record of the federal government failing to comply with this mandate. Accordingly, in the strictest sense, the Court was completely successful at altering the behavior of federal officials through this ruling. Because my theory predicts low conformity in unpopular lateral issues, I code the conservative estimate of behavior conformity as 100 percent.

It is difficult to measure the extent to which the Court's ruling affected the behavior of CLEOs because there is no comprehensive data available on how many stopped performing background checks after *Printz*. There is little reason to believe that many of these officials disagreed with the Brady Bill. Of the 2,578 CLEOs responsible for background checks in the twenty-three states affected by the Brady interim provisions, only 31 were involved in suits challenging these provisions.[17] Because background checks were probably popular among these law enforcement officials, it is not surprising that "most CLEOs in the Brady States voluntarily conducted the checks. In Brady-alternative States, checks continued in accordance with State law" (Manson et al. 1999, 10).

The most extreme estimate of the decline in CLEOs performing background checks can be obtained by examining the decline in CLEOs participating in a Bureau of Justice Statistics/Firearms Inquiry Statistical Tracking program survey. Out of 600 CLEOs surveyed, the number of respondents dropped from 311 to 244 between 1996 and 1998, a 21.5 percent decrease [(311−244)/311]. Although some of this decline is attributed to agencies discontinuing background checks after *Printz*, some of the decrease is likely due to "decreased interest in participation [in the survey] among some agencies" (Manson et al. 1999, 10).

The possibility that the *Printz* decision had a significant effect on CLEO participation in the interim Brady provisions is cast into further doubt by the fact that the number of background checks remained steady during this time period. Table 7.9 reports the number of inquiries into personal backgrounds and rejections of those applications in states originally affected by the interim provisions of the Brady Bill between 1994 and 1998. Between 1996 and 1998, the years before and after the *Printz* decision, the total number of inquires, the total number of rejections, and the rejection rate in these states all remained at similar levels. Although a few CLEOs probably did stop performing background checks after *Printz*, the effect of the Court's ruling on the total number of background checks performed in Brady states was negligible. Consequently, the generous estimate of behavior conformity is 0 percent.

---

[17] The eight sheriffs who filed separate suits and the twenty-three sheriffs in the Wyoming Sheriff's Association (GAO 1996, 47).

TABLE 7.9. *Background Checks in Original Brady States, 1994–98*

	1994	1995	1996	1997	1998
Inquires	1,696,000	1,884,000	1,213,000	1,197,000	1,248,000
Rejections	42,000	28,000	44,000	42,000	47,000
Rejection rate (%)	2.5	1.5	3.6	3.5	3.8

Note: Data based on surveys of local chief law enforcement officers as reported in Manson and Lauver (1997), Manson and Gilliard (1997), Manson and Gilliard (1998), and Manson et al. (1999).

The effect of the Court's ruling in *Printz* on the actual performance of background checks was blunted by other political actors. For example, the *Printz* decision was decided together with another challenge to the Brady Bill in a case called *Mack v. United States* (1995). Richard Mack was the sheriff of Graham County, Arizona. He challenged the interim provisions of the Brady Bill and won in federal district court on June 28, 1994; however, "[e]ffective October 1, 1994, the Arizona Department of Public Safety assumed a centralized role in conducting background checks for all residents of that state" (GAO 1996, 50). In other words, background checks in Graham County, Arizona, were interrupted for only a few months as state actors moved to counteract the effects of the district court's ruling. A similar situation occurred in Orange County, Vermont (GAO 1996, 50). In Forrest County, Mississippi, the county sheriff won in federal district court and then continued to perform background checks voluntarily.

Ultimately, the Court's ruling in *Printz* was limited by the nature of the issue at stake. The interim provisions of the Brady Bill were set to expire on November 30, 1998. After this date, the permanent provisions of the Act took effect requiring the Federal Bureau of Investigation to operate the National Instant Criminal Background Check System. Under this system, federal firearms licensees, particularly retail sales outlets, verify the identity of the purchaser and relay the purchaser's personal identification information directly to the FBI or to a designated state agency (General Accounting Office 2000, 22). Consequently, the potential effects of the Court's ruling were inherently limited to the seventeen-month period between the time of the ruling and the time that the interim provisions expired.

The Supreme Court's ruling in *Printz v. United States* achieved perfect behavior conformity, but its effects on gun control efforts were negligible. Due to strong support among the law enforcement officials responsible for implementing the interim provisions, which was likely related to the overwhelming support for the act among the public, most CLEOs continued to perform background checks after the decision. In some situations, state agencies assumed responsibility for performing background checks when CLEOs failed to do so. The decision appears to have had no effect whatsoever on the actual number of background checks performed in the United States. Once the permanent provisions of the Brady Bill took effect, the Court's ruling had no effect on behavior outcomes at all. However, despite the negligible effect of the ruling on gun control policy, my findings in this area contradict the predictions of my theory: In the Brady Bill case, the Court achieved perfect conformity to its ruling despite the fact that the ruling was unpopular and the case involved a lateral issue.

SUMMARY: UNPOPULAR LATERAL ISSUES

My study of unpopular lateral issues generally supports my theory of Supreme Court power. When Court rulings could not be directly implemented by lower courts, the successful implementation of these decisions depended on the absence of public opposition. For example, public opinion strongly influenced the Court's ability to alter behavior through rulings related to public education. In the school desegregation cases, the school prayer cases, and the censorship in public education cases, behavior tended to conform, at least partially, to the Court's preferences in those regions where the decision was more popular; however, in those regions where the Court faced strong opposition, usually the Deep South, the Court's rulings had little effect on the behavior of school boards, administrators, or teachers. However, the Court was moderately successful at exercising power through its somewhat popular decisions on minority set-aside programs. These rulings caused the discontinuation of some set-aside programs, the commissioning of numerous disparity studies, and may have caused serious economic damage to minority-owned businesses.

In two of these case studies, Congressional Exclusion and the Brady Bill, I found evidence of Court power despite the expectations of my theory. In these cases, I encountered the same dilemma that afflicted my analysis of the Gun-Free School Zones Act: It is difficult to measure the effect of the Court's preferences on behavior when the Court does not indicate a preference for a significant behavior change. Government actors complied with the specific mandate of the Court's rulings in these issue areas, but the rulings did not have a broader impact on policy or social patters. The invalidation of the Gun-Free School Zones Act was implemented by federal prosecutors, but the Court left state gun laws intact and upheld the revised version of the act. Consequently, the ruling did not significantly alter patterns of gun violence, nor would anyone expect it to. The ruling in *Powell* was implemented by the U.S. Congress: Powell was not excluded, nor was any other congressmen after the ruling. However, congress had not excluded a member for decades before the ruling, Powell had already been seated in the 91st Congress by the time the Court issued its ruling, and he soon lost reelection despite his court victory. Similarly, the *Printz* ruling stopped federal officials from forcing CLEOs to conduct background checks, but most CLEOs continued to perform the checks voluntarily, and the National Instant Criminal Background Check System became active just seventeen months after the ruling.

What do these case studies reveal about Supreme Court power? There are several ways to interpret the available evidence. First, one might measure the Court's power based on the immediate compliance to the narrow holding of the decision, as I have done, and conclude that the Court was powerful in each of these issue areas. I adopt this perspective for the purpose of coding behavior conformity because this interpretation of the evidence is the least advantageous for my theory. Indeed, the Court may be even more powerful than I have suggested; it may be able to alter the behavior of state actors even through unpopular rulings in lateral issue areas, such as *Powell* and *Printz*.

Second, one might believe, as I suggested in regard to *Lopez*, that these cases simply do not belong in this study because the Court did not indicate a preference for a significant behavior change in any of these rulings. In other words, my case selection process may have identified these cases as "important" because they signaled a significant change in legal doctrine (Commerce Clause doctrine, separation of powers doctrine, and federalism doctrine, respectively), but the change in legal doctrine did not indicate a preference for a significant behavior change. Following this logic, the findings from these case studies should be generally disregarded.

Third, one might suggest that my definition of Court power in these cases is simply too narrow. Instead, I might focus on the lack of indirect effects in these rulings: Gun violence around schools did not increase, Powell did not stay in Congress, and CLEOs continued to perform background checks. From this perspective, the Congressional Exclusion and Brady Bill cases are consistent with my theory, but the Gun-Free School Zones case is not. However, as I discussed in Chapter 2, this interpretation is oddly divorced from reality. It suggests that a rigorous test of Court power must demand far-reaching and perverse consequences from the Court's rulings: A powerful Court would cause gun violence near schools, stop CLEOs from voluntarily performing background checks, and force the people of Harlem to reelect Adam Clayton Powell. However, as I have previously stated, a proper test of judicial power evaluates the causal relationship between the expressed preferences of judges and the outcomes of their decisions; expecting the Court's rulings to also have unintended consequences would be an inappropriate test of its power.

8

Neither the Sword nor the Purse, but the Keys

> By a limited Constitution, I understand one which contains certain specified exceptions to the legislative authority; such, for instance, as that it shall pass no bills of attainder, no ex-post-facto laws, and the like. Limitations of this kind can be preserved in practice no other way than through the medium of courts of justice, whose duty it must be to declare all acts contrary to the manifest tenor of the Constitution void. Without this, all the reservations of particular rights or privileges would amount to nothing.
>
> Alexander Hamilton[1]

In this study, I have sought to identify conditions that influence the probability of the Supreme Court successfully exercising judicial power by causing the behavior of relevant actors to conform to its preferences as expressed in its rulings. My study has identified two factors that influence whether or not the Court successfully alters behavior through its rulings: the institutional position of those responsible for implementing the decision and the popularity of the decision. The Court tends to succeed at exercising power when it issues rulings in vertical issues (those in which lower courts can directly implement the decision) or popular rulings in lateral issues (all other issue areas); however, the Court tends to fail at exercising power when it issues unpopular rulings in lateral issues. Throughout the study, I have taken great care to avoid some of the methodological problems that have hampered previous examinations of Supreme Court power.[2] I summarize my findings in Table 8.1. The table reports

---

[1] Hamilton (1961).

[2] First, I have offered a clear and simple working definition of judicial power against which to test the Supreme Court: Judicial power is an actual or potential causal relation between the preferences of a judge or judges regarding the outcome of a case and the outcome itself. Second, based on this definition, I have examined the causal relationship between the preferences of Supreme Court justices, as expressed in their rulings, and the behavior of state and private actors in response to these rulings. In each case under examination, I have used a longitudinal design to measure the causal effect of the Court's ruling by comparing the behavior of relevant actors immediately before and after the ruling. Third, I have designed an objective, systematic case selection process to avoid selection bias and eliminate cases in which behavior changes could be

TABLE 8.1. *Behavior Conformity by Institutional Context and Public Opposition*

Public Opposition	Institutional Context			
	Lateral Issues		*Vertical Issues*	
	CBC*	*Issue Area*	CBC*	*Issue Area*
Less than 30% opposed	98	Reapportionment	100	Pentagon Papers
	40	Majority-minority districts	95	RFRA
	100	Legislative veto		
	100	Aid to religious schools		
	100	Affirmative action		
	29	Student religious Publications		
	95	Minimum wage		
	100	Bush v. Gore		
Between 30% and 70% opposed	38	Desegregation (Border)	63	Abortion
	93	School prayer (Northeast)	79	Capital punishment
	54	School prayer (Midwest)	40	Miranda warnings
	62	School prayer (West)	100	Warrantless eavesdropping
	18	Censorship in school libraries	25	Free press in courtroom
	31	Minority set-asides	64	Sovereign immunity
	100	Congressional exclusion		
More than 70% opposed	0	Desegregation (South)	75	Exclusionary rule
	21	School prayer (South)	52	Right to counsel
	100	Brady Bill	100	Flag desecration
			100	Obscenity
			93	Gun-Free School Zones Act

*Conservative estimates of behavior conformity, rounded to the nearest percentage point.

the conservative estimates of behavior conformity achieved by the Court in each issue area I studied, grouped together by the institutional context of the ruling and public opposition to the ruling.

PERSISTENT PUZZLES

Although my examination has illuminated several aspects of the Supreme Court's ability to implement social change, numerous questions about judicial

attributed to other factors. Whereas previous studies of Supreme Court power have usually considered, at most, three or four issue areas, my study has evaluated the Court's power in twenty-seven separate issue areas. Taken together, these methodological precautions make my findings highly reliable.

power remain unanswered. First, Court rulings may have causal effects on attitude outcomes as well as behavior outcomes. The Court may affect attitudes by educating the public (Bickel [1962] 1986, 26; Franklin and Kosaki 1989; Rostow 1952, 208), politicizing issues (Monti 1980, 237), or attracting public attention (Neier 1982, 29).[3] If the Court does have the power to alter public opinion in this manner, it means that the Court has even more influence over social change than I have suggested in this study. However, if the court does possess this power, I find it highly unlikely that such power would function in a manner similar to its power over behavior outcomes; specifically, I doubt the distinction between vertical and lateral issues would provide an effective explanation of the Court's power in this context.

Second, although I have demonstrated that the Court's success at altering behavior through its rulings in lateral issues is dependent on the absence of strong popular opposition, I have not explored how public attitudes affect implementation. I have suggested that the existence of strong public opposition compels elected officials to resist the Court's rulings in an effort to win reelection, but I have not demonstrated that this is the causal mechanism at work. It is possible that public opinion influences elected officials, who then resist the Court in an effort to curry favor with the electorate. It is also possible that public opinions merely act as a proxy for elite opinions, such as those of lawyers, judges, politicians, or public officials; strong opposition among the public may correlate with strong opposition among elites, who then resist the implementation of the Court's opinion. In other words, it may not be the case that public opposition causes policymakers to resist the Court; it may simply be the case that when the public opposes a ruling, policymakers also tend to oppose the Court for their own reasons.

Third, my study has examined the Court's ability to alter behavior in only those situations when it attempts to do so. This limitation leaves two different empirical questions unanswered. First, how often will the justices want to alter behavior? Was Dahl's first expectation accurate? Are "the policy views dominant on the Court ... never for long out of line with the policy views dominant among the lawmaking majorities of the United States" (Dahl 1957, 285)? This question is also relative to the expectations of the reader. From one standpoint, Supreme Court justices obviously share basic political ideals with the dominant political regime on a wide range of issues; it is highly unlikely that the Court would wish to subvert democracy, institute socialism, or fundamentally alter our political system in any other way. On the other hand, the last half century has witnessed the Court issuing very unpopular rulings in a wide range of controversial and prominent issue areas, including civil rights, abortion, capital punishment, and gay rights. Whether these rulings constitute a significant departure from the views of the dominant political regime or only

---

[3] See Rosenberg (2008, 25–6) for a detailed discussion of the Court's possible effects on attitude outcomes.

minor deviations from a general consensus between the Court and the elected branches remains an open question.

The second question raised by limiting my study to those situations in which the Court attempts to alter behavior is the question of strategic Court action. The Court may be able to save political capital and enhance its legitimacy by strategically ducking in situations when it knows its rulings would be ignored; accordingly, the justices may refrain from attempting to alter behavior when they foresee difficulties in implementation. It is difficult to measure how frequently this type of strategic action occurs because to do so would require knowledge of when the justices wish to act but do not. If the Court does engage in this type of strategic behavior, I believe it either does so very rarely or is rather incompetent at the task, because I have identified several issue areas in which the Court failed to alter behavior. Nonetheless, the role of strategic action by the Court to avoid implementation failures remains unexplained.

Finally, in this study I have focused entirely on those cases within the "gridlock interval"; in other words, in each of the cases identified by my case selection process, supporters of the Court's decision could not achieve their goals through the elected branches, and opponents of the decision were not powerful enough to reverse the Court's ruling. I have not considered any cases in which the Court's opponents were powerful enough to reverse the Court by passing a constitutional amendment, stripping the Court of jurisdiction, packing or shrinking the Court, or threatening to take any of these actions because my case selection process did not happen to identify any of these cases. Other scholars have included such cases in an evaluation of judicial power. For example, in his second edition of *The Hollow Hope*, Gerald Rosenberg evaluates the power of state courts to promote gay marriage. Rosenberg concludes that courts achieved little success in these cases because gay marriage opponents succeeded in amending several state constitutions to reverse the rulings (2008, 342–54). Once again, I believe this question is best considered through a separate inquiry. The dynamics that govern the implementation of rulings that are not reversed are almost certainly different than the dynamics that determine whether or not rulings will be reversed. Because Rosenberg does not clearly define the nature of his inquiry, he blurs the distinction between these two concepts.

Nonetheless, Rosenberg's argument about the possibility of constitutional reversal is a valid one. As he points out, many important decisions by state courts of last resort have been reversed by amendments to state constitutions, and, at least four times, constitutional amendments have reversed decisions by the U.S. Supreme Court.[4] The elected branches have also pressured the Court on several occasions through the use of alternative mechanisms, such as

---

[4] The Eleventh Amendment reversed the Court's ruling in *Chisholm v. Georgia* (1793). The Fourteenth Amendment reversed the Court's ruling in *Dred Scott v. Sandford* (1857). The Sixteenth Amendment reversed the Court's ruling in *Pollock v. Farmers' Loan & Trust Co.* (1895). The Twenty-Sixth Amendment reversed the Court's ruling in *Oregon v. Mitchell* (1970).

court-packing, court-shrinking, and jurisdiction-stripping. Any evaluation of the frequency with which the Court is reversed through constitutional amendment would be highly susceptible to problems involving strategic action by the Court, because the Court likely takes great efforts to avoid such reversals. Accordingly, the Court may refrain from issuing rulings in some cases because the justices anticipate reversal through one of these mechanisms.

THE SUPREME COURT AS A MECHANISM FOR SOCIAL CHANGE

My assessment of the Supreme Court's power to initiate social change runs counter to the conclusions of most empirical studies on this topic. My findings directly contradict assertions that "litigation is ineffectual" (Scheingold 1974, 130), that "U.S. courts can almost never be effective producers of significant social reform" (Rosenberg 2008, 422), that "the Court is quite constrained in its ability to secure social change" (Baum 2003), and that "the Court is almost powerless to affect the course of national policy" (Dahl 1957, 293). In direct contrast to these claims, I find that the Court possesses remarkable power to alter the behavior of state and private actors in a wide range of policy issues. In those situations in which its rulings can be directly implemented by lower-court judges, the Court commands impressive powers even when facing "serious resistance" (Rosenberg 2008, 420) "[w]ithout the support of real power holders" (Scheingold 1974, 130).

Some scholars insist that when the Court has the support of these "real power holders ... litigation is unnecessary" (Scheingold 1974, 130); my findings also contradict this claim. In those cases in which the Court could not implement its rulings through lower courts, it was only the combination of Court action with public support that induced change. Although public pressure may have eventually initiated reform without Court action, it is highly unlikely that this change would have occurred as quickly as it did without intervention from the Court in issue areas such as reapportionment, public aid to religious schools, and minority set-aside programs. In some situations, the Court is able to achieve what even broad national majorities could not accomplish through other political institutions.

Of course, the Court is not always successful at initiating change, nor would any reasonable student of the American political system expect it to be. Any statement about the Court's power is relative to the expectations of the reader; those who previously understood Court rulings to be universally implemented may be struck by the relative weakness of the Court in my study. Nonetheless, when compared to the prevailing view of the Court's power in the judicial politics literature, my study depicts the Court as a remarkably powerful institution, capable of enhancing or inhibiting political reform, enshrining or dismantling social inequalities, and expanding or suppressing individual rights.

More importantly, my study highlights an important distinction between those Court rulings that can be directly implemented by lower courts and those that cannot. This distinction, though simple and intuitive, explains vastly different behavior outcomes in different types of Court rulings. It also suggests why other empirical studies of judicial power may have been led astray; without systematic case selection procedures to ensure avoiding selection bias, other studies of judicial power may have tended to place too much emphasis on unpopular lateral issues. Although some scholars have hinted at particular elements of the distinction between vertical and lateral issues, none have fully explored the concept or suggested the significance of its many repercussions.[5]

[5] For example, Rosenberg includes as one of his conditions that may enable courts to be effective producers of significant social reform, the condition that "Court decisions allow for market implementation" (2008, 36). This concept is vaguely related to my notion of vertical issues. Specifically, Rosenberg might argue that, when lower courts refuse to convict abortionists, pornographers, or flag burners, they create a "market" that can then be filled by potential abortionists, pornographers, and flag burners, and this "market" condition explains why the Court's ruling is implemented; however, on closer analysis, my theory of vertical issues is substantially different than Rosenberg's "market" condition in several ways.

According to Rosenberg's theory of "market" response, one "condition that may allow courts to produce significant social reform" occurs when "individuals or groups are both free and able to create their own institutions to implement court decisions" (2008, 33). With this simple statement, Rosenberg implies several assumptions about the courts, without stating them explicitly. First, by referring to "courts" generally, rather than to the Supreme Court, Rosenberg implies that the judiciary is a single institution, or at least takes as assumed that lower courts will follow Supreme Court rulings. This assumption is particularly confusing because he later asserts that "[m]any lower-court judges systematically and continually abused their discretion to thwart civil rights" (2008, 89). By blurring the distinction between the Supreme Court and courts in general, Rosenberg obscures the remarkable power of the High Court to control lower-court judges; in contrast, my theory highlights this feature of Supreme Court power.

Second, Rosenberg's description of the "market" condition focuses on the ability of private actors to create their own institutions to implement court rulings. He claims that when this condition holds, "there will be two sets of institutions in existence; an older set that refuses to implement the decision and a newer one that does implement it" (2008, 33). Rosenberg's description of dual institutions may seem confusing until he invokes the "market" condition to explain his findings in the abortion case: "On the whole, in response to the Court, hospitals did not change their policies to permit abortions ... The Court's decisions allowed the market to implement the decisions. They did so, in a word, with 'clinics'" (2008, 195). The dual institutions Rosenberg seems to have in mind are hospitals and abortion clinics, but it is difficult to see how such a dual system would manifest itself in other cases. It appears as if the "market" condition Rosenberg describes is specifically tailored to explain the abortion case. By using three constraints and four conditions to explain the Court's power in three case studies, Rosenberg has guaranteed, not only that his explanatory variables will explain the results of his cases, but also that his cases will explain how he crafted his explanatory variables! In the language of statistical analysis, he has used up all of his degrees of freedom; stated more simply, he has created seven rules to explain three events. In contrast, I have suggested two independent variables to explain twenty-seven separate events.

Third, it is interesting to note that, according to Rosenberg, when the "market" condition holds, "individuals and groups are both free and able to create their own institutions ..." (2008, 33). He focuses his discussion of the "market" condition on private actors being "able to create their own institutions," but pays little notice to the idea that they are "free" to do so. In the abortion case study, Rosenberg notes, with little explanation or comment, that "[t]he Court's decisions prohibited the states from interfering with a woman's right to choose an abortion, at least in the first trimester" (2008, 196). He then proceeds to discuss the fact that "abortion reformers,

Accordingly, I must respectfully disagree with Rosenberg's assertion that "courts act as 'fly-paper' for social reformers who succumb to the 'lure of litigation'" (2008, 427). Instead, I find that social reformers have achieved great success by turning to the courts in their quest for privacy rights, free speech rights, states' rights, religious freedom, and the rights of criminal defendants. Admittedly, social reformers should think carefully about the relative advantages and disadvantages of a litigation strategy, compared to a legislative or electoral strategy for reform. My findings suggest that reformers should consider whether the institutional situation and public opinion surrounding their cause would make it likely for any favorable court ruling to be implemented. If the reform sought could be directly implemented by lower courts or if the reformers face no strong opposition from the public, the courts may offer a highly effective route to social change. If, however, reformers hope for a change that cannot be implemented by lower courts and that faces strong opposition, a litigation strategy may indeed be unwise.

Finally, it should be emphasized that the Court is not especially equipped to advance a conservative or liberal political agenda.[6] The Court's unique power to nullify legal sanctions will sometimes aid liberal movements, by protecting abortionists or flag burners. Other times, this power will be used to promote conservative causes, by shielding states from federal law suits and gun owners from federal prosecution. Nor does the Court's tendency to enact popular rulings advance one ideology over another: Whereas the reapportionment and public aid to religious schools rulings probably helped liberal causes, the affirmative action and minimum wage rulings likely promoted a conservative agenda.

---

population control groups, women's groups, and individual physicians" were *able* to set up abortion clinics; but the critical element necessary for the Court's success in this ruling, which Rosenberg seems to ignore, is that these private actors were *free* to set up abortion clinics. No police officer would arrest them, no prosecutor would charge them, and no jailer would imprison them for doing so, because all of these public actors are dependent on lower-court judges to convict abortionists. By focusing on the ability of reformers to create private institutions when free to do so, Rosenberg's analysis obscures the institutional position of lower courts that guarantee this freedom. In contrast, my study emphasizes the institutional position of lower courts as critical for the successful implementation of Supreme Court rulings in vertical issues.

Finally, if Rosenberg's "market" condition is effectively the same as my theory of vertical issues, then it has been seriously misapplied. Due to the methodological errors in Rosenberg's analysis that I discuss in Chapter Five, he concludes that "[t]here was no steep or unusual increase in the number of legal abortions following *Roe*" (2008, 179); in contrast, I find that *Roe* had a significant effect on the number of legal abortions in those states affected by the decision and caused a dramatic change in the number of women crossing state lines to get an abortion, meaning that it was both more convenient and more economical for women to obtain the procedure. Similarly, in the area of criminal law, Rosenberg concludes that the Court "was unable to achieve its stated goals," and "what the Supreme Court did simply 'did not matter much'" (2008, 334–5). In contrast, I find that the Court's rulings regarding capital punishment, the exclusionary rule, Miranda warnings, warrantless eavesdropping, and the right to counsel all had significant effects on the behavior of lower courts, prosecutors, and police officers.

[6] See Rosenberg (2008, 431) for a claim to the contrary.

JUDICIAL REVIEW IN THE AMERICAN POLITICAL SYSTEM

For the last half century, most philosophical, political, and jurisprudential discussion on the role of the U.S. Supreme Court in the American political system has revolved around what Alexander Bickel calls the countermajoritarian difficulty. However, during this same period, the most prominent studies of Supreme Court power have suggested that Bickel's difficulty is unworthy of concern because the Court possesses little real power. As Robert Dahl puts it, "the elaborate 'democratic' rationalizations of the Court's defenders and the hostility of its 'democratic' critics are largely irrelevant, for lawmaking majorities generally have had their way" (Dahl 1957, 291). Gerald Rosenberg echoes this view: "Normative and constitutional concerns about whether courts ought to be used to further social reform are misplaced if the conditions under which they can do so are so rare as to make the production of that change unlikely" (Rosenberg 2008, 428).

My findings indicate the opposite conclusion: Normative and constitutional concerns over the role of judicial review in the American political system are well founded, and the debate between the critics and apologists of judicial review should continue unabated. The Court possesses great powers over the behavior of state and private actors in our society, and conscientious academics, politicians, litigators, judges, and citizens have a responsibility to consider carefully whether the exercise of this power does more harm than good.

My study also offers a new perspective on the role of judicial review that may shed light on this critical debate. My examination of the Court's power in lateral issues generally confirms Alexander Hamilton's assertion that the judiciary "has no direction either of the strength or of the wealth of the society" (1961). When the Court seeks to control the distribution of public resources or the administration of public agencies, it is usually dependant on public support in order to accomplish its goals. In this regard, Hamilton rightly notes that "it would require an uncommon portion of fortitude in the judges to do their duty as faithful guardians of the Constitution, where legislative invasions of it had been instigated by the major voice of the community" (1961). However, the Court has initiated numerous popular social changes in lateral issue areas that may never have come to fruition absent the Court's intervention. Perhaps the most dramatic example of such intervention is reapportionment; regardless of how popular this reform may have been, it is unlikely that legislators would have initiated it without prompting from the Court.

More importantly, when its rulings can be directly implemented by lower-court judges, the High Court can instigate significant social change regardless of public opinion. These rulings almost always involve the Court designating a particular class of citizens as immune from criminal prosecution or civil action. By granting individuals new rights and liberties, the Court can have a dramatic effect on the behavior of private actors as they enjoy their new freedoms: Women freely obtain abortion procedures, protesters openly burn flags, and pornographers prosper on the Internet. In addition, the Court's creation of new rights can prompt government actors to alter their behavior by conforming to the Court's preferences in order to win criminal convictions: Police officers read Miranda warnings, law enforcement officials work to prevent illegal searches, and local governments create public defender programs. It is the Court's ability to free individuals from the punitive powers of the state that gives it real, independent power. In other words, the Court may not hold the sword or the purse of our society, but it does hold the keys to our jail, and every time it turns a key it wields great power.

This combination of strengths and weaknesses makes the Supreme Court a uniquely beneficial institution in a free society. It is perhaps this unusual and seemingly contradictory combination that has promoted the numerous conflicting understandings of Supreme Court power. The Court simultaneously holds tremendous power to influence society through the creation of individual rights and liberties, yet it remains seriously constrained from marshalling the economic and administrative powers of the state. Thanks to this brilliant combination, the framers of our constitution were able to create "courts of justice" armed with the power "to declare all acts contrary to the manifest tenor of the Constitution void," without which "all the reservations of particular rights or privileges would amount to nothing," and yet, confidently assert that "the general liberty of the people can never be endangered" by those courts (Hamilton 1961).

By endorsing this view, I do not mean to suggest that the Supreme Court possesses the power to do good for society yet lacks the power to do harm. No institution, the Court included, can be trusted to unwaveringly produce just or virtuous outcomes. Nor do I mean to suggest that the Court is capable of promoting every conception of "liberty." In fact, most controversial legal cases are properly understood as clashes between competing conceptions of liberty: Abortion cases pit the right to choose against the right to life, obscenity cases pit free expression against freedom from offensive material, and gun rights cases pit one notion of security against another. I would certainly not claim that the Court is especially equipped to promote the "true" conception of liberty, whatever that may be.

Instead, my claim is much more nuanced and much less sanguine: The Court is uniquely equipped to promote liberty only if liberty is understood as freedom from government restraint. Simply put, the Court can stop people from going to jail: The abortionist, the pornographer, and the gun owner will all go free if they win in court. This is the Court's great power: For better or worse, the Court can set them free. Understood in this light, the countermajoritarian difficulty, though unresolved, is significantly diminished; the Court can overturn the will of the majority, but only by opening the jailhouse doors.

In this study, I have not attempted to evaluate the normative value of the Court's impressive and sometimes countermajoritarian power. Undoubtedly, my findings will inspire and embolden those who hope to utilize the courts in their efforts to bring about social change, while simultaneously offering fodder to those who decry the undemocratic practice of activist judges overturning the will of elected majorities. I will not comment on this debate, except to note my agreement with Robert McCloskey's wise observation that Americans have always believed in the separate and conflicting values of popular sovereignty, embodied by the political branches, and fundamental law, embodied by the courts (1960). In my view, it is the persistent tension between these sometimes conflicting values that protects and perpetuates them both.

My findings tend to confirm the unique role of the judiciary in this delicate balance. Although the Court controls neither the economic nor the law enforcement powers of the state, it nonetheless enjoys the power to significantly alter our society by relieving private individuals and government actors from legal penalties and spurring popular change against entrenched political interests. The Supreme Court is seriously constrained when it initiates unpopular change in the administration of the state. Nevertheless, many of those who strive to reform society may hopefully turn to the Court to aid them in their struggle, and their political opponents should be wary of the institution's great power.

Appendix I

Case Selection

The most complicated criterion in my case selection process is my attempt to avoid division of labor cases by focusing on "important" Supreme Court rulings. This criterion is also critical to the relevance of my project. Understanding conditions under which the Court is capable of altering behavior is only important when the Court is issuing rulings that are important. If scholars, politicians, the media, and the public do not care about the issues at stake in a ruling, then they probably will not care about the Supreme Court's power to affect those issues. But how do we objectively identify which rulings are "important" and which are not?

To accomplish this task, I borrow methodology developed by David Mayhew for identifying "important" federal legislative enactments in his work, *Divided We Govern* (2005). I also borrow Mayhew's definition of importance: "In principle, the term 'important' will connote both innovative and consequential – or if viewed from the time of passage, thought likely to be consequential" (2005, 37). Mayhew conducts two searches for "important laws enacted": Sweep One, which utilizes "judgments that close observers of each Congress made at the time about what enactments, without regard for policy area, were particularly notable"; and Sweep Two, which uses "retrospective judgments that policy specialists have made, looking back over many Congresses, about what enactments in their own policy areas have been particularly notable" (Mayhew 2005, 37).

I create an analogous Sweep One and Sweep Two to identify "important" Supreme Court rulings using similar methodology, but my Sweep Two plays a minimal role in my case selection process. I limit my study to the years 1954 to 2005 for four reasons. First, newspaper coverage of the Supreme Court's term prior to the mid-1950s is extremely limited, which makes it impossible to extend my Sweep One before this period. Second, by selecting this time period, I cover the entire Warren, Burger, and Rehnquist Courts.[1] Third, many scholars

[1] Earl Warren was actually appointed in October of 1953; however, most major rulings are issued by the Court in the winter or spring. Regardless, Sweeps One and Two did not identify any "important" cases in 1953, so adding this year would not have altered my case selection.

claim that the nature of Supreme Court politics changed in the period following World War II (see Caldeira and Zorn 1998; Segal, Spaeth, and Epstein
2001). If this is the case, understanding the power of the Court before mid-
century may contribute little to an understanding of the Court's power today.
Finally, by limiting my analysis to the last half century, I improve my ability to
find reliable data sources for measuring behavior outcomes.

For Sweep One, I use annual end-of-term wrap-up articles about the Supreme
Court in the *New York Times* and the *Washington Post*. During the last half
century, several writers at the *Times*[2] and the *Post*[3] have developed a routine
of summarizing the Court's major rulings following the close of the term in
June or July, very similar to the end-of-session wrap-up stories Mayhew used
to evaluate congressional enactments. Using these articles, I develop a list of
"important" Supreme Court cases that includes those rulings thought especially noteworthy by Court-watchers at both the *Times* and the *Post*. Cases
given special attention in only one of the two papers are not included. This
Sweep One yields 117 Supreme Court cases.[4]

---

[2] James Reston, Luther Houston, Anthony Lewis, Fred P. Graham, Nathan Lewin, Warren Weaver,
Lesley Oelsner, Stuart Taylor, and Linda Greenhouse.

[3] Richard Lyons, James E. Clayton, Morton Mintz, John P. MacKenzie, Morton Mintz, Fred
Barbash, Al Kamen, Ruth Marcus, Joan Biskupic, Edward Walsh, and Charles Lane.

[4] In order for a journalist's mention of a case to count for inclusion in Sweep One:

1. The case must be mentioned in the text of the main article and in any list of cases following
   the article. If the article did not include a list of cases, a case must be given special attention in
   the first section of the article. The *Washington Post* does not usually split the summary article
   clearly between the discussion section and lists, but many articles begin discussing a series
   of minor cases about halfway through, sometimes using bullet points. Cases listed after this
   point in an article were not included. Also, about halfway through many of the *Washington
   Post* articles, the writer stops discussing major rulings and begins discussing the role of certain
   justices or voting patterns, often quoting from legal experts. Cases after the halfway point
   are sometimes described as "important" but usually prefaced with the words "for example"
   as if merely illustrative of a larger point. Some cases were described as "exceptions" as if less
   important but interesting because they were breaking a pattern. Rulings mentioned after this
   halfway point were not included. See the 1988 *Washington Post* article as an especially good
   example of why this division makes sense.

2. The case must be described in enough detail to clearly identify the case and explain the issue
   at stake. References to general legal issues did not count as a mention of case (i.e., stating that
   the Court "upheld free speech rights" does not count).

3. The case must not be mentioned briefly to illustrate a point. This requirement applies especially to cases mentioned in a list after the words, "For example."

4. The case must be a full written opinion that sets national precedent (i.e., I eliminated a 4–4
   tie in 1973).

5. The description of the case must explain how the Court ruled, not just the question posed
   and not just which side won (i.e., the description of a particular justice's vote in a particular
   case does not count for inclusion because such a mention is usually meant to highlight the
   justice's ideology rather than the importance of the case; the statement that the Court voted
   with a property owner fighting a zoning law in the *Washington Post* in 1992 does not count
   for inclusion because it does not explain the issue in the case; the statement that the Court
   "upheld affirmative action" in the *Washington Post* in 1986 does not count because it does
   not explain the context or details of the case).

For Sweep Two, I borrow the list of cases Jerry Goldman identified as the "Canon of Constitutional Law"[5] in order to utilize the retrospective judgments of legal experts about what Supreme Court rulings have been particularly important (Goldman 2005). Goldman and his research team[6] conducted a survey of major constitutional law textbooks, identifying cases that were given special attention in each text. Next, he identified his "canon" as those cases that were given special attention in the vast majority of textbooks. Goldman identified only twenty-two cases as canonical for the entire history of the Supreme Court. Again following Mayhew, I enlarge this list to a size comparable to that in my Sweep One. Building on Goldman's technique, I expand the list of cases to all those given special attention in at least four textbooks. Sweep Two yields 181 cases, 149 of which were issued between 1954 and 2005.

There is a great deal of overlap between Sweep One and Sweep Two; 57 of the 117 Sweep One cases are also in Sweep Two (49%). Most variation between Sweep One and Sweep Two can be attributed to the imprecise nature

Other notes on Sweep One:

1. Variation in the number of special attention cases from year to year is sometimes due to the fact that the *New York Times* did not focus on many cases as important. In other years, it is because most or all of the special attention cases were upholding federal laws or did not decide the constitutionality of a law.

2. The 1972 *Washington Post* article discussed the death penalty case several times and mentions the nine separate opinions, but it does not clearly state the Court's ruling in the case. I nonetheless include the case because the article's lack of specificity about the ruling is probably due to the lack of clarity in the ruling itself, which the article highlighted by referring to the nine separate opinions.

3. In the 1984 *Washington Post* article, there were no cases listed before the laundry list of cases; therefore, I coded as important those rulings that were described in the general discussion at the beginning of the article and included in the laundry list. Including these cases was irrelevant to my final case selection because there was no overlap between these cases and those listed in the *New York Times*.

4. In the 1970 *Washington Post* article, I coded only one case as important. This case barely qualifies because it appears to be mentioned simply as an example of Burger's ideology; the case is not mentioned in the *New York Times*. The *New York Times* 1970 article yielded only one case, which was not the same. My final case selection includes no 1970 cases because there is no overlap.

5. For the *Washington Post* in 1965, I use an article that centers entirely on *Griswold v. Connecticut*. Although the use of this article may eliminate other important cases, this is unlikely because the *Washington Post* writers decided not to write a summary article that year and the *Griswold* article emphasizes that it was the most important case of the term.

6. In 1966, MacKenzie wrote several large articles on four cases rather than one summary article at the end of the year. I included only these four cases in the *Washington Post* Sweep One for 1966.

[5] Although I highly value Professor Goldman's work, I have written elsewhere about the importance of clearly distinguishing "canonical" cases or "super precedents" from other important cases. (See Hall 2010). Following Mayhew's lead, I use the shorthand "important" to describe innovative and consequential (or thought likely to be consequential) Supreme Court cases.

[6] I was fortunate to have the opportunity to work on Professor Goldman's research team for this project. I thank him for that opportunity and for his thoughtful assistance in this project.

of both selection processes.[7] For example, Sweep Two identifies the 1982 case *New York v. Ferber*, in which the Court upheld a New York statute prohibiting child pornography. This case is not identified by Sweep One, but Sweep One did identify five other Supreme Court cases regarding the regulation of pornography, one of which is also in Sweep Two. It is unlikely that the Court's power was substantially different in these cases, so it is unlikely that this sort of error will produce any bias in my findings. Regardless, *Ferber* would have been removed from my case selection because the Court upheld the New York law in this case. There are some minor systematic differences between Sweep One and Sweep Two, but on the whole, both lists highlight the same constitutional issues.[8]

Nonetheless, cases identified by Sweep Two should be considered cautiously for the purposes of this study. The textbooks Goldman uses in his study may be focusing on those cases in which the Court was especially successful; in other words, Sweep Two may be capturing cases that were innovative and consequential and missing those that were innovative and could have been consequential. As a result, using Sweep Two cases may bias my study in favor of finding more judicial power than actually exits. To avoid this problem, I use Sweep One cases for my study with a few exceptions. For a few years in my date range (1954–56 and 1969), neither the *Times* nor the *Post* published a term summary article on the Supreme Court. For these years, I use cases identified by Sweep Two for my case selection.[9] Combining these cases with those identified by Sweep One produces a list of 126 cases.

---

[7] Several factors in the case selection process artificially deflate the amount of overlap between Sweep One and Sweep Two. First, the textbooks used for Sweep Two were all published before 2005, and a few were published before 2000. This means that Sweep Two under-represents important cases after the turn of the century. As a result, only 5 of 21 post-2000 cases in Sweep One are also in Sweep Two. Second, although for most years Sweep One reflects cases in which both the *New York Times* and *Washington Post* focus on a case, the *Post* did not publish a review article for every year that the *Times* did. The overlap requirement tended to filter out less important cases that were mentioned in the articles. Without this overlap requirement, the number of cases in Sweep One may be inflated for the years without *Post* articles (1956–59, 1962, 1968, and 1974). In other words, some of the Sweep One cases in these years may not deserve to be on the list. As a result, only 5 of the 17 Sweep One cases for these years are also in Sweep Two. Without considering years affected by these concerns, 47 out of 79 cases in Sweep One are also in Sweep Two (59%).

[8] I have chosen to use Goldman's study of the "Canon of Constitutional Law" (2005)because I am only interested in cases in which the Court invalidated policy on constitutional grounds. Although my Sweep One yields mostly constitutional cases, it is not restricted to this category by definition. This factor may also decrease the overlap between Sweep One and Sweep Two. Thanks to Professor Andrew Martin for highlighting this aspect of my Sweep Two process.

[9] The following cases were added to my case selection list from Sweep Two: *Brown v. Board I* (1954), *Bolling v. Sharpe* (1954), *Brown v. Board II* (1955), *Williamson v. Lee Optical* (1955), *Pennsylvania v. Nelson* (1956), *Brandenburg v. Ohio* (1969), *Shapiro v. Thompson* (1969), *Powell v. McCormack* (1969), *Tinker v. Des Moines Independent School District* (1969), *Chimel v. California* (1969).

Next, in order to avoid "legitimation" cases, I limit my case list to those cases in which the Court invalidated a law or practice on constitutional grounds. This step reduces the list to 77 cases. Finally, in order to avoid "regime enforcement" cases, I eliminate cases in which the Court invalidated a state law or practice maintained in only a few states. My final list includes 59 Supreme Court cases. I then group these cases into twenty-seven issue areas for investigation.

As in any study, readers should be conscious of potential case selection bias. If the selection criteria are correlated with both the independent variables (institutional context and popularity) and other unobserved factors that affect Court power, it will create the potential for biased results. My selection of "important" cases is threatened by several potential sources of bias.

The first source of bias is the possibility that legal analysts at the *Times* and the *Post* may focus on cases in which they expect the Court to be particularly powerful. If so, my study may indicate that the Court is more powerful than it actually is. This concern is mitigated by several factors. First, the *Times* and the *Post* cover a wide variety of cases on a range of topics with varying levels of support both on and off the Court. Second, it is not clear how the journalists at the *Times* and the *Post* could possibly predict the Court's power in particular cases. Third, if the journalists were able to perfectly predict when the Court would be successful and were only focusing on these cases, all of my results would show the Court making a significant impact on behavior change; however, my results show that the Court's power is severely limited in certain contexts. Fourth, although my results suggest the Court is more powerful in general than other scholars have argued, my main goal is to establish the conditions under which the Court is powerful. Unless the case selection process is also correlated with my independent variables, focus on cases in which the Court is more powerful would not bias these results. Finally, though my Sweep One may be biased towards cases in which journalists expect the Court to be powerful, it is much more likely that journalists tend to focus on controversial Court decisions. One would expect the Court to be less powerful, not more powerful, when implementing controversial decisions. Assuming journalists' ability and interest in predicting the Court's power is less significant than their interest in controversy, my results may actually underestimate the power of the Court.

Mayhew mentions several concerns with his Sweep One for congressional enactments that may also apply to my Sweep One.[10] I consider each of these in turn.

My Sweep One may focus more on dramatic thrusts in policy change while missing important gradual changes. This tendency may bias the study toward particular policy areas in which the Court is more likely to make sudden,

---

[10] Mayhew also lists several concerns that do not apply to my study. These include the possibility that some cases did not have later impact (this is exactly what I am testing), the concern that attention is linked to importance, the 1980s budget bills, and the early focus on the president's agenda.

dramatic changes. Because I will rely on longitudinal studies to establish causality in the Court's actions, my project depends on the sudden nature of the Court's decisions. However, anyone using my Sweep One in another context should be aware of this possibility. (Mayhew 2005, 39)

The methodology used to create my Sweep One may conflate importance with controversy; rather than highlighting cases that are innovative and thought likely to be consequential, the media may focus only on cases over which the public is deeply divided or strongly opposed to the Court. An examination of the cases identified by Sweep One does not appear to confirm this possibility; there are numerous popular decisions on the list. However, after eliminating cases in which the Court did not invalidate a state or federal law, most of the decisions on the list are unpopular. Fortunately, this selection bias is not problematic for my study because few scholars dispute that popular Court decisions are implemented. The more challenging task, and the main contribution of my study, is to explain the variation in implementation between different types of unpopular Supreme Court rulings.

My Sweep One may also fall victim to a "top ten list" problem. Rather than identifying cases that overcome a certain objective threshold of importance, the media may simply be listing the most important cases of the year, regardless of how important they are compared to other years. The data do not appear to support this hypothesis. My case selection process does not identify any important cases for thirteen of the years between 1954 and 2005.[11] In each of three years, the process identifies four different cases.[12] In addition, the concern seems unwarranted given the large correlation between Sweep One and Sweep Two. I may have avoided this concern by requiring agreement between the *New York Times* and *Washington Post*; if each paper had to stretch to fill in a "top ten list" of cases, it is unlikely they would include the exact same cases in their efforts to fill the list. Finally, the rejection of a "top ten list" mentality is evidenced by the explicit recognition in some articles that the Court made no important rulings during that term.[13]

Finally, Sweep One may suffer from ideological bias if the journalists writing the summary articles held such biases. Although it appears that some authors may have possessed an ideological bias, it does not appear that this affected the selection of cases. Biased writers were just as eager to lament the issuing of unfavorable rulings as to trumpet friendly decisions.

---

[11] 1959, 1968, 1970, 1975, 1977, 1979, 1981, 1984, 1986, 1988, 1991, 1993, and 1998.

[12] 1967, 1995, and 2000.

[13] For example, in the 1970 *Washington Post* summary article, the headline read "First Term of the Burger Court Is Notable for What Wasn't Done" (MacKenzie 1970, A6).

Appendix II

Survey Information and Citations

Unless noted otherwise, the survey results reported here were obtained from searches of the iPOLL Databank and other resources provided by the Roper Center for Public Opinion Research, University of Connecticut.

THE RELIGIOUS FREEDOM RESTORATION ACT

State of The First Amendment Survey [July 1997][1]
"Even though the US (United States) Constitution guarantees freedom of religion, government has placed some restrictions on it. Overall, do you think Americans have too much religious freedom, too little religious freedom, or is the amount of religious freedom people have about right?"

6%	Too much freedom
21	Too little freedom
71	About right
2	Don't know/Refused

Columbus Day Survey: Looking For America [July 1997][2]
"(Please tell me if you think this country goes too far or not far enough in protecting the following individual rights and freedoms – or is about right in its efforts.) Do you think this country goes too far or not far enough in protecting ... freedom of religion ... or is it about right in its efforts?"

---

[1] Survey by Freedom Forum. Methodology: Conducted by Center for Survey Research and Analysis, University of Connecticut, July 17–August 1, 1997, and based on telephone interviews with a national adult sample of 1,026. [USCSRA.97AMEND.RA09]
[2] Survey by Wisconsin Public Television. Methodology: Conducted by Princeton Survey Research Associates, July 31–August 17, 1997, and based on telephone interviews with a national adult sample of 800. [USPSRA.97COLM.Q05B]

10%	Goes too far
21	Not far enough
67	About right
2	Don't know/Refused

THE PENTAGON PAPERS CASE

Harris Survey [July 1971][3]

"Do you agree or disagree with the decision of the U.S. Supreme Court on the Pentagon Papers case?"

43%	Agree with decision
23	Disagree with decision
34	Not sure

ABORTION

See Survey by SurveyUSA, July 2007.[4]

Harris Survey [March 1973][5]

"The U.S. Supreme Court recently decided that state laws which make it illegal for a woman to have an abortion up to three months of pregnancy are unconstitutional, and that the decision on whether a woman should have an abortion up to three months of pregnancy should be left to a woman and her doctor to decide. In general, do you favor or oppose the U.S. Supreme Court decision making abortions up to three months of pregnancy legal?"

52%	Favor
41	Oppose
7	Not sure

Gallup Poll (AIPO) [March 1974][6]

---

[3] Methodology: Conducted by Louis Harris & Associates during July 1971 and based on personal interviews with a national adult sample of 1,600. [USHARRIS.71JUL.R23]

[4] Retrieved January 20 from the SurveyUSA Web site. http://www.surveyusa.com/50State2005/50StateAbortion0805SortedbyProLife.htm Adults age eighteen and older in each of the fifty states were interviewed by SurveyUSA August 12–14, 2005. You must credit SurveyUSA of Verona, New Jersey, if you broadcast, print, or cite these results in whole or part. Click on each state to open a link that contains the margin of sampling error for each state, a complete statement of methodology, and fully crosstabbed data.

[5] Methodology: Conducted by Louis Harris & Associates, March 15–23, 1973, and based on personal interviews with a national adult sample of 1,472. [USHARRIS.041973.R1]

[6] Methodology: Conducted by Gallup Organization, March 8–18, 1974, and based on personal interviews with a national adult sample of 1,582. Combined results of AIPO894 (3/8–11/74) and 895 (3/15–18/74). [USGALLUP.894-5.R02]

"The U.S. Supreme Court has ruled that a woman may go to a doctor to end pregnancy at any time during the first three months of pregnancy. Do you favor or oppose this ruling?"

47%	Favor
44	Oppose
9	No opinion

Overturning Roe v. Wade Survey [April 2007][7]

"Roe versus Wade prohibits states from restricting abortion during the first six months of pregnancy for any reason, including all of those we just discussed. If Roe were overturned, states could make abortion policies that would permit abortion for some reasons and bar it for others. Knowing that, would you like the Supreme Court to overturn Roe versus Wade, or not? (If Yes/No, ask:) Do you feel that way strongly, or just somewhat?"

31%	Yes, overturn/Strongly
12	Yes, overturn/Somewhat
11	No, not overturn/Somewhat
37	No, not overturn/Strongly
9	Don't know/Refused

FLAG DESECRATION

Harris Study [1989][8]

"Do you agree or disagree with a recent Supreme Court decision that said that while the flag was a symbol of patriotism, one of the freedoms an individual has is the right to desecrate and even burn the flag, as part of the First Amendment guaranteeing freedom of expression?"

23.9%	Agree
74.6	Disagree
1.5	Not sure

OBSCENITY

Pew News Interest Index Poll [April 1997][9]

[7] Survey by Ethics and Public Policy Center, Judicial Confirmation Network. Methodology Conducted by Ayers, McHenry & Associates, April 26–May 2, 2007, and based on telephone interviews with a national registered voters sample of 1,000. [USAYRES.051407.R3]
[8] Harris study no. 891105. Survey Date: 08/1989. Sample: National Sample of Persons 18 or older. Question: 5d. Number of Valid Cases: 1250. SAS/SPSS Variable Name: Q5D. Retrieved January 21, 2008, from the iPOLL Databank, The Roper Center for Public Opinion Research, University of Connecticut. http://www.ropercenter.uconn.edu/ipoll.html.
[9] Survey by Pew Research Center for the People & the Press. Methodology: Conducted by Princeton Survey Research Associates, April 3–6, 1997, and based on telephone interviews with a national adult sample of 1,206. [USPSRA.041197.R30]

"(I'd like to ask you about some things that have been in the news recently. Not everyone will have heard about them.) ... Have you heard about a recent Supreme Court case challenging a federal law which makes it illegal to send indecent or obscene materials to minors on the Internet?"

77%	Yes, have heard
22	No, have not heard
1	Don't know/Refused

Pew News Interest Index Poll [April 1997][10]

"(Please tell me if you approve or disapprove of the following policies or proposals.) ... A federal law which makes it illegal to send indecent or obscene material to children under 18 through the Internet."

83%	Approve
16	Disapprove
1	Don't know/Refused

THE EXCLUSIONARY RULE

American National Election Study [1964][11]

"We are all pretty busy these days and can't be expected to keep up on everything. Have you had time to pay any attention to what the Supreme Court of the United States has been doing in the past few years. (Yes.) Is there anything in particular that it has done that you have liked or disliked? (What is that?) (Anything else?)"

Things R likes about the Supreme Court (# of responses):

6	Protection of rights of criminals, communists, law enforcement.

Things R dislikes about the Supreme Court (# of responses):

145	Civil rights (general mention or other specific issues)
253	Prayers in the schools
46	Protection of rights of criminals, communists

[10] Survey by Pew Research Center for the People & the Press. Methodology: Conducted by Princeton Survey Research Associates, April 3–6, 1997, and based on telephone interviews with a national adult sample of 1,206. [USPSRA.041197.R32C]

[11] VAR 640357A, Q. 43, 43A, 43B. Var. 640358A. Political Behavior Program, the Survey Research Center of the Institute of Social Research, University of Michigan. NATIONAL ELECTION STUDIES, 1964: PRE-/POST-ELECTION STUDY [dataset]. Ann Arbor, MI: University of Michigan, Center for Political Studies [producer and distributor], 1999.

MIRANDA WARNINGS

Harris Survey [1966][12]

"Another decision of the U.S. Supreme Court was to (READ LIST). Do you personally think that decision of the U.S. Supreme Court was right or wrong? (RECORD BELOW)"

Item: "Rule that the police could not question a criminal unless he had a lawyer with him."

30.0%	Right
56.6	Wrong
13.4	Not sure

PSRA/Newsweek Poll [June 2000][13]

"(As I read you a list of some recent decisions by the Supreme Court, please tell me if you generally agree or disagree with each one.) What about ... the recent decision upholding 'Miranda Rules' requiring police to inform arrested suspects of their rights to remain silent and to have a lawyer present during any questioning? Do you generally agree or disagree with this decision?"

86%	Agree
11	Disagree
3	Don't know

WARRANTLESS EAVESDROPPING

Harris Survey [March 1974][14]

"Do you feel the federal government should be allowed to engage in wiretapping and electronic surveillance, if in each case it had to go to court beforehand to obtain court permission, or don't you feel the federal government should ever be allowed to engage in wiretapping or electronic surveillance?"

63%	Should be allowed
28	Should not
9	Not sure

---

[12] Survey Collection: Harris/1643. IRSS Study Number: S1643. Date: 09/1966. Sample: VOTERS. Question Number: 15b. Number of Valid Cases: 1176. SAS/SPSS Variable Name: Q15B_4. Retrieved January 21, 2008, from the iPOLL Databank, The Roper Center for Public Opinion Research, University of Connecticut. http://www.ropercenter.uconn.edu/ipoll.html.

[13] Survey by Newsweek. Methodology: Conducted by Princeton Survey Research Associates, June 29–30, 2000, and based on telephone interviews with a national adult sample of 752. [USPSRNEW.070100.R10E]

[14] Methodology: Conducted by Louis Harris & Associates, March 24–29, 1975, and based on personal interviews with a national adult sample of 1,495. [USHARRIS.090574.R3]

THE RIGHT TO COUNSEL

American National Election Study [1964][15]

"Is there anything in particular that the Supreme Court has done that you have disliked? What is that? Is there anything else that the Court has done that you have disliked? What is that?"

Things R dislikes about the Supreme Court (# of responses):

235	Civil Prayers in the schools decision
140	Protection of rights of accused criminals: right to counsel, fair trial, no forced confessions (Gideon, Esposito, Miranda cases)

CAPITAL PUNISHMENT

Nixon Poll [July 1972][16]

"The Supreme Court has recently ruled that capital punishment as now administered in the United States is unconstitutional. Do you agree or disagree with the ruling of the Supreme Court?"

Harris Survey [July 1976][17]

"The U.S. Supreme Court recently handed down a series of very important decisions. Let me read off for you some of those decisions. For each, tell me if you tend to agree or disagree with that decision." (READ STATEMENTS AND RECORD BELOW FOR EACH)

Item: "The Supreme Court reversed its previous decision that declared the death penalty for murder was so arbitrarily imposed that it was unconstitutional. Now the Court says that the death penalty is not 'cruel and unusual punishment,' but should still not be automatically applied."

63.9%	Agree
26.3	Disagree
9.8	Not Sure

[15] VAR 660140A. C35, C38. C35A, C38A. C35C, C38C. C35D, C38D. Walter Murphy, Joseph Tanenhaus, and the Political Behavior Program of the University of Michigan NATIONAL ELECTION STUDIES, 1966: POST-ELECTION STUDY [dataset]. Ann Arbor, MI: University of Michigan, Center for Political Studies [producer and distributor], 1999.

[16] Methodology: Conducted by Opinion Research Corporation, July 19–20, 1972, and based on telephone interviews with a national adult sample of 1,038. One of a series of surveys conducted for Richard Nixon while he was President. [USORC.072072.R08]

[17] Survey Collection: Harris / 2628, PUBLIC. IRSS Study Number: S2628. Date: 07/1976. Sample: National Sample of Persons 18 or older. Question Number: P3a.
Survey by Louis Harris & Associates, July 1976.

FREE PRESS IN THE COURTROOM

Public Image of Courts [October 1977][18]
"(How strongly do you agree or disagree with each of the statements on this card?) ... Reporters should be prohibited from publishing/broadcasting information which might affect fair trial."

69%	Strongly agree/Somewhat agree
31	Somewhat disagree/Strongly disagree/Uncertain

Speaker and the Listener [December 1979][19]
"(So far we've talked about newspapers and television, but now I'd like to talk about the broader areas of freedom of speech and freedom of the press or what I'll combine and call freedom of expression. Freedom of expression means different things to different people, now I'm interested in what it means to you. I'll read you some statements about the right of freedom of expression, about what it protects and how far it goes. For each one, tell me whether you agree if this is a freedom of expression right or not. If you're not sure, just say so.) ... A judge has a right to prevent newspapers from covering a trial if he thinks such coverage would make a fair trial impossible. Agree or disagree?"
Harris Survey [July 1976][20]

80%	Agree
14	Disagree
7	Not sure

"The U.S. Supreme Court recently handed down a series of very important decisions. Let me read off for you some of those decisions. For each, tell me if you tend to agree or disagree with that decision. (READ STATEMENTS AND RECORD BELOW FOR EACH) The Court ruled that judges generally cannot bar newspapers and the media from reporting on a trial as it happens."

[18] Survey by National Center for State Courts. Methodology: Conducted by Yankelovich Clancy Shulman, October 1–December 31, 1977, and based on personal interviews with a national adult sample of 1,931. The Study also had three other samples of influentials, 317 lawyers, 194 state and local judges, and 278 community leaders. The responses of these samples are available from the Roper Center. [USYANK.COURTS.R07D]

[19] Methodology: Conducted by Public Agenda Foundation, December 8–23, 1979, and based on telephone interviews with a national adult sample of 1,000. [USPAF.80SP.R038]

[20] Harris study no. 2628. Survey Date: 07/1976. Sample: National Sample of Persons 18 or older. Question: P3a. Number of Valid Cases: 1488. SAS/SPSS Variable Name: P3A_2. Retrieved January 21, 2008, from the iPOLL Databank, The Roper Center for Public Opinion Research, University of Connecticut. http://www.ropercenter.uconn.edu/ipoll.html

71.4%	Agree
19.0	Disagree
9.6	Not sure

SOVEREIGN IMMUNITY

Gallup/CNN/USA Today Poll [June 1996][21]

"(As you may know, some states legalize betting so that the state can raise revenues. Please tell me whether you would approve or disapprove of each of the following types of betting as a way to help your state raise revenue.) Would you approve or disapprove of ... casino gambling on Indian reservations?"

57%	Approve
38	Disapprove
6	Don't know/Refused

THE GUN-FREE SCHOOL ZONES ACT

Gallup/PDK Poll of Public Attitudes Toward the Public Schools [May 1994][22]

"How effective do you think each of the following measures would be in reducing violence in the public schools – very effective, somewhat effective, not very effective, or not at all effective? ... stronger penalties for possession of weapons by students."

86%	Very effective
8	Somewhat effective
3	Not very effective
2	Not at all effective
1	Don't know

Time to Move On: An Agenda for Public Schools Survey [March 1998][23]

"How important is it for a school to ... be free from weapons, drugs, and gangs? Is that absolutely essential, important but not essential, or not too important?"

[21] Survey by Cable News Network, USA Today. Methodology: Conducted by Gallup Organization, June 27–30, 1996, and based on telephone interviews with a national adult sample of 1,004. [USGALLUP.96JU27.R16G]

[22] Survey by Phi Delta Kappa. Methodology: Conducted by Gallup Organization, May 10–June 8, 1994, and based on telephone interviews with a national adult sample of 1,326. [USGALLUP.94PDK.R03A]

[23] Methodology: Conducted by Public Agenda Foundation, March 26–April 17, 1998, and based on telephone interviews with a national adult African-American & white parents sample of

Black responses:

93%	Absolutely essential
7	Important but not essential/Not too important/Don't know

White responses:

97%	Absolutely essential
3	Important but not essential/Not too important/ Don't know

American Association of University Women Education Survey [June 1998][24]
"(Let me read you some areas people have given for federal government involvement and for each one please tell me, regardless of whether you favor or oppose the idea, if you think the federal government should play a very strong role in that area, somewhat of a strong role, not too strong of a role, or no role at all.) ... Helping to guarantee that schools are safe from violence, guns, and drugs."

69%	Strong role
15	Somewhat strong role
9	Not strong role
6	No role at all
1	Don't know

REAPPORTIONMENT

Harris Survey [September 1966][25]
"Another decision of the U.S. Supreme Court was to (READ LIST). Do you personally think that decision of the U.S. Supreme Court was right or wrong?"

Item: "Rule all Congressional Districts had to have an equal number of people in them so each person's vote would count equally."

　　1,600. The sample included 800 African-American parents and 800 white parents of children in grades K-12. The survey was done in conjunction with the Public Education Network. [USPAF.98RACE.R14A]

24 Survey by American Association of University Women. Methodology: Conducted by Lake, Snell, Perry & Associates during June 1998 and based on telephone interviews with a national registered women voters sample of 600. [USLAKESP.98AAUW.R32] Subpopulation/ Note: Asked of Form A half sample.

25 Survey Collection: Harris/1643. IRSS Study Number: S1643. Date: 09/1966. Sample: VOTERS. Question Number: 15b. Number of Valid Cases: 1175. SAS/SPSS Variable Name: Q15B_2. Retrieved January 21, 2008, from the iPOLL Databank, The Roper Center for Public Opinion Research, University of Connecticut. http://www.ropercenter.uconn.edu/ipoll.html

57.0%	Right
18.6	Wrong
24.4	Not sure

Harris Survey [November 1966][26]

"Another decision of the U.S. (United States) Supreme Court was to ... rule all Congressional Districts had to have an equal number of people in them so each person's vote would count equally. Do you personally think that decision of the U.S. Supreme Court was right or wrong?"

74%	Right
24	Wrong

MAJORITY-MINORITY CONGRESSIONAL DISTRICTS

ABC News/Washington Post Poll [July 1995][27]

"As you may know, a recent ruling by the Supreme Court has made it harder for states to create congressional districts where blacks make up the majority of residents. Do you approve or disapprove of this ruling making it harder to create majority-black congressional districts?"

31%	Approve
61	Disapprove
8	Don't know/No opinion

Washington Post/Kaiser/Harvard Racial Attitudes Survey [March 2001][28]

"In order to elect more minorities to public office, do you think race should be a factor when boundaries for US (United States) Congressional voting districts are drawn, or should it not be a factor?"

11%	Race should be a factor
86	Race should not be a factor
12	Don't know

[26] Methodology: Conducted by Louis Harris & Associates during November 1966 and based on personal interviews with a national adult sample of 1,250. Sample size is approximate. As reported in the Philadelphia Inquirer. [USHARRIS.111466.R2B]

[27] Methodology: Conducted by ABC News/Washington Post, July 14–17, 1995, and based on telephone interviews with a national adult sample of 1,548. [USABCWP.5729.Q033]

[28] Survey by Washington Post, Henry J. Kaiser Family Foundation, Harvard University. Methodology: Conducted by Washington Post, March 8–April 22, 2001, and based on telephone interviews with a national adult with an oversample of minority groups sample of 1,709. The sample included 779 whites, 323 African-Americans, 315 Hispanics, and 254 Asians. Results are weighted to be representative of a national adult population. [USWASHP.01RACE.R52B]

PUBLIC AID TO RELIGIOUS SCHOOLS

Gallup/Kettering Poll of Public Attitudes Toward the Public Schools 1970 [April 1970][29]
"It has been proposed that some government tax money be used to help parochial schools make ends meet. How do you feel about this? Do you favor or oppose giving some government tax money to help parochial schools?"

48%	Favor
44	Oppose
8	Don't Know/No Answer

Gallup/Kettering Poll of Public Attitudes Toward the Public Schools 1974 [May 1974][30]
"These proposals are being suggested to amend the U.S. Constitution. As I read each one, will you tell me if you favor or oppose it: An amendment to the Constitution that would permit government financial aid to parochial schools?"

53%	Favor
35	Oppose
13	Don't Know/No Answer

Associated Press/Media General Poll [September 1985][31]
"Do you think tax funds should be used to send public school teachers into religious private schools to teach non-religious courses not available in the private school, or not?"

29%	Should be used
61	Should not
10	Don't Know/No Answer

AFFIRMATIVE ACTION IN COLLEGE ADMISSIONS

Pew News Interest Index Poll [April 2003][32]

[29] Survey by Charles F. Kettering Foundation. Methodology: Conducted by Gallup Organization, April 15–20, 1970, and based on personal interviews with a national adult sample of 1,592. [USGALLUP.70EDUC.Q022]

[30] Survey by Charles F. Kettering Foundation. Methodology: Conducted by Gallup Organization, May 10–12, 1974, and based on personal interviews with a national adult sample of 1,543. [USGALLUP.74EDUC.Q016B]

[31] Methodology: Conducted by Associated Press/Media General, September 1–7, 1985, and based on telephone interviews with a national adult sample of 1,412. [USAPMGEN.8.R33]

[32] Survey by Pew Research Center for the People & the Press. Methodology: Conducted by Princeton Survey Research Associates, April 30–May 4, 2003, and based on telephone interviews with a national adult sample of 1,201. [USPSRA.050703.R16]

"All in all, do you think these programs are a good thing or a bad thing? (If respondent needs question repeated, ask in full) All in all, do you think affirmative action programs designed to increase the number of black and minority students on college campuses are a good thing or a bad thing?"

60%	Good thing
30	Bad thing
10	Don't know/Refused

Pew News Interest Index Poll [April 2003][33]
"All in all, do you think affirmative action programs designed to increase the number of black and minority students on college campuses are fair, or unfair?"

47%	Fair
42	Unfair
11	Don't know/Refused

Gallup/CNN/USA Today Poll [August 2001][34]
"Do you favor or oppose affirmative action programs for minorities and women for admission to colleges and universities?"

56%	Favor
39	Oppose
6	Don't know/Refused

Associated Press Poll [February 2003][35]
"Do you think affirmative action programs that provide advantages or preferences for blacks, Hispanics and other minorities in hiring, promoting and college admissions should be continued, or do you think these affirmative action programs should be abolished?"

53%	Should be continued
35	Should be abolished
12	Don't know/Refused

[33] Survey by Pew Research Center for the People & the Press. Methodology: Conducted by Princeton Survey Research Associates, April 30–May 4, 2003, and based on telephone interviews with a national adult sample of 1,201. [USPSRA.050703.R15]
[34] Survey by Cable News Network, USA Today. Methodology: Conducted by Gallup Organization, August 3–5, 2001, and based on telephone interviews with a national adult sample of 1,017. [USGALLUP.200127.Q34]
[35] Methodology: Conducted by Associated Press, February 28–March 4, 2003, and based on telephone interviews with a national adult sample of 1,013. Interviews were conducted by ICR – International Communications Research. [USAP.031003.R1]

CBS News/New York Times Poll [January 2003][36]
"Do you think affirmative action programs in hiring, promoting, and college admissions should be continued, or do you think these affirmative action programs should be abolished?"

54%	Continued
37	Abolished
9	Don't know

New Models National Brand Poll [January 2003][37]
"Recently President (George W.) Bush took a position opposing the affirmative action admissions policies of the University of Michigan. In his statement he said that University's use of race in their admissions policy is in conflict with the constitution. Would you say that you agree or disagree with the President's position?"

58%	Agree
29	Disagree
13	Don't know/Refused

Los Angeles Times Poll [January 2003][38]
"President (George W.) Bush stated publicly that he opposes a program of racial preferences for minority applicants at the University of Michigan. The Bush administration urged the Supreme Court to declare the University of Michigan's admissions system unconstitutional. Do you approve or disapprove of the Bush administration decision to oppose the University of Michigan's racial preference admissions program? (If Approve/Disapprove ask:) Do you approve/disapprove strongly or do you approve/disapprove somewhat?"

38%	Approve strongly
18	Approve somewhat
9	Disapprove somewhat
17	Disapprove strongly
18	Don't know

Quinnipiac University Poll [February 2003][39]

[36] Methodology: Conducted by CBS News/New York Times, January 19–22, 2003, and based on telephone interviews with a national adult sample of 997. [USCBSNYT.012303B.R46]
[37] Survey by New Models. Methodology: Conducted by Winston Group during January 2003 and based on telephone interviews with a national registered voters sample of 1,000. [USWG.03JAN.R24]
[38] Methodology: Conducted by Los Angeles Times, January 30–February 2, 2003, and based on telephone interviews with a national adult sample of 1,385. [USLAT.020603.R1]
[39] Methodology: Conducted by Quinnipiac University Polling Institute, February 26–March 3, 2003, and based on telephone interviews with a national adult sample of 1,448. [USQUINN.030503.R34]

"As you may know, the Supreme Court will be deciding whether public universities can use race as one of the factors in admissions to increase diversity in the student body. Do you favor or oppose this practice?"

28%	Favor
67	Oppose
5	Don't know/No answer

NBC News/Wall Street Journal Poll [January 2003][40]
"As you may know, the U.S. (United States) Supreme Court will be deciding whether public universities can use race as one of the factors in admissions to increase diversity in the student body. Do you favor or oppose this practice?"

26%	Favor
65	Oppose
9	Not sure

Time/CNN/Harris Interactive Poll [February 2003][41]
"Do you approve or disapprove of affirmative action admissions programs at colleges and law schools that give racial preferences to minority applicants?"

39%	Approve
49	Disapprove
12	Not sure

Princeton Survey Research Associates/Newsweek Poll [January 2003][42]
"Please tell me whether you think colleges and universities should or should not give preferences in admissions for each of the following groups. What about ... Blacks? Should there be preferences in admissions for this group, or not?"

26%	Should
68	Should not
6	Don't know

[40] Survey by NBC News, Wall Street Journal. Methodology: Conducted by Hart and Teeter Research Companies, January 19–21, 2003, and based on telephone interviews with a national adult sample of 1,025. [USNBCWSJ.03JAN.R40A] Subpopulation/Note: Asked of Form A half sample.
[41] Survey by Time, Cable News Network. Methodology: Conducted by Harris Interactive, February 19–20, 2003, and based on telephone interviews with a national adult sample of 1,299. [USHARRIS.Y030403.R32]
[42] Survey by Newsweek. Methodology: Conducted by Princeton Survey Research Associates, January 16–17, 2003, and based on telephone interviews with a national adult sample of 1,002. [USPSRNEW.011803.R17A]

Princeton Survey Research Associates/Newsweek Poll [January 2003][43]

"(Please tell me whether you think colleges and universities should or should not give preferences in admissions for each of the following groups.) What about ... Hispanics? Should there be preferences in admissions for this group, or not?"

25%	Should
70	Should not
3	Don't know

Princeton Survey Research Associates/Newsweek Poll [January 2003][44]

"(Please tell me whether you think colleges and universities should or should not give preferences in admissions for each of the following groups.) What about ... Asians? Should there be preferences in admissions for this group, or not?"

23%	Should
71	Should not
6	Don't know

NBC News/Wall Street Journal Poll [March 1995][45]

"(Here are some specific affirmative action programs. For each one, please tell me if you strongly favor, somewhat favor, somewhat oppose, or strongly oppose that program.) College scholarship programs available only to black or minority students ..."

7%	Strongly favor
12	Somewhat favor
22	Somewhat oppose
56	Strongly oppose
3	Not sure

MINIMUM WAGE FOR STATE EMPLOYEES

Cambridge Reports/National Omnibus Survey [April 1977][46]

---

[43] Survey by Newsweek. Methodology: Conducted by Princeton Survey Research Associates, January 16–17, 2003, and based on telephone interviews with a national adult sample of 1,002. [USPSRNEW.011803.R17B]

[44] Survey by Newsweek. Methodology: Conducted by Princeton Survey Research Associates, January 16–17, 2003, and based on telephone interviews with a national adult sample of 1,002. [USPSRNEW.011803.R17C]

[45] Survey by NBC News, Wall Street Journal. Methodology: Conducted by Hart and Teeter Research Companies, March 4–7, 1995, and based on telephone interviews with a national adult sample of 1,011. [USNBCWSJ.031095.R27C3]

[46] Methodology: Conducted by Cambridge Reports/Research International during April 1977 and based on personal interviews with a national adult sample of 1,500. Sample size is approximate. [USCAMREP.77APR.R021]

"Recently the (Carter) Administration made a proposal to raise the minimum wage from $2.30 an hour to $2.70 an hour. The AFL-CIO (American Federation of Labor – Congress of Industrial Organizations) argues that the minimum wage should be raised to $3.00 per hour. Which of these is closest to your opinion? ...01. Don't raise it at all 02. Raise it to $2.70 03. Raise it to $3.00."

15%	Don't raise it at all
31	Raise it to $2.70
49	Raise it to $3.00
5	Other (vol.)/Don't know

Roper Report 79–3 [February 1979][47]
"On January 1 (1979) the minimum wage went up from $2.65 an hour to $2.90 an hour. Do you think the minimum wage should have been raised or left where it was?"

15%	Should have been raised
31	Left where it was
49	Don't know

Roper Report 81–3 [February 1981][48]
"On January 1, (1981) the minimum wage went up from $2.90 an hour to $3.35 an hour. Do you think the minimum wage should have been raised or left where it was?"

76%	Should have been raised
19	Left where it was
5	Don't know

Knowledge of Business and The Economy [July 1984][49]
"Do you think: No one should be paid less than the minimum wage set by the federal government? There ought to be exceptions allowed to the minimum wage law, so that under some circumstances people could be paid at less than minimum wage?"

---

[47] Methodology: Conducted by Roper Organization, February 10–24, 1979, and based on personal interviews with a national adult sample of 2,004. [USROPER.79–3.R15]

[48] Methodology: Conducted by Roper Organization, February 14–28, 1981, and based on personal interviews with a national adult sample of 2,005. [USROPER.81–3.R19Y]

[49] Survey by Hearst Corporation. Methodology: Conducted by Research & Forecasts, July 27–August 9, 1984, and based on telephone interviews with a national adult sample of 1,006. [USRF.84BUS.R41]

63%	No one should be paid less than the minimum wage set by the federal government
35	There ought to be exceptions allowed to the minimum wage law, so that under some circumstances people could be paid at less than minimum wage
2	Don't know/No answer

Gallup Poll [April 1987][50]
"As you may know, a bill has been introduced in Congress that would gradually raise the minimum wage from the present $3.35 per hour to $4.65 per hour over the next three years. Those in favor point out that the minimum wage has not been increased since 1981 while consumer prices have gone up by about 20 percent. Those opposed say that increasing the cost of labor would lead to fewer jobs, higher unemployment, and higher inflation. All things considered, do you favor or oppose increasing the minimum wage to $4.65 per hour over the next three years?"

63%	Favor
35	Oppose
2	Don't Know

Service Sector Issues [May 1987][51]
"(Let me read you some things people have said about the minimum wage, and for each one could you tell me whether you agree a lot, agree a little, disagree a little or disagree a lot?) ... Wages should be set by the market and not by the government."

49%	Agree a lot
20	Agree a little
11	Disagree a little
11	Disagree a little
8	Don't know

Service Sector Issues [May 1987][52]

[50] Methodology: Conducted by Gallup Organization, April 10–13, 1987, and based on personal interviews with a national adult sample of 1,571. [USGALLUP.871274.Q05B]
[51] Survey by Service Employees International Union. Methodology: Conducted by Fingerhut/Granados on May 25, 1987, and based on telephone interviews with a national registered voters sample of 724. [USFHUT.87SEIU.R049]
[52] Survey by Service Employees International Union. Methodology: Conducted by Fingerhut/Granados on May 25, 1987, and based on telephone interviews with a national registered voters sample of 724. [USFHUT.87SEIU.R051]

"Having heard a few of these arguments, do you think you would strongly support, somewhat support, somewhat oppose, or strongly oppose an increase in the minimum wage?"

57%	Strongly support
27	Somewhat support
6	Somewhat oppose
7	Strongly oppose
3	Don't know

BUSH V. GORE

Gallup/CNN/USA Today Poll [December 2000][53]

"As you may know, the US (United States) Supreme Court reached a decision last night (December 12, 2000) which effectively ended the (2000 presidential election) vote recount in Florida, meaning that George W. Bush will be the next president ... Do you agree or disagree with the US Supreme Court's decision?"

52%	Agree
42	Disagree
6	No opinion

ABC News/Washington Post Poll [December 2000][54]

"From what you've heard or read about it, do you approve or disapprove of the U.S. (United States) Supreme Court's decision rejecting the (2000 presidential election) recount in Florida?"

50%	Approve
48	Disapprove
2	Don't know/no opinion

CBS News Poll [December 2000][55]

"As you may know, on Tuesday (December 12, 2000), the United States Supreme Court ruled in George W. Bush's favor and stopped the manual recounting of (2000 presidential election) votes in Florida that had been ordered by the Florida Supreme Court. Do you approve or disapprove of the US Supreme Court's ruling that stopped the manual recount?"

---

[53] Survey by Cable News Network, USA Today. Methodology: Conducted by Gallup Organization on December 13, 2000, and based on telephone interviews with a national adult sample of 633.

[54] Methodology: Conducted by ABC News/Washington Post, December 14–15, 2000, and based on telephone interviews with a national adult sample of 807. [USABCWP.16219.Q002]

[55] Methodology: Conducted by CBS News, December 14–16, 2000, and based on telephone interviews with a national adult sample of 1,048. [USCBS.121700.R27]

54%	Approve
42	Disapprove
2	Don't know/No answer

ABC News/Washington Post Poll [December 2000][56]

"As you may know, the United States Supreme Court on Tuesday, (December 12, 2000) rejected a recount in the (2000) presidential election in Florida and said it was too late for a new recount. The ruling means George W. Bush wins the election and the presidency. Al Gore conceded on Wednesday night (December 13, 2000). Do you approve or disapprove of Gore's decision to concede the presidential race to Bush?"

73%	Approve
26	Disapprove
2	No opinion

ABC News/Washington Post Poll [December 2000][57]

"As you may know, the United States Supreme Court on Tuesday (December 12, 2000) rejected a recount in the presidential election in Florida and said it was too late for a new recount. The ruling means George W. Bush wins the election and the presidency. Al Gore conceded on Wednesday night. Do you approve or disapprove of Gore's decision to concede the presidential race to Bush?"

72%	Approve
26	Disapprove
2	Don't know/No opinion

Gallup/CNN/USA Today Poll [December 2000][58]

"In his speech tonight (December 13, 2000), Al Gore is likely to accept the ruling of the US (United States) Supreme Court and acknowledge that George W. Bush will be the next president, even though Gore believes he got more votes in Florida. Do you think Gore should – concede that he lost, or should he withdraw from the race without conceding?"

[56] Methodology: Conducted by ABC News/Washington Post on December 14, 2000, and based on telephone interviews with a national adult sample of 603. [USABCWP.121400.R01]

[57] Methodology: Conducted by ABC News/Washington Post, December 14–15, 2000, and based on telephone interviews with a national adult sample of 807. [USABCWP.16219. Q001]

[58] Survey by Cable News Network, USA Today. Methodology: Conducted by Gallup Organization on December 13, 2000, and based on telephone interviews with a national adult sample of 633. [USGALLUP.00DC13.R07]

59%	Concede that he lost
32	Withdraw without conceding
9	No opinion

SCHOOL DESEGREGATION

Gallup Poll (AIPO) [May 1954][59]
"The U.S. Supreme Court has ruled that racial segregation in all public schools is illegal. This means that all children, no matter what their race, must be allowed to go to the same schools. Do you approve or disapprove of this decision?"

55%	Approve
40	Disapprove
5	No opinion

SCHOOL PRAYER

Hopes and Fears [September 1964][60]
"The U.S. Supreme Court has held that prayers in public schools are unconstitutional because they violate the doctrine of separation of church and state. Would you favor or oppose a constitutional amendment to legalize prayers in public schools?"

77%	Favor
19	Oppose
5	Don't know

Harris Survey [September 1966][61]
"Another decision of the U.S. Supreme Court was to (READ LIST). Do you personally think that decision of the U.S. Supreme Court was right or wrong? (RECORD BELOW)
    Item: Rule that children could not be required to recite a prayer in school."

26.9%	Right
65.5	Wrong
7.6	Not sure

[59] Survey by Gallup Organization, May 21–26, 1954. Retrieved January 21, 2008, from the iPOLL Databank, The Roper Center for Public Opinion Research, University of Connecticut.

[60] Survey by Institute for International Social Research. Methodology: Conducted by Gallup Organization during September 1964 and based on personal interviews with a national adult sample of 1,611.

[61] Survey Collection: Harris/1643. IRSS Study Number: S1643. Top of Form. Date: 09/1966. Sample: VOTERS. Question Number: 15b. Number of Valid Cases: 1171. SAS/SPSS Variable

Harris Survey [November 1966][62]
"Another decision of the U.S. (United States) Supreme Court was to ... rule that children could not be required to read a prayer in school. Do you personally think that decision of the U.S. Supreme Court was right or wrong?"

30%	Right
70	Wrong

Gallup Poll (AIPO) [October, 1971][63]
"The U.S. Supreme Court has ruled that no state or local government may require the reading of the Lord's Prayer or Bible verses in public schools. What are your views on this – do you approve of disapprove of this?"

27%	Approve
67	Disapprove
5	No opinion

GSS Bible Prayer in Public Schools[64]
"The United States Supreme Court has ruled that no state or local government may require the reading of the Lord's Prayer or Bible verses in public schools. What are your views on this – do you approve or disapprove of the court ruling?"

	GSS School Prayer Poll, 1974								
	New Eng.	Mid Atl.	E. N. Cen.	W.N. Cen.	S. Atl.	E. S. Cen.	W.S. Cen.	Mtn.	Pac.	Row Total
Approve	38.3	30.6	26.5	44.7	24.8	26.7	40.2	33.3	40.9	31.7
Dis.	61.7	69.4	73.5	55.3	75.2	73.3	59.8	66.7	59.1	68.3

CENSORSHIP IN PUBLIC EDUCATION

Roper Report 82–3 [February 1982][65]

Name: Q15B_3. Retrieved January 21, 2008, from the iPOLL Databank, The Roper Center for Public Opinion Research, University of Connecticut. http://www.ropercenter.uconn.edu/ipoll.html.

[62] Methodology: Conducted by Louis Harris & Associates during November 1966 and based on personal interviews with a national adult sample of 1,250. Sample size is approximate. As reported in the Philadelphia Inquirer. [USHARRIS.111466.R2F]

[63] Methodology: Conducted by Gallup Organization, October 8–11, 1971, and based on personal interviews with a national adult sample of 1,526. [USGALLUP.838.Q002]

[64] Q. 119a. Selected Study: General Social Surveys, 1972–2006 [Cumulative File].

[65] Methodology: Conducted by Roper Organization, February 12–27, 1982, and based on personal interviews with a national adult sample of 2,000. [USROPER.82–3.R07YB] Subpopulation/Note: Response of Y half of sample.

"(Asked of 'Y' half of sample) (Here is a list of changes some people favor, but that others oppose. [Card shown respondent] Would you read down that list, and for each one tell me whether it is a change that you favor or oppose?) ... Banning in schools and libraries books that some people consider objectionable."

28%	Favor
66	Oppose
6	Don't know

Roper Report 82–3 [February 1982][66]

"(Asked of 'X' half of sample) (Here is a list of changes some people favor on the grounds that they are needed for the good of our society, but that others oppose on the grounds that they violate various Constitutional guarantees, such as freedom of the press, separation of church and state, the right of privacy, etc. [Card shown respondent] Would you read down that list, and for each one tell me whether it is a change that you favor or oppose?) ... Banning in schools and libraries books that some people consider objectionable."

31%	Favor
63	Oppose
6	Don't know

Merit Report [March 1982][67]

"Which one of the following groups, if any, do you think should have the most to say about what books are available in public school libraries ... school teachers, school librarians, superintendents and school principles, school boards, or none of the above?"

24%	School teachers
9	School librarians
7	Superintendents and school principles
26	School boards
26	None of the above
8	No opinion

People, The Press & Politics Poll [April 1987][68]

[66] Methodology: Conducted by Roper Organization, February 12–27, 1982, and based on personal interviews with a national adult sample of 2,000. [USROPER.82–3.R07XB] Subpopulation/Note: Response of X half of sample.

[67] Survey by Merit. Methodology: Conducted by Audits & Surveys, March 8–11, 1982, and based on telephone interviews with a national adult sample of [sample number was not provided by the iPOLL databank]. [USAS.14.R07]

[68] Survey by Times Mirror. Methodology: Conducted by Gallup Organization, April 25–May 10, 1987, and based on personal interviews with a national adult sample of 4,244. [USGALLUP. TM09PR.R402AG]

"Books that contain dangerous ideas should be banned from public school libraries."

24%	Completely agree
26	Mostly agree
25	Mostly disagree
19	Completely disagree
6	Don't know

People, The Press & Politics Poll [May 1988][69]
"Books that contain dangerous ideas should be banned from public school libraries."

29%	Completely agree
22	Mostly agree
22	Mostly disagree
12	Completely disagree
6	Don't know

People, The Press & Politics Poll [January 1989][70]
"Books that contain dangerous ideas should be banned from public school libraries."

26%	Completely agree
24	Mostly agree
23	Mostly disagree
13	Completely disagree
4	Don't know

People, The Press & Politics Poll 1990 [May 1990][71]
"(Here are some statements on a different topic. Please tell me how much you agree or disagree with each of these statements.) ... Books that contain dangerous ideas should be banned from public school libraries."

[69] Survey by Times Mirror. Methodology: Conducted by Gallup Organization, May 13–22, 1988, and based on personal interviews with a national adult sample of 3,021. [USGALLUP.588TM. R203G]
[70] Survey by Times Mirror. Methodology: Conducted by Gallup Organization, January 27–February 5, 1989, and based on personal interviews with a national adult sample of 2,048. Report also contains comparative data from an American leadership sample and from samples of foreign investors from Japan, United Kingdom, Netherlands, and Canada. [USGALLUP. JF88TN.R059BKK]
[71] Survey by Times Mirror. Methodology: Conducted by Princeton Survey Research Associates, May 1–31, 1990, and based on personal interviews with a national adult sample of 3,004. There was a re-interview of 1,000 of these respondents August 19–25, 1990, to update the Persian Gulf crisis data. These data are reported separately. [USPSRA.90TM2A.R402G]

29%	Completely agree
21	Mostly agree
24	Mostly disagree
21	Completely disagree
5	Don't know

GSS Allow Antireligious Book in Library[72]

"There are always some people whose ideas are considered bad or dangerous by other people. For instance, somebody who is against churches and religion ... c. If some people in your community suggested a book he wrote against churches and religion should be taken out of your public library, would you favor removing this book or not?"

GSS Antireligious Book Poll, 1974										
	New Eng.	Mid Atl.	E. N. Cen.	W.N. Cen.	S. Atl.	E. S. Cen.	W.S. Cen.	Mtn.	Pac.	Row Total
Remove	30.0	26.8	32.2	40.6	42.1	57.6	57.4	18.7	30.1	36.4
Not Remove	70.0	73.2	67.8	59.4	57.9	42.4	42.6	81.3	69.9	63.6

GSS Allow Communist's Book in Library[73]

"Now, I should like to ask you some questions about a man who admits he is a Communist: c. Suppose he wrote a book which is in your public library. Somebody in your community suggests that the book should be removed from the library. Would you favor removing it, or not?"

GSS Communist's Book Poll, 1974										
	New Eng.	Mid Atl.	E. N. Cen.	W.N. Cen.	S. Atl.	E. S. Cen.	W.S. Cen.	Mtn.	Pac.	Row Total
Remove	40.6	34.9	43.0	46.1	47.3	60.5	62.5	36.9	35.9	44.0
Not Remove	59.4	65.1	57.0	53.9	52.7	39.5	37.5	63.1	64.1	56.0

GSS Allow Homosexual's Book in Library[74]

"And what about a man who admits that he is a homosexual? c. If some people in your community suggested that a book he wrote in favor of homosexuality should be taken out of your public library, would you favor removing this book, or not?"

---

[72] Q. 76. Selected Study: General Social Surveys, 1972–2006 [Cumulative File].
[73] Q. 79. Selected Study: General Social Surveys, 1972–2006 [Cumulative File].
[74] Q. 81. Selected Study: General Social Surveys, 1972–2006 [Cumulative File].

GSS Homosexual's Book Poll, 1974									
	New Eng.	Mid Atl.	E. N. Cen.	W.N. Cen.	S. Atl.	E. S. Cen.	W.S. Cen.	Mtn.	Pac.	Row Total
Remove	35.2	36.8	42.2	50.2	60.9	62.9	44.9	31.8	33.6	44.5
Not Remove	64.8	63.2	57.8	49.8	39.1	37.1	55.1	68.2	66.4	55.5

GSS Allow Racist's Book in Library[75]
"Or consider a person who believes that Blacks are genetically inferior. c. If some people in your community suggested that a book he wrote which said Blacks are inferior should be taken out of your public library, would you favor removing this book, or not?"

GSS Racist's Book Poll, 1974									
	New Eng.	Mid Atl.	E. N. Cen.	W.N. Cen.	S. Atl.	E. S. Cen.	W.S. Cen.	Mtn.	Pac.	Row Total
Remove	21.3	32.8	38.0	33.9	49.8	51.9	39.3	27.6	34.3	38.1
Not Remove	78.7	67.2	62.0	66.1	50.2	48.1	60.7	72.4	65.7	61.9

MINORITY SET-ASIDE PROGRAMS

ABC News/Washington Post Poll [July 1995][76]
"The Supreme Court also has ruled that federal affirmative action programs cannot give preferences to all minority contractors, but only to those who can prove their company has been discriminated against in the past. Do you approve or disapprove of this ruling?"

55%	Approve
41	Disapprove
4	Don't know/No opinion

NBC News/Wall Street Journal Poll [March 1995][77]
"(Here are some specific affirmative action programs. For each one, please tell me if you strongly favor, somewhat favor, somewhat oppose, or strongly

[75] Q. 78. Selected Study: General Social Surveys, 1972–2006 [Cumulative File].
[76] Methodology: Conducted by ABC News/Washington Post, July 14–17, 1995, and based on telephone interviews with a national adult sample of 1,548. [USABCWP.5729.Q034]
[77] Survey by NBC News, Wall Street Journal. Methodology: Conducted by Hart and Teeter Research Companies, March 4–7, 1995, and based on telephone interviews with a national adult sample of 1,011. [USNBCWSJ.031095.R27C4]

oppose that program.) Set aside programs that guarantee a certain percentage of government contracts to minority-owned firms."

11%	Strongly favor
23	Somewhat favor
25	Somewhat oppose
34	Strongly oppose
7	Not sure

CONGRESSIONAL EXCLUSION

Gallup Poll (AIPO) [January 1967][78]
"A congressional committee is now investigating the question of whether Representative Adam Clayton Powell should be allowed to keep his seat in Congress. How do you, yourself, feel – do you think Powell should be allowed to keep his seat or not?"

21%	Yes, allowed to keep
61	No
19	Don't know

Harris Survey [January 1967][79]
"As you know Congress is now holding an investigation over whether or not Congressman (Adam Clayton) Powell should be seated in Congress. Do you think Representative Powell should or should not be given his seat in Congress?"

18%	Should
54	Should not
28	Should not

THE BRADY BILL

Gallup/CNN/USA Today Poll [June 1997][80]
"Do you support or oppose the Brady Bill, which establishes a five-day waiting period for the purchase of handguns in order to conduct background checks?"

[78] Methodology: Conducted by Gallup Organization, January 26–31, 1967, and based on personal interviews with a national adult sample of 2,366. [USGALLUP.740.Q09B] Subpopulation/Note: HEARD/READ OF INVESTIGATION (85%)
[79] Methodology: Conducted by Louis Harris & Associates during January 1967 and based on personal interviews with a national adult sample of 1,250. Sample size is approximate. As reported in The Washington Post. [USHARRIS.020667.R4]
[80] Survey by Cable News Network, USA Today. Methodology: Conducted by Gallup Organization, June 23–24, 1997, and based on telephone interviews with a national adult sample of 1,030. [USGALLUP.97JN23.R21]

84%	Support
15	Oppose
2	Don't know/Refused

CBS News/New York Times Poll [February 1995][81]
  "Do you favor or oppose the national law, known as the Brady Act, that requires a five-day waiting period between the time a person applies to buy a handgun and the time it is sold to them?"

87%	Favor
11	Oppose
2	Don't know/No answer

Gallup Poll [February 1999][82]
  "Please tell me whether you would generally favor or oppose each of the following proposals which some people have made to reduce the amount of gun violence ... The Brady bill, which requires a five-day waiting period on the purchase of all guns in order to determine whether the prospective buyer has been convicted of a felony."

89%	Favor
10	Oppose
1	Don't know/No answer

[81] Survey by Cable News Network, USA Today. Methodology: Conducted by Gallup Organization, June 23–24, 1997, and based on telephone interviews with a national adult sample of 1,030. [USGALLUP.97JN23.R21]

[82] Methodology: Conducted by Gallup Organization, February 8–9, 1999, and based on telephone interviews with a national adult sample of 1,054. [USGALLUP.99FEB8.R27A] Subpopulation/Note: * = less than .5 percent.

Appendix III

Supporting Data for Figures

TABLE A3.1. *Supporting Data for Figure 5.1*

Year	# of Legal Abortions	Year	# of Legal Abortions
1969	93	1987	1,353,671
1970	193,491	1988	1,371,285
1971	485,816	1989	1,396,658
1972	586,760	1990	1,429,247
1973	615,831	1991	1,388,937
1974	763,476	1992	1,359,146
1975	854,853	1993	1,330,414
1976	988,267	1994	1,267,415
1977	1,079,430	1995	1,210,883
1978	1,157,776	1996	1,225,937
1979	1,251,921	1997	1,186,039
1980	1,297,606	1998	884,273
1981	1,300,760	1999	861,789
1982	1,303,980	2000	857,475
1983	1,268,987	2001	853,485
1984	1,333,521	2002	854,122
1985	1,328,570	2003	848,163
1986	1,328,112		

Note: Data compiled by CDC (1969–2003).

TABLE A3.2. *Supporting Data for Figure 5.2*

Year	Number of Legal Abortions	
	No or Light Restrictions	Heavy Restrictions
1969	93	0
1970	175,508	0
1971	451,444	28,815
1972	530,858	55,902
1973	474,707	141,124
1974	490,066	273,410
1975	505,046	349,807
1976	561,796	426,471
1977	613,188	466,242
1978	666,239	491,537
1979	724,586	527,335
1980	759,068	538,538
1981	768,421	532,339
1982	764,649	539,331
1983	754,493	514,494
1984	916,906	416,615
1985	921,365	406,711
1986	930,141	422,612
1987	954,690	398,063
1988	972,628	398,657
1989	996,910	399,748
1990	924,948	504,629
1991	915,692	473,245
1992	898,622	460,523
1993	874,384	456,030
1994	743,745	423,670
1995	806,198	404,685
1996	817,909	403,676
1997	793,182	392,857
1998	505,481	378,792
1999	501,836	359,953
2000	491,415	366,060
2001	486,561	366,924
2002	491,569	362,553
2003	492,781	355,382

Note: Data compiled by CDC (1969–2003).

TABLE A3.3. *Supporting Data for Figure 5.3*

Year	No or Light Restrictions	Heavy Restrictions
1969	.2	0
1970	177.8	0
1971	332.0	66.4
1972	422.9	91.8
1973	337.5	91.8
1974	344.3	162.7
1975	356.1	205.6
1976	390.3	247.6
1977	407.0	257.4

Note: Data compiled by CDC (1969–2003).

TABLE A3.4. *Supporting Data for Figure 5.4*

Year	Percent of Abortions Obtained by Out-of-State Residents, 1971–2002	Year	Percent of Abortions Obtained by Out-of-State Residents, 1971–2002
1971	42.2	1987	8.3
1972	43.8	1988	8.6
1973	25.2	1989	9.0
1974	13.4	1990	8.2
1975	10.8	1991	8.4
1976	10.0	1992	8.0
1977	10.0	1993	8.6
1978	10.7	1994	8.5
1979	10.0	1995	8.3
1980	7.4	1996	8.1
1981	7.5	1997	8.1
1982	7.1	1998	8.6
1983	6.7	1999	8.8
1984	8.0	2000	8.7
1985	7.6	2001	8.7
1986	7.6	2002	8.8

Note: Data compiled by CDC (1969–2003).

TABLE A3.5. *Supporting Data for Figure 5.5*

Year	Reports of Flag Desecration	Year	Reports of Flag Desecration
1963	1	1985	0
1964	0	1986	0
1965	0	1987	1
1966	4	1988	3
1967	4	1989	3
1968	3	1990	
1969	3	1991	
1970	7	1992	
1971	2	1994	3
1972	0	1995	9
1973	0	1996	31
1974	1	1997	16
1975	0	1998	14
1976	1	1999	11
1977	0	2000	1
1978	0	2001	14
1979	2	2002	11
1980	4	2003	7
1981	1	2004	3
1982	0	2005	10
1983	0	2006	11
1984	1	2007	6

Note: Data compiled by Goldstein (1995, 68–75) and reports collected by the Citizens Flag Alliance.

TABLE A3.6. *Supporting Data for Figure 5.6*

Year	Arrests in Baltimore			
	Stolen property	Weapons	Narcotics	Gambling
1956	166	1,341	324	434
1957	144	1,324	239	512
1958	241	1,343	435	849
1959	350	1,452	239	577
1960	488	1,559	502	623
1961	294	936	221	345
1962	274	1,031	275	467
1963	163	1,120	314	328
1964	171	1,326	368	192
1965	168	1,030	378	996

Note: Data based on research conducted by Canon (1974, 705, figure 2).

TABLE A3.7. *Supporting Data for Figure 5.7*

Year	Arrests in Buffalo			
	Stolen property	Weapons	Narcotics	Gambling
1956	41	148	76	91
1957	46	137	62	90
1958	68	152	68	93
1959	67	108	87	126
1960	72	125	112	171
1961				
1962	57	97	69	222
1963	44	94	110	137
1964	65	113	80	154
1965	81	127	83	102
1966	81	147	173	92

Note: Data based on research conducted by Canon (1974, 705, figure 3).

TABLE A3.8. *Supporting Data for Figure 5.11*

Year	Number of Executions	Year	Number of Executions
1930	155	1969	0
1931	153	1970	0
1932	140	1971	0
1933	160	1972	0
1934	168	1973	0
1935	199	1974	0
1936	195	1975	0
1937	147	1976	0
1938	190	1977	1
1939	160	1978	0
1940	124	1979	2
1941	123	1980	0
1942	147	1981	1
1943	131	1982	2
1944	120	1983	5
1945	117	1984	21
1946	131	1985	18
1947	153	1986	18
1948	119	1987	25
1949	119	1988	11
1950	82	1989	16
1951	105	1990	23
1952	83	1991	14
1953	62	1992	31
1954	81	1993	38
1955	76	1994	31
1956	65	1995	56
1957	65	1996	45
1958	49	1997	74
1959	49	1998	68
1960	56	1999	98
1961	42	2000	85
1962	47	2001	66
1963	21	2002	71
1964	15	2003	65
1965	7	2004	59
1966	1	2005	60
1967	2	2006	53
1968	0		

Note: Data compiled by Bureau of Justice Statistics (2006).

TABLE A3.9. *Supporting Data for Figure 5.12*

Year	Prisoners under Death Sentence	Year	Prisoners under Death Sentence
1953	131	1970	631
1954	147	1971	642
1955	125	1972	334
1956	146	1973	134
1957	151	1974	244
1958	147	1975	488
1959	164	1976	420
1960	212	1977	423
1961	257	1978	482
1962	267	1979	593
1963	297	1980	692
1964	315	1981	860
1965	331	1982	1,066
1966	406	1983	1,209
1967	435	1984	1,420
1968	517	1985	1,575
1969	575		

Note: Data compiled by Bureau of Justice Statistics (2006).

TABLE A3.10. *Supporting Data for Figure 5.13*

Year	Tribal-State Compacts		Year	Tribal-State Compacts	
	Revenue Sharing	No Revenue Sharing		Revenue Sharing	No Revenue Sharing
1989	0	5	1998	5	13
1990	0	4	1999	44	2
1991	0	15	2000	5	7
1992	2	23	2001	1	8
1993	1	27	2002	1	3
1994	2	9	2003	6	0
1995	12	16	2004	6	1
1996	0	8	2005	7	1
1997	4	1	2006	2	0

Note: Data compiled by Scalia (2000, 13).

TABLE A3.11. *Supporting Data for Figure 5.14*

| Year | Defendants Charged with Possession of a Firearm in a School Zone | |
	# of Charges	# of Charges Per 10,000 Firearm Charges
1992	55	72
1993	28	40
1994	4	5
1995	9	12
1996	59	95
1997	64	107
1998	80	125
1999	108	151

Note: Data compiled by Scalia (2000, 13).

TABLE A3.12. *Supporting Data for Figure 6.1*

Year	Average % Difference Between Least and Most Populous Congressional District	Year	Average % Difference Between Least and Most Populous Congressional District
1953–54	90.16009	1969–70	24.17076
1955–56	90.16009	1971–72	24.17076
1957–58	90.16009	1973–74	2.300706
1959–60	90.16009	1975–76	1.905191
1961–62	90.16009	1977–78	1.905191
1963–64	106.5705	1979–80	1.905191
1965–66	82.50745	1981–82	1.905191
1967–68	26.03942	1983–84	1.092303

Note: Data based on reports of censorship in ALA (1970–1995).

TABLE A3.13. *Supporting Data for Figure 6.2*

Year	Majority-Black Districts	Majority-Hispanic Districts	Year	Majority-Black Districts	Majority-Hispanic Districts
1962	4		1984	17	9
1964	6		1986	17	9
1966	6		1988	17	9
1968	7		1990	17	9
1970	7		1992	32	20
1972	12	3	1994	32	20
1974	12	3	1996	27	19
1976	12	3	1998	26	18
1978	12	3	2000		
1980	12	3	2002		
1982	14	9	2004	25	25

Note: Data based on data compiled by Adler (2003).

TABLE A3.14. *Supporting Data for Figure 6.3*

Congressional Session	# of Congressional Vetoes	Congressional Session	# of Congressional Vetoes
93rd	4	102nd	0
94th	51	103rd	0
95th	12	104th	0
96th	14	105th	0
97th	18	106th	0
98th pre-6/83	12	107th	0
98th post-6/83	0	108th	0
99th	0	109th	0

Note: Data based on a search of the THOMAS search engine on the Library of Congress Web site.

TABLE A3.15. *Supporting Data for Figure 6.4*

Year	Number of Private School Students Receiving Title I Services
1984–85	185,000
1985–86	123,000
1986–87	138,000
1987–88	142,000
1988–89	151,000
1989–90	160,000
1990–91	159,000
1991–92	168,000

Note: Data based on a study conducted by GAO (1993, 32).

TABLE A3.16. *Supporting Data for Figure 6.5*

Year	# of Employees	% of Employees
1982	396	5.4
1983	396	5.4
1984	401	5.3
1985	7,695	100
1986	7,938	100
1987	8,107	100
1988	8,286	100
1989	8,494	100

Note: Data compiled by the Employment Standards Administration (1983–1990).

TABLE A3.17. *Supporting Data for Figure 7.1*

School Year	% of Blacks in School with Whites	
	Border States	Southern States
1954–55	2.9	0.001
1955–56	11.3	0.115
1956–57	39.6	0.144
1957–58	41.4	0.151
1958–59	44.3	0.132
1959–60	45.4	0.051
1960–61	49	0.162
1961–62	52.5	0.241
1962–63	51.8	0.453
1963–64	54.8	1.17
1964–65		
1965–66	65.6	7.5
1966–67	67.8	24.4

Note: Data based on Rosenberg (1991).

TABLE A3.18. *Supporting Data for Figure 7.2*

Year	Reports of Censorship in NIF	Year	Reports of Censorship in NIF
1970	6	1983	17
1971	11	1984	13
1972	7	1985	17
1973	9	1986	11
1974	16	1987	9
1975	18	1988	9
1976	22	1989	9
1977	16	1990	8
1978	19	1991	10
1979	12	1992	20
1980	13	1993	25
1981	16	1994	15
1982	18	1995	17

Note: Data based on reports of censorship in ALA (1970–1995).

TABLE A3.19. *Supporting Data for Figure 7.3*

Year	Reports of Censorship		Year	Reports of Censorship	
	Non-South	South		Non-South	South
1977	3	13	1987	6	3
1978	5	14	1988	2	7
1979	2	10	1989	5	4
1980	6	7	1990	0	8
1981	4	12	1991	2	8
1982	7	11	1992	10	10
1983	4	13	1993	4	21
1984	3	10	1994	5	10
1985	4	13	1995	7	10
1986	4	7			

Note: Data based on reports of censorship in ALA (1970–1995).

Appendix IV

Statistical Analysis on the Effects of the *Pico* Ruling

TABLE A4.1. *Regression Estimates of Books Censored on* Pico *Ruling*

	Model 1	Model 2
Pico ruling	−7.52**	−7.34*
	(3.64)	(3.68)
# of years since *Pico* ruling	–	−.35
		(.35)
# of years since reports started	.56**	.74**
	(.24)	(.35)
Constant	10.71***	9.66***
	(1.94)	(2.45)
R-squared	.189	.208
Sample size	26	26
F-test	.090	.156

Note: This table reports coefficient estimates for regressions of reports of book censorship on the *Pico* ruling, the number of years since the *Pico* ruling, and the number of years since the reports started. The dependent variable is the number of reports of book censorship each year as reported in the *Newsletter on Intellectual Freedom* (NIF); ALA 1970–1995). Standard errors listed in parentheses.
*p < .10 **p < .05 ***p < .01.

Appendix V

Behavior Conformity Calculations

THE RELIGIOUS FREEDOM RESTORATION ACT

Conservative estimate: 95.2%
  11.8 (percentage point decrease in successful free exercise claims after
  Boerne) / 12.4 (percentage point difference between free exercise success rate before and after *Smith*)
Generous estimate: 98.5%
  129 (number of cases in which courts of appeals complied with *Boerne*
  ruling) / 131 (number of cases in which courts of appeals considered
  free exercise claims after *Boerne*)

THE PENTAGON PAPERS CASE

Conservative and generous estimates: 100%
  The Pentagon Papers were freely published

ABORTION

Conservative estimate: 54.6%
  180.62 (decrease in difference between abortion rates in states with no
  or light restrictions and states with heavy or total restriction from 1972
  to 1975) / 331.08 (difference between abortion rates in states with no
  or light restrictions and states with heavy or total restriction in 1972) =
  54.6%
Generous estimate: 100%
  No convictions under abortion statutes after *Roe*

FLAG DESECRATION

Conservative estimate: 100%
> Drastic increase in frequency of flag burning incidents after *Texas v. Johnson*

Generous estimate: 100%
> No convictions under flag desecration statutes after *Texas v. Johnson*

OBSCENITY

Conservative and generous estimates: 100%
> No convictions under the CDA after *Reno v. ACLU* and no convictions under COPA after *Ashcroft v. ACLU*

THE EXCLUSIONARY RULE

Conservative estimate: 75%
> Officers reporting more adherence to legality in searches after *Mapp* = 75%

Generous estimate: 100%
> The ruling was "wholly successful" at imposing the exclusionary rule on those states not yet applying it

MIRANDA WARNINGS

Conservative estimate: 40%
> 40 (percentage point increase in suspects read Miranda warnings after *Miranda* according to Wald [1967]) / 100 (percent of suspects not read warnings before *Miranda* according to Wald [1967]) = 40%

Generous estimate: 100%
> 50 (number of suspects read Miranda warnings after *Miranda*) / 50 (all defendants) = 100%

WARRANTLESS EAVESDROPPING

Conservative estimate and generous estimate: 100%
> No wiretaps conducted after *Berger* except for intelligence purposes and no wiretaps conducted after U.S. District Court except for intelligence purposes involving a foreign power

THE RIGHT TO COUNSEL

Conservative estimate: 54.2%
> 39 (percentage point increase in population served by public defender office after *Gideon*) / 72 (percent of population not served by public defender office before *Gideon*) = 54.2%

Generous estimate: 100%
> No reports of defendants denied counsel after *Gideon*

CAPITAL PUNISHMENT

Conservative estimate: 79%
> 134 (people on death row after *Furman*) / 642 (people on death row before *Furman*) = 79%

Generous estimate: 99%
> 633 (people reported released from death row by Radelet [n.d.]) / 642 (people on death row before *Furman*) = 99%

FREE PRESS IN THE COURTROOM

Conservative estimate: 23.5%
> 2.7 (decrease in average monthly courtroom closures after *Richmond Newspapers*) / 11.8 (average monthly courtroom closures before *Richmond Newspapers*)

Generous estimate: 100%
> Assumes the decrease was exactly the type of small change the Court intended

SOVEREIGN IMMUNITY

Conservative estimate: 63.9%
> 61.4 (percentage point decrease in tribal-state compacts without revenue-sharing agreements after *Seminole Tribe*) / 96.1 (percent of tribal-state compacts without revenue-sharing agreements before *Seminole Tribe*)

Generous estimate: 100%
> Drastic increase in tribal-state compacts with revenue-sharing provisions

THE GUN-FREE SCHOOL ZONES ACT

Conservative estimate: 93%
> 51 (decrease in the annual number of federal charges for possession of a firearm on school property after Fifth Circuit ruling in *Lopez*) / 55 (annual number of federal charges for possession of a firearm on school property before Fifth Circuit ruling in *Lopez*)

Generous estimate: 100%
> No federal convictions for possession of a firearm on school property after *Lopez*

REAPPORTIONMENT

Conservative and generous estimates: 97.9%
> 104.3 (percentage point decrease in average percent difference between least and most populous congressional district in each state after *Wesberry*) / 107 (average percent difference between least and most populous congressional district in each state before *Wesberry*) = 97.9%

MAJORITY-MINORITY CONGRESSIONAL DISTRICTS

Conservative estimate: 40%
  6 (decrease in number of majority-black congressional districts after *Miller*) / 15 (increase in majority-black congressional districts after 1990 census) = 40%
Generous estimate: 100%
  All congressional districts ordered redrawn were redrawn

THE LEGISLATIVE VETO

Conservative and generous estimates: 100%
  No resolutions disapproving of executive actions after the *Chadha* ruling

PUBLIC AID TO RELIGIOUS SCHOOLS

Conservative and generous estimates: 100%
  Every school district studied complied with the *Aguilar* ruling

AFFIRMATIVE ACTION IN COLLEGE ADMISSIONS

Conservative and generous estimates: 100%
  3 (number of schools ending use of point systems after *Gratz*) / 3 (number of schools using point systems before *Gratz*) = 100%

STUDENT RELIGIOUS PUBLICATIONS AT PUBLIC UNIVERSITIES

Conservative and generous estimates: 29%
  Percent of schools that excluded religious groups from their funding pools before *Rosenberger* that stopped this practice after the ruling

MINIMUM WAGE FOR STATE EMPLOYEES

Conservative and generous estimates: 94.7%
  Percent of state and local government employees excluded from application of the FLSA after *National League of Cities*

BUSH V. GORE

Conservative and generous estimate: 100%
  The recount stopped, and George Bush became President of the United States

SCHOOL DESEGREGATION

Border States:
Conservative and generous estimates: 37.8%

36.7 (percentage point increase in blacks in school w/whites after *Brown II*) / 97.1 (percent of blacks not in school w/whites before *Brown II*) = 37.8%

Deep South:

Conservative and generous estimates: 0.14%

0.144 (percentage point increase in blacks in school w/whites after *Brown II*) / ~100 (percent of blacks not in school w/whites before *Brown II*) = 0.14%

SCHOOL PRAYER

Conservative estimate for each region calculated by Dolbeare and Hammond (1971):

North = 93%
Midwest = 54%
West = 62%
South = 21%

Generous estimate calculated for each region by dividing percentage point reduction in reports of school prayer from Way (1968) by percent reporting school prayer before ruling:

North = 81.4%
Midwest = 44.7%
West = 64.3%
South = 26.4%

CENSORSHIP IN PUBLIC EDUCATION

Conservative estimate: 18.3%

1.3 (percentage point decrease in schools reporting restriction or removal per year after *Pico*) / 5.8 (percent of schools reporting restriction of removal per year before *Pico*)

Generous estimate: 41.7%

7.5 (estimate of the effect of the *Pico* ruling on decrease in reports of censorship reported in the *NIF* [ALA 1970–1995]) / 18 (number of reports of censorship in the *NIF* [ALA 1970–1995] the year *Pico* was issued)

MINORITY SET-ASIDE PROGRAMS

Conservative estimate: 31%

73 (number of jurisdictions reported complying with *Croson*) / 236 (number of jurisdictions operating minority set-aside programs before *Croson*) = 31%

Generous estimate: 100%

Every city surveyed complied with *Croson* ruling

CONGRESSIONAL EXCLUSION

Conservative and generous estimates: 100%

Powell retained his seat, and Congress never excluded a member for reasons other than age, citizenship, and residency requirements after the *Powell* ruling

THE BRADY BILL

Conservative estimate: 21.5%

67 (decrease in responses to survey of CLEOs regarding background checks after *Printz*) / 311 (number of responses to survey of CLEOs before *Printz*)

Generous estimate: 0%

No significant decrease in background checks after *Printz*

Appendix VI

Statistical Analysis of Behavior Conformity

In Chapter 3, I hypothesize that the probability of the Supreme Court achieving high behavior conformity when issuing a ruling will increase when one of the following conditions has been met:

(1) The Court issues a ruling in a vertical issue area, or
(2) The Court issues a popular ruling in a lateral issue area.

However, the probability of the Court achieving high behavior conformity will decrease when:

(3) The Court issues an unpopular ruling in a lateral issue area.

This hypothesis can be formally stated as:

$$\mu_i = \alpha + \beta_1 \, lateral + \beta_2 \, lateral \times popularity + \varepsilon$$

where μ is the average behavior conformity, α is a constant, *lateral* is an indicator variable for lateral issues, *lateral* $\times$ *popularity* is an interaction term between an indicator variable for lateral issues and a trichotomous indicator variable indicating the popularity of the Court's ruling, β_1 and β_2 are coefficients for the effects of these two variables, and ε is the unobserved disturbance. I code the trichotomous indicator variable as 1 if less than 30 percent of respondents in national public opinion surveys indicate opposition to the Court's ruling; as 0 if more than 70 percent of respondents indicate opposition, and as 0.5 otherwise. For those Supreme Court cases in which no national public opinion poll was conducted, I assume the Court faces little public opposition and code the trichotomous indicator variable as 1.

For each of the issue areas studied in Chapters 4, 5, 6, and 7, I calculate the degree to which behavior conformed to the Court's preferences;[1] my measure of behavior conformity is an estimate of the Court's causal effect on the most relevant behavior outcome in that issue area. In order to formulate a skeptical test of judicial power, I always choose the conformity rate least supportive

[1] See Appendix 5.

of my theory to use as the conservative estimate of behavior conformity. I use more generous estimates of conformity to run an alternate regression analysis. This alternate analysis offers a more generous evaluation of my theory.

Behavior conformity was calculated in three different ways depending on the issue area studied. First, for cases in which the Court ordered government actors to cease a particular behavior, I used the best measure of that behavior immediately before the decision as a baseline and calculated the percentage decrease after the ruling. For example, in order to calculate behavior conformity to the Court's capital punishment ruling, I measure the number of people on death row the year before the ruling (642) and compare it to the number of people on death row the year after the ruling (134). This change reflects a 79 percent decrease in the behavior proscribed by the Court, so I code the behavior conformity to the capital punishment ruling as 79 percent. Note that this is a very conservative estimate of the Court's effect. I could argue that because Radelet (n.d.) reports 633 people having their sentences commuted after the *Furman* ruling, the correct behavior conformity is 99 percent (633/642). I could also argue that the correct behavior conformity is 100 percent because the Court ordered no one be executed between 1972 and 1976, and no one was executed during this period.

Second, for cases in which the Court ordered government actors to engage in a particular behavior, I use the best measure of those not engaged in that behavior before the ruling and calculate the percentage point increase in the behavior after the ruling. For example, in order to calculate behavior conformity to the Court's desegregation ruling in the Border States, I measure the percent of African-American students not in school with whites the year before *Brown II* (97.1%) and compare it to the percentage point increase of African-American students in school with whites after the ruling (36.6 percentage points). This change reflects a 37.8 percent increase (36.6/97.1 = 37.8%) in the behavior prescribed by the Court, so I code the behavior conformity to the desegregation ruling as 37.8 percent in the Border States. I repeat this process to calculate behavior conformity to the desegregation ruling in the Deep South.

Third, for cases in which the Court prohibited the criminalization of a particular behavior, I measure the difference between the frequency of this behavior in places where the behavior was legal and places where it was not before the ruling and calculate the percentage decrease in this difference after the ruling. For example, in order to calculate behavior conformity to the Court's abortion ruling, I measure the difference between abortion rates in states with no or light abortion restrictions and states with heavy abortion restrictions before *Roe* (331.08) and compare it to the difference in abortion rates between these two groups of states after *Roe* (150.46). This change reflects a 54.6 percent decrease (180.62/331.08 = 54.6%) in the difference between these groups, so I code behavior conformity to the abortion ruling as 54.6 percent. Once again, this is an extremely conservative estimate of behavior conformity because there is no reason to assume that the underlying propensity to obtain an abortion once the practice is legalized is uniform across these two groups.

TABLE A6.1. *Regression Estimates of Behavior Conformity on Issue Type and Popularity*

	Conservative Behavior Conformity Regressions		Generous Behavior Conformity Regressions	
Lateral issue	−38.3*	−38.7*	−75.5***	−77.6***
	(21.1)	(21.1)	(12.0)	(11.3)
Popularity	0.9	–	5.4	–
	(18.2)		(6.0)	
Lateral* popularity	43.5	44.3***	68.8***	74.2***
	(31.3)	(25.1)	(16.0)	(14.6)
Constant	75.5***	75.8***	95.8***	97.9***
	(9.4)	(7.2)	(4.1)	(1.9)
R-squared	.179	.179	.650	.648
N	31	31	31	31
F-test	.359	.195	.000	.000

Note: This table reports coefficient estimates for regressions on Supreme Court power cases. The dependent variable is the conservative or generous estimate of behavior conformity as indicated. Standard errors, clustered by ruling, listed in parentheses.
*p < .05 **p < .01 ***p < .001.

For my generous estimate of behavior conformity, I code the abortion issue area as having 100 percent conformity because there is no record of a doctor being convicted under a criminal abortion code in violation of *Roe*.

The regression analysis of behavior conformity is presented in Table A6.1. The first two columns report regression results using conservative behavior conformity as the dependent variable; the third and fourth columns report results using generous behavior conformity as the dependant variable. The regression analyses reported in the first and third columns include an independent variable for the popularity of each ruling; because the coefficients for this variable are not substantively or statistically significant in either model, they are not included in the analyses reported in the second and fourth columns.

As reported in the second column of Table A6.1, both independent variables of interest are substantively significant. The results near conventional levels of statistical significance for conservative estimates of conformity and easily meet these levels for generous estimates. Because Court rulings in vertical issues are the excluded category, the constant represents the average conformity rate in those issue areas. Based on this regression analysis, when the Court issues a ruling in a vertical issue area, on average it causes 75.5 percent of relevant behavior to conform to its preferences (using conservative conformity estimates). When the Court issues a popular ruling in a lateral issue area, on average it causes 80.7 percent of relevant behavior to conform to its preferences (75.5 − 38.3 + 43.5 = 80.7). When it issues an unpopular ruling in a lateral issue area, on average it causes only 37.2 percent of relevant behavior to conform to its preferences (75.5 − 38.3 = 17). Not surprisingly, the results of the regression analyses based on generous estimates of behavior conformity provide even stronger support for my theory of Supreme Court power. It is also worth noting that the size and statistical significance of the coefficients greatly improve if the rather unusual Brady Bill case is thrown out (the Brady Bill case is unusual because the conservative estimate of behavior conformity is 100%, whereas the generous estimate is 0%, causing radically different interpretations of the case's fit with the expectations of the model).

Appendix VII

The Effects of Unanimity on Behavior Conformity

Some scholars have suggested that the Supreme Court may wield greater influence when the justices are more united in their rulings.[1] The Court may be most powerful when it issues unanimous rulings and least powerful when the Court is sharply divided. This expectation is inconsistent with my theory of Supreme Court power because the divisions on the Court are unrelated to the institutional context of the ruling and the popularity of the ruling. Nonetheless, in this appendix I test the relationship between unanimity on the Court and behavior conformity to the Court's rulings in order to test this alternate theory.

To test this relationship, I repeat the analysis conducted in Appendix VI and add a new independent variable, # of Dissenters, to the regression analysis. The # of Dissenters variable is coded as the number of justices who dissented from the critical Supreme Court ruling studied in each issue area (i.e., the # of Dissenters variable is coded as a 2 for the abortion issue area because there were two dissenting justices in Roe v. Wade). Table A7.1 reports the results of regressing conservative and generous estimates of behavior conformity on the # of Dissenters with and without controls for the institutional context and popularity of the ruling. A negative coefficient for # of Dissenters would indicate that more unanimity on the Court is associated with greater behavior conformity; however, the coefficient for # of Dissenters is not statistically significant, nor is the sign in the expected direction in any of the regression models reported in the table. Based on these findings, I conclude that there is no relationship between unanimity on the Supreme Court and the Court's power.

[1] See Johnson (1979) for an analysis and rejection of this theory.

TABLE A7.1. *Regression Estimates of Behavior Conformity on Number of Dissenters, Issue Type and Popularity*

	Conservative Behavior Conformity Regressions		Generous Behavior Conformity Regressions	
# of dissenters	4.0	−0.8	5.4	−0.4
	(4.4)	(3.9)	(5.0)	(2.3)
Lateral issue	–	−59.5**	–	−78.9**
		(14.9)		(11.1)
Popularity	–	1.3	–	5.6
		(19.0)		(6.3)
Lateral* popularity	–	74.9*	–	80.4**
		(22.2)		(11.3)
Constant	58.8**	77.4**	68.9	96.6**
	(12.7)	(14.7)	(15.8)	(6.4)
R-squared	.038	.452	.074	.786
N	30	30	30	30
F-test	.371	.000	.292	.000

Note: This table reports coefficient estimates for regressions on Supreme Court power cases. The dependent variable is the conservative or generous estimate of behavior conformity as indicated. Standard errors, clustered by ruling, are listed in parentheses.
*p < .01 **p < .001.

Case References

Abington School District v. Schempp. 1963. 374 U.S. 203.
Adarand Constructors v. Pena. 1995. 515 U.S. 200.
Agostini v. Felton. 1997. 521 U.S. 203.
Aguilar v. Felton. 1985. 521 U.S. 203.
Alden v. Maine. 1999. 527 U.S. 706.
American Civil Liberties Union v. Ashcroft. 2003. 322 F.3d 240 (3rd Cir.)
American Civil Liberties Union v. Reno. 2000. 217 F.3d 162 (3rd Cir.)
Argersinger v. Hamlin. 1972. 407 U.S. 25.
Ashcroft v. American Civil Liberties Union. 2002. 535 U.S. 564.
Ashcroft v. American Civil Liberties Union. 2004. 542 U.S. 656.
Baker v. Carr. 1962. 369 U.S. 186.
Benton v. Maryland. 1969. 395 U.S. 784.
Berger v. New York. 1967. 388 U.S. 41.
Betts v. Brady. 1942. 316 U.S. 455.
Board of Education of Westside Community Schools v. Mergens. 1990. 496 U.S. 226.
Board of Education v. Allen. 1968. 392 U.S. 236.
Board of Education v. Pico. 1982. 457 U.S. 853.
Bolling v. Sharpe. 1954. 347 U.S. 497.
Boyd v. United States. 1886. 116 U.S. 616.
Brandenburg v. Ohio. 1969. 395 U.S. 444.
Brown v. Board of Education (I). 1954. 347 U.S. 483.
Brown v. Board of Education (II). 1955. 349 U.S. 294.
Burdeau v. McDowell. 1921. 256 U.S. 465.
Bush v. Gore. 2000. 531 U.S. 98.
Bush v. Vera. 1996. 517 U.S. 952.
Califano v. Westcott. 1972. 443 U.S. 76.
California v. Cabazon Band of Indians. 1987. 480 U.S. 202.
Cantwell v. Connecticut. 1940. 310 U.S. 296.
Chimel v. California. 1969. 395 U.S. 752.
Chisholm v. Georgia. 1793. 2 U.S. 419.
Christians v. Crystal Evangelical Free Church. 1998. 141 F.3d 854.
City of Alexandria v. United States. 1984. 737 F.2d 1022 (C.A.F.C.)
City of Boerne v. Flores. 1997. 521 U.S. 507.

City of Richmond v. J.A. Croson Co. 1989. 422 U.S. 358.
Civil Rights Cases. 1883. 109 U.S. 3.
Clinton v. New York. 1998. 524 U.S. 417.
Coleman v. Alabama. 1970. 377 U.S. 129.
Dickerson v. United States. 2000. 530 U.S. 428.
Douglas v. California. 1963. 372 U.S. 353.
Dred Scott v. Sandford. 1857. 60 U.S. 393.
Employment Division v. Smith. 1990. 494 U.S. 872.
Engel v. Vitale. 1959. 191 N.Y.S.2d 453.
Engel v. Vitale. 1962. 370 U.S. 421.
Escobedo v. Illinois. 1964. 378 U.S. 478.
Everson v. Board of Education. 1947. 330 U.S. 1.
Ex Parte McCardle. 1869. 74 U.S. 506.
Fitzpatrick v. Bitzer. 1976. 427 U.S. 445.
Furman v. Georgia. 1972. 408 U.S. 238.
Gagnon v. Scarpelli. 1973. 411 U.S. 778.
Garcia v. San Antonio Transit Authority. 1985. 469 U.S. 528.
Gideon v. Wainwright. 1963. 372 U.S. 335.
Gitlow v. New York. 1925. 268 U.S. 652.
Gore v. Harris. 2000. 777 So. 2d 1243.
Grand Rapids v. Ball. 1985. 473 U.S. 373.
Gratz v. Bollinger. 2003. 539 U.S. 244.
Gregg v. Georgia. 1976. 428 U.S. 153.
Grutter v. Bollinger. 2003. 539 U.S. 306.
Home Building & Loan Association v. Blaisdel. 1934. 290 U.S. 398.
Immigration and Naturalization Service v. Chadha. 1983. 462 U.S. 919.
In re Gault. 1967. 387 U.S. 1.
Katz v. United States. 1967. 389 U.S. 347.
Katzenbach v. Morgan. 1966. 384 U.S. 641.
Lamb's Chapel v. Center Moriches School District. 1993. 508 U.S. 384.
Lamont v. Postmaster General. 1965. 381 U.S. 301.
Lawrence v. Texas. 2003. 539 U.S. 558.
Lee v. Weisman. 1992. 505 U.S. 577.
Lemon v. Kurtzman. 1971. 403 U.S. 602.
Lucas v. Forty-Fourth General Assembly of Colorado. 1964. 377 U.S. 713.
Mack v. United States. 1995. 66 F.3d 1025.
Malloy v. Hogan. 1964. 378 U.S. 1.
Mapp v. Ohio. 1961. 367 U.S. 643.
Marbury v. Madison. 1803. 5 U.S. 137.
Miller v. California. 1973. 413 U.S. 15.
Miller v. Johnson. 1995. 515 U.S. 900.
Miranda v. Arizona. 1966. 384 U.S. 436.
Morrissey v. Brewer. 1972. 408 U.S. 471.
Nardone v. United States. 1937. 302 U.S. 379.
National Labor Relations Board v. Jones & Laughlin Steel Corp. 1937. 301 U.S. 1.
National League of Cities v. Usery. 1975. 426 U.S. 833.
Near v. Minnesota. 1931. 283 U.S. 697.
Nebraska Press Association v. Stuart. 1976. 427 U.S. 539.

New York v. Ferber. 1982. 458 U.S. 747.
New York Times v. Sullivan. 1964. 376 U.S. 254.
New York Times v. United States. 1971. 403 U.S. 713.
Olmstead v. United States. 1928. 277 U.S. 438.
Oregon v. Mitchell. 1970. 400 U.S. 112.
Palko v. Connecticut. 1937. 302 U.S. 319.
Parents Involved in Community Schools v. Seattle School District No. 1. 2007. 127
    S. Ct. 2738.
Pennsylvania v. Nelson. 1956. 350 U.S. 497.
People v. Dorado. 1965. 62 Cal. 2d 338.
Plaut v. Spendthrift Farm, Inc. 1995. 514 U.S. 211.
Pollock v. Farmers' Loan & Trust Co. 1895. 157 U.S. 429.
Powell v. McCormack. 1969. 395 U.S. 486.
Printz v. United States. 1997. 521 U.S. 898.
Regents of the University of California v. Bakke. 1978. 438 U.S. 265.
Reno v. American Civil Liberties Union. 1997. 521 U.S. 844.
Reynolds v. Sims. 1964. 377 U.S. 533.
Richmond Newspapers, Inc. v. Virginia. 1980. 448 U.S. 555.
Rios v. United States. 1960. 364 U.S. 253.
Roe v. Wade. 1973. 410 U.S. 113.
Roper v. Simmons. 2005. 543 U.S. 551.
Rosenberger v. University of Virginia. 1995. 515 U.S. 819.
Santa Fe Independent School District v. Doe. 2000. 530 U.S. 290.
Seminole Tribe v. Florida. 1996. 517 U.S. 44.
Seminole Tribe of Florida v. Butterworth. 1981. 658 F.2d 310 (5th Cir).
Shapiro v. Thompson. 1969. 394 U.S. 618.
Shaw v. Hunt. 1996. 517 U.S. 899.
Shaw v. Reno. 1993. 509 U.S. 630.
Sherbert v. Verner. 1963. 374 U.S. 398.
Silverman v. United States. 1961. 365 U.S. 505.
South Carolina v. Katzenbach. 1966. 383 U.S. 301.
Steward Machine Co. v. Davis. 1937. 301 U.S. 548.
Sutton v. Providence St. Joseph Medical Center. 1999. 192 F. 3d. 826.
Texas v. Johnson. 1989. 491 U.S. 397.
Thomas v. Collins. 1945. 323 U.S. 516.
Tinker v. Des Moines Independent School District. 1969. 393 U.S. 503.
United States v. Eichman. 1990. 496 U.S. 310.
United States v. Lee. 1982. 455 U.S. 252.
United States v. Lopez. 1993. 2 F.3d 1342 (5th Cir).
United States v. Lopez. 1995. 514 U.S. 549.
United States v. Morrison. 2000. 529 U.S. 598.
United States v. U.S. District Court. 1972. 407 U.S. 297.
United States v. Wade. 1967. 388 U.S. 218.
Wallace v. Jaffree. 1985. 472 U.S. 38.
Walz v. Tax Commission of the City of New York. 1970. 397 U.S. 664.
Weeks v. United States. 1914. 232 U.S. 383.
Wesberry v. Sanders. 1964. 376 U.S. 1.
West Coast Hotel v. Parrish. 1937. 300 U.S. 379.

West Virginia Board of Education v. Barnette. 1943. 319 U.S. 624.
Widmar v. Vincent. 1981. 454 U.S. 263.
Williamson v. Lee Optical. 1955. 348 U.S. 483.
Wolf v. Colorado. 1949. 338 U.S. 25.
Worcester v. Georgia. 1831. 31 U.S. 515.

References

Abel, C. F., and Hans J. Hacker. 2006. "Local Compliance with Supreme Court Decisions: Making Space for Religious Expression in Public Schools." *Journal of Church and State* 48(2):355–77.

Ackerman, Bruce, ed. 2002. *Bush v. Gore: The Question of Legitimacy.* New Haven: Yale University Press.

Adamany, David. 1973. "Legitimacy, Realigning Elections and the Supreme Court." *Wisconsin Law Review* 1973:790–846.

Adamczyk, Amy, John Wybraniec, and Roger Finke. 2004. "Religious Regulation and the Courts: Documenting the Effects of *Smith* and RFRA." *The Journal of Church and State* 46:237–62.

Adler, Scott. 2003. "Congressional District Data File." University of Colorado, Boulder, CO. http://socsci.colorado.edu/~esadler/districtdatawebsite/Congressional-DistrictDatasetwebpage.htm.

American Library Association (ALA). 1970–95. *The Newsletter on Intellectual Freedom.* Chicago: Intellectual Freedom Committee of the American Library Association.

Ansolabehere, Stephen, Alan Gerber, and James Snyder. 2002. "Equal Votes, Equal Money: Court-Ordered Redistricting and Public Expenditures in the American States." *American Political Science Review* 96(4):767–77.

Ansolabehere, Stephen and James Snyder. 2008. *The End of Inequality: One Person, One Vote, and the Transformation of American Politics.* New York: Norton.

Arkes, Hadley. 1992. *First Things.* Princeton: Princeton University Press.

Association of American Publishers, American Library Association, Association for Supervision and Curriculum Development (AAP). 1981. *Limiting What Students Shall Read: Books and Other Learning Materials in Our Public Schools: How they Are Selected and How They Are Removed.* Washington: Association of American Publishers.

Ball, Howard. 2000. *The Bakke Case: Race, Education, and Affirmative Action.* University Press of Kansas.

Ban, Michael. 1973a. "The Impact of *Mapp v. Ohio* on Police Behavior." Paper presented at the annual meeting of the Midwest Political Science Association, Chicago, IL, May.

1973b. "Local Courts v. The Supreme Court: The Impact of *Mapp v. Ohio.*" Paper presented at the annual meeting of the American Political Science Association, New Orleans, LA, September.

Banks, Christopher P., Michael E. Cohen, and John Clifford Green, eds. 2005. *The Final Arbiter: The Consequences of* Bush v. Gore *for Law and Politics.* Albany: State University of New York Press.

Barreto, Matt A., Gary M. Segura, and Nathan D. Woods. 2004. "The Mobilizing Effect of Majority-Minority Districts on Latino Turnout." *American Political Science Review* 98(1):65–75.

Bartley N. V. 1969. *The Rise of Massive Resistance: Race and Politics in the South during the 1950's.* Baton Rouge: Louisiana State University Press.

Baum, Lawrence. 2003. "The Supreme Court in American Politics." *Annual Review of Political Science* 6:161–80.

Bazelon, David. L. 1976. "The Realities of *Gideon* and *Argersinger.*" *Georgetown Law Journal* 64:811–38.

Beaney, William M. and Edward N. Beiser. 1964. "Prayer and Politics: The Impact of *Engel* and *Schempp* on the Political Process." *Journal of Public Law* 13:475–503.

Bedau, Hugo Adam. 1998. The Death Penalty in America: Current Controversies. Oxford University Press.

Benesh, Sarah C. and Malia Reddick. 2002. "Overruled: An Event History Analysis of Lower Court Reaction to Supreme Court Precedent." *Journal of Politics* 64(2):534–50.

Benjamin, Roger W. and Theodore B. Pedeliski. 1969. "The Minnesota Public Defender System and the Criminal Law Process: A Comparative Study of Behavior at the Judicial District Level." *Law & Society Review* 4(2):279–320.

Benner, Laurance A. 1975. "Tokenism and the American Indigent: Some Perspectives on Defense Services." *American Criminal Law Review* 12:667–88.

Berutti, Ronald A. 1992. "The Cherokee Cases: The Fight to Save the Supreme Court and the Cherokee Indians." *American Indian Law Review* 17:291.

Bickel, Alexander. [1962] 1986. *The Least Dangerous Branch.* New Haven: Yale University Press.

Birkby, Robert H. 1966 "The Supreme Court and the Bible Belt: Tennessee Reaction to the 'Schempp' Decision." *Midwest Journal of Political Science* 10(3):304–19.

Bitler, Marianne and Madeline Zavodny. 2002. "Did Abortion Legalization Reduce the Number of Unwanted Children? Evidence from Adoptions." *Perspectives on Sexual and Reproductive Health* 34(1):25–33.

Black, Charles. 1960. *The People and the Court: Judicial Review in a Democracy.* New York: Macmillan.

Blatnik, Edward J. W. 1998. "No RFRAF Allowed: The Status of the Religious Freedom Restoration Act's Federal Application in the Wake of *City of Boerne v. Flores.*" *Columbia Law Review* 98(6):1410–60.

Bradley, Craig. 1993. *The Failure of the Criminal Procedure Revolution.* Philadelphia: University of Pennsylvania Press.

Bravin, Jesse. 2005. "Voting Cases Could Shape Debate Over Alito." *The Wall Street Journal,* November 21.

Brent, James. 1999. "An Agent and Two Principals: U.S. Court of Appeals Reponses to *Employment Division, Department of Human Resources v. Smith* and the Religious Freedom Restoration Act." *American Politics Quarterly* 27(2):236–66.

2003. "A Principal-Agent Analysis of the U.S. Courts of Appeals Responses to *Boerne v. Flores.*" *American Politics Research* 31(5):557–70.

Brosi, Kathleen B. 1979. *A Cross-City Comparison of Felony Case Processing.* Washington: Institute for Law and Social Research.

Bruni, Frank. 2000. "Bush Remains Upbeat as the Tension Mounts." *The New York Times,* November 8.

Bureau of Justice Statistics. 2006. "Capital Punishment, 2006 – Statistical Tables." Washington: Bureau of Justice Statistics. http://www.ojp.usdoj.gov/bjs/glance/exe.htm.

Burress, Lee. 1989. *Battle of the Books: Literary Censorship in the Public Schools, 1950–1985.* Metuchen, NJ: Scarecrow Press.

Caldeira, Gregory A. and James L. Gibson. 1992. "The Etiology of Public Support for the Supreme Court." *American Journal of Political Science* 36(3):635–664.

Caldeira, Gregory A. and Christopher J. W. Zorn. 1998. "Of Time and Consensual Norms in the Supreme Court." *American Journal of Political Science* 42(3): 874–902.

Cameron, Charles, David Epstein, and Sharyn O'Halloran. 1996. "Do Majority-Minority Districts Maximize Substantive Black Representation in Congress?" *American Political Science Review* 90(4):794–812.

Canon, Bradley C. 1974. "Is the Exclusionary Rule in Failing Health? Some New Data and a Plea against a Precipitous Conclusion." *Kentucky Law Journal* 62:703–7.

1977. "Testing the Effectiveness of Civil Liberties Policies at the State and Federal Levels: The Case of the Exclusionary Rule." *American Politics Quarterly* 5(1):57–82.

Canon, Bradley C. and Charles A. Johnson. 1999. *Judicial Policies: Implementation and Impact.* 2nd Ed. Washington, DC: CQ Press.

Casper, Jonathan D. 1976. "The Supreme Court and National Policy Making." *American Political Science Review* 70(1):50–63.

Cassell, Paul G. 1996a. "*Miranda's* Social Costs: An Empirical Reassessment." *Northwestern University Law Review* 90(2): 387.

1996b. "All Benefits, No Costs: The Grand Illusion of *Miranda's* Defenders." *Northwestern University Law Review* 90(3):1084–124.

1997. "*Miranda's* 'Negligible' Effect on Law Enforcement: Some Skeptical Observations." *Harvard Journal of Law and Public Policy* 20(2):327–46.

Cassell, Paul G. and Richard Fowles. 1998a. "Handcuffing the Cops? A Thirty-Year Perspective on *Miranda's* Harmful Effects on Law Enforcement." *Stanford Law Review* 50:1055–2245.

1998b. "Falling Clearance Rates After *Miranda*: Coincidence or Consequence?" *Stanford Law Review* 50:1181–92.

Centers for Disease Control. 1969–2003. "Abortion Surveillance Report." Washington: National Center for Chronic Disease Prevention and Health Promotion, Division of Reproductive Health.

Clayton, Cornell W. and J. Mitchell Pickerill. 2006. "The Politics of Criminal Justice: How the New Right Regime Shaped the Rehnquist Court's Criminal Justice Jurisprudence." *Georgetown Law Journal* 94(June):1385–425.

Clegg, Roger. 2005. "Time Has Not Favored Racial Preferences." *Chronicle of Higher Education* 51(19):B10. January 14.

Comptroller General of the United States. 1979. "Impact of the Exclusionary Rule on Federal Criminal Prosecutions." Washington: General Accounting Office, Rep. No. CDG-79-45.

Congressional Record. 1956. 84th Cong., Vol. 102.

Cox, Gary W. and Jonathon N. Katz. 1999. "The Reapportionment Revolution and Bias in U.S. Congressional Elections." *American Journal of Political Science* 43(3):812–41.

2002. *Elbridge Gerry's Salamander: The Electoral Consequences of the Reapportionment Revolution.* New York: Cambridge University Press.

Cushman, Barry. 1998. *Rethinking the New Deal Court.* New York: Oxford University Press.

Dahl, Robert. 1957. "Decision-Making in a Democracy: The Supreme Court as a National Policy-Maker." *Journal of Public Law* 6:279.

Davies, Thomas Y. 1982. "Affirmed: A Study of Criminal Appeals and Decision-Making Norms in a California Court of Appeal." *American Bar Foundation Research Journal* 7(3):543–648.

1983. "A Hard Look at What We Know (And Still Need to Learn) about the 'Costs' of the Exclusionary Rule: The NIJ Study and Other Studies of 'Lost' Arrests." *American Bar Foundation Research Journal* 8(3):611–90.

Davis, James A., Tom W. Smith, and Peter V. Marsden. 2007. *General Social Surveys, 1972–2006.* Chicago, IL: National Opinion Research Center. Storrs, CT: Roper Center for Public Opinion Research, University of Connecticut / Ann Arbor, MI: Inter-university Consortium for Political and Social Research / Berkeley, CA: Computer-assisted Survey Methods Program (http://sda.berkeley.edu), University of California.

DeFrances, Carol J. 2001. "State-Funded Indigent Defense Services, 1999." Bureau of Justice Statistics. NCJ 188464.

DeVoe, Jill F., Katharin Peter, Phillip Kaufman, Amanda Miller, Thomas D. Snyder, and Katrina Baum. 2004. "Indicators of School Crime and Safety." Washington: National Center for Education Statistics, NCES 2005–002; Bureau of Justice Statistics, NCJ 205290.

Dierenfield, R. B. 1962. *Religion in American Public Schools.* Washington: Public Affairs Press.

DiNardo, John. 2007. "Interesting Questions in *Freakonomics*." *Journal of Economic Literature* XLV:973–1000.

Dionne, E. J., Jr., and William Kristol. 2001. Bush v. Gore: *The Court Cases and the Commentary.* Washington: Brookings Institution Press.

Dolbeare, Kenneth M. and Phillip E. Hammond. 1971. *The School Prayer Decisions: From Court Policy to Local Practice.* Chicago: University of Chicago Press.

Donohue, John J., III. 1998. "Did *Miranda* Diminish Police Effectiveness?" *Stanford Law Review* 50:1147–80.

Donohue, John J., III, and Steven D. Levitt. 2001. "The Impact of Legalized Abortion on Crime." *Quarterly Journal of Economics* CXVI(2):379–420.

2008. "Measurement Error, Legalized Abortion, and the Decline in Crime: A Response to Foote and Goetz." *Quarterly Journal of Economics* 123(1):425–40.

Douglas, William O. 1956. *We, the Judges: Studies in American and Indian Constitutional Law from Marshal to Mukherjea.* Garden City, NY: Doubleday.

Drecksel, Paul Calvin. 1991. "The Crisis in Indigent Defense Systems." *Arkansas Law Review* 44:363–408.

Dreyfuss, Joel and Charles Lawrence. 1979. *The Bakke Case: Politics of Inequality.* New York: Harcourt Brace Jovanovich.

Dudley, Louise M. 1995. "Board Changes Funding Guidelines: Student Religious Publications Now Eligible." *U VaToday*, August 25.

Dworkin, Ronald, ed. 2002. *A Badly Flawed Election: Debating* Bush v. Gore, *the Supreme Court, and American Democracy*. New York: New Press.

Edwards, George C., III. 1980. *Presidential Influence in Congress*. San Francisco: W.H. Freeman.

———. 1985. "Measuring Presidential Success in Congress: Alternative Approaches." *Journal of Politics* 47:667–85.

Employment Standards Administration. 1983–90. "Minimum Wage and Maximum Hours Standards under the Fair Labor Standards Act." Washington: U.S. Department of Labor.

Enemark, Christine E. 1997. "*Adarand Constructors, Inc. v. Pena*: Forcing the Federal Communications Commission into a New Constitutional Regime." *Columbia Journal of Law and Social Problems* 30(2):215–66.

Engel, Stephen. 2009. "A Mere Party Machine"? Judicial Authority, Party Development, and the Changing Politics of Attacking the Courts. Dissertation, Yale University.

Epstein, Lee and Jack Knight. 1998. *The Choices Justices Make*. Congressional Quarterly Press.

Epstein, Lee and Joseph F. Kobylka. 1992. *The Supreme Court and Legal Change: Abortion and the Death Penalty*. Chapel Hill: The University of North Carolina Press.

Epstein, Lee, and Thomas G. Walker. 1995. Constitutional Law for a Changing America: Institutional Powers and Constraints. 2nd ed. Washington, DC: CQ Press.

Eskridge, William N. 1991a. "Reneging on History? Playing the Court/Congress/President Civil Rights Game." *California Law Review* 79(3):613–84.

———. 1991b. "Overriding Supreme Court Statutory Interpretation Decisions." *Yale Journal* 101(2):331–455.

Feeley, Malcom M. 1973. "Power, Impact, and the Supreme Court." In *The Impact of Supreme Court Decisions*, ed. Theodore L. Becker and Malcolm M. Feeley. 2d ed. New York: Oxford University Press.

Feeney, Floyd, Forrest Dill, and Adriane Weir. 1983. "Arrests Without Conviction: How Often They Occur and Why." Washington: National Institute of Justice.

Ferejohn, John. 2002. "Judicializing Politics, Politicizing Law." *Law and Contemporary Problems* 65(3):41–68.

Fisher, Louis. 1993. "The Legislative Veto: Invalidated, It Survives." *Law and Contemporary Problems* 56(4):273–92.

———. 2005. "Legislative Vetoes After *Chadha*." Washington: Congressional Research Service, RS22132.

Fletcher, Matthew L.M. 2007. "Bringing Balance to Indian Gaming." *Harvard Journal on Legislation* 44:39.

Fletcher, William A. 1982. The Discretionary Constitution: Institutional Remedies and Judicial Legitimacy." *Yale Law Journal* 91(4):635–97.

Foote, Christopher L. and Christopher F. Goetz. 2008. "The Impact of Abortion on Crime: Comment." *Quarterly Journal of Economics* 123(1):407–23.

Forst, Brian, Judith Lucianovic, and Sarah J. Cox. 1977. "What Happens After Arrest? A Court Perspective of Police Operations in the District of Columbia." PROMIS Research Project Publication. Washington: Institute for Law and Social Research.

———. 1982. "Arrest Convictability as a Measure of Police Performance." Washington: National Institute of Justice.

Frankfurter, Felix. 1954. *Some Observations on Supreme Court Litigation and Legal Education (The Ernst Freund Lecture)*. University of Chicago Press.

Franklin, Charles H. and Liane C. Kosaki. 1989. "Republican Schoolmaster: the U.S. Supreme Court, Public Opinion, and Abortion." *American Political Science Review* 83(3):751–71 .

Frymer, Paul. 2003. "Acting When Elected Officials Won't: Federal Courts and Civil Rights Enforcement in U.S. Labor Unions." *American Political Science Review* 97(3):483–99.

Funston, Richard. 1975. "The Supreme Court and Critical Elections." *American Political Science Review* 69(3): 795–811.

Gay, Claudine. 2001. "The Effect of Minority Districts and Minority Representation on Political Participation in California." San Francisco, CA: Public Policy Institute of California.

General Accounting Office. 1987. "Compensatory Education: Chapter 1 Services Provided to Private Sectarian School Students." Washington: General Accounting Office, GAO/HRD-87–128BR.

    1989. "Compensatory Education: *Aguilar v. Felton* Decision's Continuing Impact on Chapter 1 Program." Washington: General Accounting Office, GAO/HRD-89–131BR.

    1993. "Compensatory Education: Additional Funds Help More Private School Students Receive Chapter 1 Services." Washington: General Accounting Office, GAO/HRD-93–65.

    1996. "Gun Control: Implementation of the Brady Handgun Violence Prevention Act." Washington: General Accounting Office, GAO/GGD-96–22.

    2000. "Options for Improving the National Instant Criminal Background Check System." Washington: General Accounting Office, GAO/GGD-00–56.

    2001. "Status of Small Disadvantaged Business Certifications." Washington: General Accounting Office, GAO-01–273.

Gillman, Howard. 1993. *The Constitution Besieged: The Rise and Demise of* Lochner *Era Police Powers Jurisprudence*. Durham and London: Duke University Press.

    2000. *The Votes That Counted: How the Court Decided the 2000 Presidential Election*. University of Chicago Press.

    2002. "How Political Parties Can Use the Courts to Advance Their Agendas: Federal Courts in the United States, 1875–1891." *American Political Science Review* 96(3):511–24.

Glater, Jonathan D. 2006. "Colleges Open Minority Aid to All Comers." *The New York Times*, March 14.

Goldman, Jerry. 2005. "The Canon of Constitutional Law Revisited." *Law and Politics Book Review* 15(8):648–56.

Goldstein, Robert Justin. 1995. "Two Centuries of Flagburnings in the United States." *The Flag Bulletin* 163:65–77.

Graber, Mark A. 1993. "The Nonmajoritarian Difficulty: Legislative Deference to the Judiciary." *Studies in American Political Development* 7(Spring):35–73.

    1998. "Establishing Judicial Review? Schooner Peggy and the Early Marshall Court." *Political Research Quarterly* 51(1): 221–3.

    1999. "The Problematic Establishment of Judicial Review." In *The Supreme Court in American Politics: New Institutionalist Interpretations*, ed. Howard Gillman, Cornell Clayton. Lawrence: University of Kansas Press.

2005. "Constructing Judicial Review." *Annual Review of Political Science* 8:425–51.

Grigg, Delia and Jonathan N. Katz. 2005. "The Impact of Majority-Minority Districts on Congressional Elections." Paper presented at the annual meeting of the Midwest Political Science Association, April 7–10, 2005, Chicago, IL.

Grose, Christian R. 2005. "Disentangling Constituency and Legislator Effects in Legislative Representation: Black Legislators or Black Districts?" *Social Science Quarterly* 86(2):427–43.

Gruhl, John. 1980. "The Supreme Court's Impact on the Law of Libel: Compliance by Lower Federal Courts." *Western Political Quarterly* 33(4):502–19.

Gruhl, John and Susan Welch. 1990. "The Impact of the *Bakke* Decision on Black and Hispanic Enrollment in Medical and Law Schools." *Social Science Quarterly* 71(3):458–73.

Hall, Matthew E. K. 2010. "Bringing Down Brown: Super Precedents, Myths of Rediscovery and the Retroactive Canonization of *Brown v. Board of Education.*" *Journal of Law and Policy* 16(3):655–99.

Hamilton, Alexander. 1961. *The Federalist 78.*

Hand, Learned. 1960. "The Spirit of Liberty," speech at an "I Am an American Day" ceremony, Central Park, New York City, May 21, 1944. In *The Spirit of Liberty,* ed. Irving Dilliard. 3d ed. New York: Knopf.

Handberg, Roger and Harold F. Hill, Jr. 1980. "Court Curbing, Court Reversals, and Judicial Review: The Supreme Court versus Congress." *Law & Society Review* 14(2):309–22.

Hansen, Susan B. 1980. "State Implementation of Supreme Court Decisions: Abortion Rates Since Roe v. Wade." *Journal of Politics* 42(2):372–95.

Hill, Kevin. 1995. "Does the Creation of Black Majority Districts Aid Republicans: An Analysis of the 1992 Congressional Elections in Eight Southern States." *Journal of Politics* 57(2):384–415.

Hirschl, Ran. 2004. *Toward Juristocracy: The Origins and Consequences of the New Constitutionalism.* Cambridge: Harvard University Press.

Hoekstra, Valerie J. 2000. "The Supreme Court and Local Public Opinion." *American Political Science Review* 94(1):89–100.

Hoekstra, Valerie. 2005. "Competing Constraints: State Court Responses to Supreme Court Decisions and Legislation on Wages and Hours." *Political Research Quarterly* 58(2):317–28.

Hopkins, Dianne McAfee. 1995. "Challenges to Library Materials from Principals in United States Secondary Schools – A 'Victory' of Sorts." *School Libraries Worldwide* 1(2)8–29.

1996. "The Library Bill of Rights and School Library Media Programs." *Library Trends* 45(1):61.

Horowitz, Donald L. 1977. *The Courts and Social Policy.* Washington: The Brookings Institution.

Hulse, Carl. 2008. "Democrats Seek to Block Appointee to Obama's Seat, but Authority Is in Question." *The New York Times,* December 31.

2009. "Democrats Open Way to Seat Illinois Pick for Senate." *The New York Times,* January 8.

Intellectual Freedom Committee of the American Library Association. 1970–95. *Newsletter on Intellectual Freedom.* Chicago: Intellectual Freedom Committee of the American Library Association.

Irons, Peter. 2006. *A People's History of the Supreme Court: The Men and Women Whose Cases and Decisions Have Shaped Our Constitution*. Revised Edition. New York: Penguin Books.

Johnson, Charles A. 1979. "Lower Court Reactions to Supreme Court Decisions." *American Journal of Political Science* 23(4):792–804.

1987. "Law, Politics, and Judicial Decision Making: Lower Federal Court Uses of Supreme Court Decisions." *Law & Society Review* 21(2):325–40.

Johnson, Charles A., and Bradley, C. Canon 1984. *Judicial Policies: Implementation and Impact*. Washington: CQ Press.

Johnson, Richard M. 1967. "Compliance and Supreme Court Decision-Making." *Wisconsin Law Review* 1967:170–85.

Johnston, Henry P., ed., 4 vols. 1890–93. *The Correspondence and Public Papers of John Jay*. Vol. 4. New York and London: G. P. Putnam's Sons.

Joyce, Ted. 2004. "Did Legalized Abortion Lower Crime?" *Journal of Human Resources* 39(1):1–28.

Katz, Ellis. 1965. "Patterns of Compliance with the Schempp Decision." *Journal of Public Law* 14:396–408.

Keck, Thomas M. 2007. "Party Politics or Judicial Independence? The Regime Politics Literature Hits the Law Schools." *Law & Social Inquiry* 32(3):511–44.

2009. "Beyond Backlash: Assessing the Impact of Judicial Decisions on LGBT Rights." *Law & Society Review* 42(1):151–85.

Klarman, Michael. 1996. "Rethinking the Civil Rights and Civil Liberties Revolutions." *Virginia Law Review* 82(1):1–67.

2004. *From Jim Crow to Civil Rights: The Supreme Court and the Struggle for Racial Equality*. New York: Oxford University Press.

Klien, Richard. 1986. "The Emperor *Gideon* Has No Clothes: The Empty Promise of the Constitutional Right to Effective Assistance of Counsel." *Hastings Constitutional Law Quarterly* 13:625–93.

Korn, Jessica. 1996. *The Power of Separation: American Constitutionalism and the Myth of the Legislative Veto*. Princeton, NJ: Princeton University Press.

Kramer, Larry D. 2004. *The People Themselves: Popular Constitutionalism and Judicial Review*. New York: Oxford University Press.

Lambert, Ken. 2007. "High Court Rejects School Integration Plans." *The Seattle Times*, 28 June.

Lasser, William. 1988. *The Limits of Judicial Power*. Chapel Hill: University of North Carolina Press.

Laubach, John H. 1969. *School Prayers: Congress, the Courts, and the Public*. Washington: Public Affairs.

Lax, Jeffrey. 2003. "Certiorari and Compliance in the Judicial Hierarchy." *Journal of Theoretical Politics* 15(1):61–86.

Leiken, Lawrence S. 1970. "Police Interrogation in Colorado: The Implementation of *Miranda*." *Denver Law Journal* 47(1):1–53.

Leo, Richard A. 1996. "The Impact of *Miranda* Revisited." In *The* Miranda *Debate*, ed. Richard A. Leo and George C. Thomas, III. Boston: Northeastern University Press.

Leuchtenburg, William. 1995. *The Supreme Court Reborn*. New York: Oxford University Press.

Levi, Edward H. 1975. "Prepared Statement of Hon. Edward H. Levi, Attorney General of the United States." Testimony to the Senate Select Committee to Study Governmental Operations with Respect to Intelligence Activities. November 6.

Levinson, L. Harold. 1987. "The Decline of the Legislative Veto: Federal/State Comparisons and Interactions." *Publius* 17(1):115–32.

Light, Steven Andrew, and Kathryn R.L. Rand. 2007. *Indian Gaming & Tribal Sovereignty: The Casino Compromise.* Lawrence: University of Kansas Press.

Lovell, George I. 2003. *Legislative Deferrals: Statutory Ambiguity, Judicial Power, and American Democracy.* New York: Cambridge Press.

Lublin, David. 1997. *The Paradox of Representation.* Princeton: Princeton University Press.

  1999. "Racial Redistricting and African-American Representation: A Critic of 'Do Majority-Minority Districts Maximize Substantive Black Representation in Congress?'" *American Political Science Review* 93(1):183–6.

Lublin, David and D. Stephen Voss. 2000. "Boll-Weevil Blues: Polarized Congressional Delegations into the 21st Century." *American Review of Politics* 21(Winter): 427–50.

  2003. "The Missing Middle: Why Median-Voter Theory Can't Save Democrats from Singing the Boll-Weevil Blues." *Journal of Politics* 65(1):227–37.

MacKenzie, John P. 1970. "First Term of the Burger Court is Notable for What Wasn't Done." *The Washington Post,* July 7, p. A6.

Manson, Donald A. and Darrell K. Gilliard. 1997. "Presale Handgun Checks, 1996." Washington: Bureau of Justice Statistics.

  1998. "Presale Handgun Checks, 1997." Washington: Bureau of Justice Statistics.

Manson, Donald A., Darrell K. Gilliard, and Gene Lauver. 1999. "Presale Handgun Checks, the Brady Interim Period, 1994–1998." Washington: Bureau of Justice Statistics.

Manson, Donald A., and Gene Lauver. 1997. "Presale Firearm Checks." Washington: Bureau of Justice Statistics.

Manwaring, David. 1972. "The Impact of *Mapp v. Ohio.*" In *The Supreme Court as Policy-Maker: Three Case Studies on the Impact of Judicial Decisions,* ed. D. Everson. Carbondale: Public Affairs Research Bureau Southern Illinois University at Carbondale.

Marshall, Thomas R. 1989. "Policymaking and the Modern Court: When Do Supreme Court Rulings Prevail?" *Western Political Quarterly* 42(4):493–507.

Mayhew, David. 1974. "Congressional Elections: The Case of the Vanishing Marginals." *Polity* 6:295–317.

  2004. *Congress: The Electoral Connection.* 2nd ed. New Haven: Yale University Press.

  2005. *Divided We Govern: Party Control, Lawmaking, and Investigations, 1946–2002.* 2nd Ed. New Haven, CT: Yale University Press.

McCann, Michael W. 1994. *Rights at Work: Pay Equity Reform and the Politics of Legal Mobilization.* Chicago: University of Chicago Press.

  1999. "How the Supreme Court Matters in American Politics: New Institutionalist Perspectives." In *The Supreme Court in American Politics: New Institutionalist Interpretations,* ed. Howard Gillman, Cornell Clayton. Lawrence: University of Kansas Press.

McCloskey, Robert G. 1960. *The American Supreme Court.* University of Chicago Press.

McCubbins, Mathew and Thomas Schwartz. 1988. "Congress, the Courts, and Public Policy: Consequences of the One Man, One Vote Rule." *American Journal of Political Science* 32(2):388–415.

McMahon, Kevin J. 2004. *Reconsidering Roosevelt on Race: How the Presidency Paved the Road to* Brown. Chicago: University of Chicago Press.

McManus, Doyle and Alan C. Miller. 2000. "Lawyers Push for Final Appeal, but Gore Passes." *The Los Angeles Times*, December 14.

Medalie, Richard J., Leonard Zeitz, and Paul Alexander. 1968. "Custodial Police Interrogation in our Nation's Capital: The Attempt to Implement *Miranda*." *Michigan Law Review* 66:1347–422.

Miller, Arthur Selwyn. 1968. *The Supreme Court and American Capitalism*. New York: The Free Press.

Miller, Arthur Selwyn and Alan W. Scheflin. 1967. "The Power of the Supreme Court in the Age of the Positive State: A Preliminary Excursus. Part Two: On the Need for Adaptation to Changing Reality." *Duke Law Journal* 1967(3):522–51.

Milner, Neal A. 1970. Comparative Analysis of Patterns of Compliance." *Law & Society Review* 5(1):119–34.

Mondak, Jeffrey J. 1990. "Perceived Legitimacy of Supreme Court Decisions: Three Functions of Source Credibility." *Political Behavior* 12(4):363–84.

    1991. "Substantive and Procedural Aspects of Supreme Court Decisions as Determinants of Approval." *American Politics Quarterly* 19(2):174–88.

    1992. "Institutional Legitimacy, Policy Legitimacy, and the Supreme Court." *American Politics Quarterly* 20(2):457–77.

Monti, Daniel J. 1980. "Administrative Forces in Educational Chicken Coops." *Law and Policy Quarterly* 2:233.

Moran, John Thomas, ed. 1982. "Gideon Undone: The Crisis in Indigent Defense Funding." American Bar Association in cooperation with the National Legal Aid and Defender Association.

Mounts, Suzanne E. 1982. "Public Defender Programs, Professional Responsibility, and Competent Representation." *Wisconsin Law Review* 473–533.

Mounts, Suzanne E., and Richard J. Wilson. 1986. "Systems for Providing Indigent Defense: An Introduction." *New York University Review of Law and Social Change* 14:193–201.

Murphy, Michael. 1966. "The Problem of Compliance by Police Departments." *Texas Law Review* 44:939–46.

Murphy, Walter. 1964. *Elements of Judicial Strategy*. University of Chicago Press.

Nagel, Jack. 1975. *The Descriptive Analysis of Power*. New Haven: Yale University Press.

Nagel, Robert F. 2001. "Judicial Power and the Restoration of Federalism." *Annals of the American Academy of Political and Social Science* 574:57.

Nagel, Stuart S. 1965. "Law and Society: Testing the Effects of Excluding Illegally Seized Evidence." *Wisconsin Law Review* 1965:283–310.

Nardulli, Peter F. 1983. "The Societal Costs of the Exclusionary Rule: An Empirical Assessment." *American Bar Foundation Research Journal* 8(3):585–609.

    1987. "The Societal Costs of the Exclusionary Rule Revisited." *University of Illinois Law Review* 1987:223–39.

National Association for College Admission Counseling (NACAC). 2003. "Diversity and College Admission in 2003: A Survey Report." Alexandria, VA: National Association for College Admission Counseling.

National Institute of Justice, United States Department of Justice. 1982. "Criminal Justice Research Report – The Effects of the Exclusionary Rule: A Study in California." Washington: National Institute of Justice.

Neier, Aryeh. 1982. *Only Judgment: The Limits of Litigation in Social Change*. Middletown: Wesleyan University Press.

Note. 1968. "Effect of *Mapp v. Ohio* on Police Search-and-Seizure Practices in Narcotics Cases." *Columbia Journal of Law and Social Problems* 4:87–104.

2000. "*Gideon's* Promise Unfulfilled: The Need for Litigated Reform of Indigent Defense." *Harvard Law Review* 113:2062–79.

Oaks, Dallin H. 1970. "Studying the Exclusionary Rule in Search and Seizure." *University of Chicago Law Review* 37:665–757.

Orfield, Myron W., Jr. 1987. "The Exclusionary Rule and Deterrence: An Empirical Study of Chicago Narcotics Officers." *University of Chicago Law Review* 54(3):1016–69.

Peltason J. W. 1971. *Fifty-Eight Lonely Men: Southern Federal Judges and School Desegregation*. Urbana: University of Illinois Press, Revised Edition.

People for the American Way (PAW). 1982–93. *Attacks on the Freedom to Learn*. Washington: People for the American Way.

Peretti, Terri J. 1999. *In Defense of a Political Court*. Princeton: Princeton University Press.

Perrin, L. Timothy, H. Mitchell Caldwell, Carol A. Chase, and Ronald W. Fagan. 1997. "If It's Broken, Fix It: Moving Beyond the Exclusionary Rule." *Iowa Law Review* 38:669.

Perry, Barbara A. 2007. *The Michigan Affirmative Action Cases*. Lawrence: University Press of Kansas.

Petrocik, John R. and Scott E. Desposato. 1998. "The Partisan Consequences of Majority-Minority Redistricting in the South, 1992 and 1994." *Journal of Politics* 60(3):613–33.

Pickerill, J. Mitchell and Cornell W. Clayton. 2004. "The Rehnquist Court and the Political Dynamics of Federalism." *Perspectives on Politics* 2(2):233–48.

Plaus, Stephen A. 1991. "Judicial Versus Legislative Charting of National Economic Policy: Plotting a Democratic Course for Minority Entrepreneurs." *Loyola of Los Angeles Law Review* 24:655–89.

Prucha, Francis Paul. 1984. *The Great Father: The United States Government and the American Indians*, volume I. Lincoln: University of Nebraska Press.

Radelet, Michael L. n.d. "Thirty Years After *Gregg*." Manuscript prepared for Amnesty International. http://www.amnestyusa.org/abolish/greggvgeorgia/study_guide .pdf.

Reed, Douglas S. 2001. *On Equal Terms: The Constitutional Politics of Educational Opportunity*. Princeton, NJ: Princeton University Press.

Reich, D. 1968. "The Impact of Judicial Decision Making: The School Prayer Cases." In *The Supreme Court as Policy-Maker: Three Case Studies on the Impact of Judicial Decisions*, ed. D. Everson. Carbondale: Public Affairs Research Bureau Southern Illinois University.

Reichman, Henry. 1993. *Censorship and Selection: Issues and Answers for Schools*. Chicago: American Library Association.

Reporters Committee for Freedom of the Press. 1979. "Court Watch Summary." *The News Media and the Law*, June/July, p. 18.

1980. "Court Watch Summary." *The News Media and the Law*, October/November, p. 34.

1981. "Court Watch Summary." *The News Media and the Law*, June/July, p. 18.

Rice, Mitchell F. 1999. "Federal Set-Aside Policy and Minority Business Contracting: Understanding the *Adarand* Decision." *International Journal of Public Administration* 22(7):1001–16.

Richardson, James T. 1995. "Legal Status of Minority Religions in the United States." *Social Compass* 42:249.

Robinson, Cyril D. 1968. "Police and Prosecutor Practices and Attitudes Relating to Interrogation as Revealed by Pre- and Post-*Miranda* Questionnaires: A Construct of Police Capacity to Comply." *Duke Law Journal* 1968(3):425–524.

Rosen, Jeffrey. 2006. *The Most Democratic Branch: How the Courts Serve America.* New York: Oxford University Press.

2007 "Can a Law Change a Society?" *The Nation,* 1 July.

Rosenberg, Gerald. 2008. *The Hollow Hope: Can Courts Bring About Social Change?* 2d ed. University of Chicago Press.

Rostow, Eugene V. 1952. "The Democratic Character of Judicial Review." *Harvard Law Review* 66:193.

Rudenstine, David. 1996. *The Day the Presses Stopped: A History of the Pentagon Papers Case.* Berkeley: University of California Press.

Sack, Kevin and Frank Bruni. 2000. "How Gore Stopped Short On His Way to Concede." *The New York Times,* November 9.

Safra, Seth J. 2000. "The Amended Gun-Free School Zones Act: Doubt as to its Constitutionality Remains." *Duke Law Journal* 50:637–62.

Saikowski, Charlotte. 1987. "The Power of Judicial Review." *Christian Science Monitor,* February 11.

Scalia, John. 2000. "Federal Firearm Offenders, 1992–98." Washington: Bureau of Justice Statistics.

Scheingold, Stuart A. 1974. *The Politics of Rights: Lawyers, Public Policy, and Political Change.* New Haven, CT: Yale University Press.

Schmidt, Peter. 2004. "Since Court Ruled, Fewer Black Students Have Applied to Michigan and Ohio State." *Chronicle of Higher Education* 50(26):A22. March 5.

Schmidt, Peter and Jeffrey R. Young. 2003. "MIT and Princeton Open 2 Summer Programs to Students of All Races." *Chronicle of Higher Education* 49(24):A31. February 21.

Schulhofer, Stephen J. 1987. "Reconsidering *Miranda.*" *University of Chicago Law Review* 54(2):435–61.

1996a. "*Miranda's* Practical Effect: Substantial Benefits and Vanishingly Small Social Costs." *Northwestern University Law Review* 90(2):500–63.

1996b. "*Miranda* and Clearance Rates." *Northwestern University Law Review* 91(1): 278.

1997. "Reconsidering Miranda." *University of Chicago Law Review* 54(2): 435–61.

Schultz, D. A., ed. 1998. *Leveraging the Law: Using the Courts to Achieve Social Change.* New York: Peter Lang.

Seeburger, Richard H. and R. Stanton Wettick, Jr. 1967. "Miranda in Pittsburgh – A Statistical Study." *University of Pittsburgh Law Review* 29:1–16.

Segal, Jeffery A. and Harold J. Spaeth. 2002. *The Supreme Court and the Attitudinal Model Revisited.* Cambridge University Press.

Segal, Jeffrey A., Harold J. Spaeth, and Lee Epstein. 2001. "The Norm of Consensus on the U.S. Supreme Court." *American Journal of Political Science* 45(2):362–77.

Select Committee to Study Governmental Operations. 1976. "Warrantless F.B.I. Electronic Surveillance." *Supplementary Detailed Staff Reports on Intelligence Activities and the Rights of Americans.*

Selingo, Jeffrey. 2005. "Michigan: Who Really Won?" *Chronicle of Higher Education* 51(19):A21. January 14.

Senate Committee on the Judiciary. 2005. Confirmation Hearing on the Nomination of John G. Roberts, Jr. To Be Chief Justice of the United States: Hearing Before the S. Comm. on the Judiciary. 109th Cong. 144–5.

"Senate lets Reapportionment Ruling Stand." 1966. *CQ Press Electronic Library, CQ Almanac Online Edition*, cqal66–1301890. Originally published in *CQ Almanac 1966* (Washington: Congressional Quarterly). http://library.cqpress.com/ cqalmanac/cqal66–1301890 (28 January 2009).

Sharpe, Christine Leveaux and James C. Garand. 2001. "Race, Roll Calls, and Redistricting: The Impact of Race-Based Redistricting on Congressional Roll-Call." *Political Research Quarterly* 54(1):31–51.

Shotts, Kenneth W. 2001. "The Effect of Majority-Minority Mandates on Partisan Gerrymandering." *American Journal of Political Science* 45(1):120–35.

2002. "Gerrymandering, Legislative Composition, and National Policy Outcomes." *American Journal of Political Science* 46(2):398–414.

2003a. "Does Racial Redistricting Cause Conservative Policy Outcomes? Policy Preferences of Southern Representatives in the 1980s and 1990s." *Journal of Politics* 65(1):216–26.

2003b. "Racial Redistricting's Alleged Perverse Effects: Theory, Data and 'Reality'." *The Journal of Politics* 65(1):238–43.

Simms, M.C. 1990. "Rebuilding Set-Aside Programs." *Black Enterprise* 21(2).

Skolnick, Jerome H. 1966. *Justice Without Trial: Law Enforcement in Democratic Society*. New York: Wiley.

Skowronek, Stephen. 1982. *Building a New American State: The Expansion of National Administrative Capacities 1877–1920*. New York: Cambridge University Press.

1997. *The Politics President Make: Leadership from John Adams to Bill Clinton*. Cambridge: The Belknap Press of Harvard University.

Smith, Steven K. and Carol J. DeFrances. 1996. "Indigent Defense." Bureau of Justice Statistics. NCJ-158909.

Songer, Donald R. 1987. "The Impact of the Supreme Court on Trends in Economic Policy Making in the United States Courts of Appeals." *Journal of Politics* 49(3):830–41.

1988. "Alternative Approaches to the Study of Judicial Impact: *Miranda* in Five State Courts." *American Politics Research* 16:245–444.

Songer, Donald R., Jeffrey A. Segal, and Charles M. Cameron. 1994. "The Hierarchy of Justice: Testing a Principal-Agent Model of Supreme Court-Circuit Court Interactions." *American Journal of Political Science* 38(3): 673–96.

Songer, Donald R. and Reginald S. Sheehan. 1990. "Supreme Court Impact on Compliance and Outcomes: *Miranda* and *New York Times* in the United States Courts of Appeals." *Western Political Quarterly* 43(2):297–316.

Spangenberg, Robert L. and Marea L. Beeman. 1995. "Indigent Defense Systems in the United States." *Law and Contemporary Problems* 58(1):31–49.

Specter, Arlen. 1962. "*Mapp v. Ohio*: Pandora's Problems for the Prosecutor." *University of Pennsylvania Law Review* 111:4.

Spiotto, James E. 1973. "Search and Seizure: An Empirical Study of the Exclusionary Rule and Its Alternatives." *Journal of Legal Studies* 2(1):243–78.

Spriggs, James F. 1997. "Explaining Federal Bureaucratic Compliance with Supreme Court Opinions." *Political Research Quarterly* 50(3):567–93.

Stephens, Otis H. Jr. 1965. "Police Interrogation and the Supreme Court: An Inquiry into the Limits of Judicial Policy-Making." *Journal of Public Law* 17:241–57.

Strazzella, James A. 1977. "Ineffective Assistance of Counsel Claims: New Uses, New Problems." *Arizona Law Review* 19:443–84.

Tocqueville, Alexis de. 1945. *Democracy in America, Volume I.* New York: Random House, Inc.

Tushnet, Mark. 1999. *Taking the Constitution Away from the Courts.* Princeton: Princeton University Press.

Twetten, Daniel. 2000. "Public Law 280 and the Indian Gaming Regulatory Act: Could Two Wrongs Ever Be Made into a Right?" *Journal of Criminal Law and Criminology* 90(4):1317–52.

Uchida, Craig D. and Timothy S. Bynum. 1991. "Search Warrants, Motions to Suppress and 'Lost Cases': The Effects of the Exclusionary Rule in Seven Jurisdictions." *Journal of Criminal Law and Criminology* 81(4):1034–66.

U.S. Congress. House. 1995. Proposed Legislation: "The Gun-Free School Zones Amendments Act of 1995." 104th Cong., 1st sess. H.Doc. 104–72.

United States Commission on Civil Rights. 2005. "Federal Procurement after *Adarand.*" Washington: U.S. Commission on Civil Rights.

Van Zwaluwenburg, Pamela Joy. 2004. *Wide Awake or Sound Asleep? Universities and the Implementation of* Rosenberger v. University of Virginia. Dissertation, Miami University, 2004.

Wald, Michael S., Richard Ayres, David W. Hess, Michael Schantz, and Charles H. Whitebread II. 1967. "Interrogations in New Haven: The Impact of *Miranda.*" *Yale Law Journal* 76:1519–648.

Waldron, Jeremy. 1999. *Law and Disagreement.* New York: Oxford University Press.

Ward, James D. 1994. "Response to *Croson.*" *Public Administration Review* 54(5): 483–5.

Wasby, Stephen L. 1970. *The Impact of the United States Supreme Court: Some Perspectives.* Homewood, IL: Dorsey.

———. 1976. *Small Town Police and the Supreme Court.* Lexington, MA: Lexington Books.

Way, H. Frank. 1968. "Survey Research on Judicial Decisions: The Prayer and Bible Reading Cases." *Western Political Quarterly* 21(2):189–205.

Wayne, Stephen J. 1978. *The Legislative Presidency.* New York: Harper and Row.

Wechsler, Herbert. 1959. "Toward Neutral Principles of Constitutional Law." *Harvard Law Review* 73:1.

Wetstein, Matthew E. 1995. "The Abortion Rate Paradox: The Impact of National Policy Change on Abortion Rates." *Social Science Quarterly* 76(3):607–18.

Whittington, Keith E. 2001. "Once More Unto the Breach: Post-Behavioralist Approaches to Judicial Politics." *Law & Social Inquiry* 25: 601.

———. 2005. "'Interpose Your Friendly Hand': Political Supports for the Exercise of Judicial Review by the United States Supreme Court." *American Political Science Review* 99(4):583–96.

———. 2007. *Political Foundations of Judicial Supremacy: The Presidency, the Supreme Court, and Constitutional Leadership in U.S. History.* Princeton University Press.

Index

Made in the USA
Middletown, DE
02 August 2018